Belly Dance
Around the World

Belly Dance Around the World

New Communities, Performance and Identity

Edited by CAITLIN E. MCDONALD *and* BARBARA SELLERS-YOUNG

McFarland & Company, Inc., Publishers
Jefferson, North Carolina, and London

LIBRARY OF CONGRESS CATALOGUING-IN-PUBLICATION DATA

Belly dance around the world : new communities, performance and identity / edited by Caitlin E. McDonald and Barbara Sellers-Young.
    p.   cm.
Includes bibliographical references and index.

ISBN 978-0-7864-7370-0
softcover : acid free paper ∞

1. Belly dance — Social aspects. 2. Dance and transnationalism. I. McDonald, Caitlin E. II. Sellers-Young, Barbara.
GV1798.5.B43 2013
793.3 — dc23   2013018394

BRITISH LIBRARY CATALOGUING DATA ARE AVAILABLE

© 2013 Caitlin E. McDonald and Barbara Sellers-Young. All rights reserved

No part of this book may be reproduced or transmitted in any form or by any means, electronic or mechanical, including photocopying or recording, or by any information storage and retrieval system, without permission in writing from the publisher.

On the cover: Lynette Harper and Rahma Haddad explored their shared Lebanese roots and Arab-Canadian identities through dance and storytelling in *Bekaa Valley Girls: A Lebanese Saga* at Vancouver's Dance Centre (photograph courtesy Harry Brewster)

Manufactured in the United States of America

McFarland & Company, Inc., Publishers
  Box 611, Jefferson, North Carolina 28640
  www.mcfarlandpub.com

Table of Contents

Preface and Acknowledgments   1

Introduction: The Interplay of Dance and the Imagined Possibilities of Identity
    BARBARA SELLERS-YOUNG   3

What Is *Baladi* about *al-Raqs al-Baladi*? On the Survival of Belly Dance in Egypt
    NOHA ROUSHDY   17

Finding "the Feeling": Oriental Dance, *Musiqa al-Gadid*, and *Tarab*
    CANDACE BORDELON   33

Performing Identity/Diasporic Encounters
    LYNETTE HARPER   48

1970s Belly Dance and the "How-To" Phenomenon: Feminism, Fitness and Orientalism
    VIRGINIA KEFT-KENNEDY   68

Dancing with Inspiration in New Zealand and Australian Dance Communities
    MARION COWPER *and* CAROLYN MICHELLE   93

Local Performance/Global Connection: American Tribal Style and Its Imagined Community
    TERESA CUTLER-BROYLES   106

The Use of Nostalgia in Tribal Fusion Dance
    CATHERINE MARY SCHEELAR   121

"I mean, what is a Pakeha New Zealander's national dance? We don't have one": Belly Dance and Transculturation in New Zealand
    BRIGID KELLY   138

Quintessentially English Belly Dance: In Search of an English Tradition
    SIOUXSIE COOPER   152

Delilah: Dancing the Earth
    BARBARA SELLERS-YOUNG   168

Negotiating Female Sexuality: Bollywood Belly Dance, "Item Girls" and Dance Classes
    SMEETA MISHRA   181

Digitizing *Raqs Sharqi*: Belly Dance in Second Life
    CAITLIN E. MCDONALD   197

About the Contributors   211

Index   213

Preface and Acknowledgments

We live in an era of globalization. Socially, culturally and economically, flows of commodities and power cut across physical and geographic boundaries; in particular the power of technology, including but not limited to the internet, creates new communities which transcend geographic boundaries. Thus, it is necessary to raise new lines of inquiry to examine the ways in which communities form in this globalizing era. Studying these emerging communities requires engaging with them in multiple physical localities as well as understanding how these groups contact one another, and how they transmit and address questions of legitimacy about the identity-forming subject that brings them together.

A popular cultural performance form within the framework of global culture is a dance form referred to in Egypt as *raks sharqi*, but known popularly as belly dance. This dance form is the practice of individuals who trace their heritage to North Africa and the Middle East and many others who have no biological roots there but trace their creative identity and fictive bodily presence to this part of the world. As such, it participates in the global flows of images of men and women dancing within the expressive frames of their bodies to images associated with popular conceptions of North Africa and the Middle East.

As a dance form moves across cultural boundaries, it participates in dialogues between the forces of globalization and a resistance to alterations of existing power structures, specifically in reference to masculinity and femininity and related gender roles. This tension results in two emergent tropes: first, an attempt to suppress the influences of globalization by restricting its effects and returning to older, more traditional ways of life that make cross-geographic flows of cultural and economic capital (and the types of community formation resulting from these flows) far more difficult than current technologies allow. Second, an endeavor to appropriate all the advantages of globalization while leaving behind some of the less desirable elements and replacing these with more highly valued elements of "local" culture; in other words creating a new process of "glocalization" in which local themes are superimposed on global themes, creating new localisms. Belly dance becomes in this volume of essays a way to examine these global/local forces through the lens of a popular dance form.

This book would not be possible if it were not for the support of families and friends who have listened to the ideas over coffee and extended dinners or read versions presented at conferences. This manuscript would also not be possible without the generosity of the global belly dance community.

Caitlin: would like to thank her parents who have been an unwavering source of support and encouragement in continuing to seek out new, interesting, and bold questions about the human experience. Special thanks are also due to Professor Kristin Zahra Sands, who first allowed me to explore belly dance in an academic context; Professor Mike Siff, who brought the discipline of human-computer interaction to my attention; Professor Julie Abraham, who introduced unexpected questions about the boundaries and vagaries of gender; Professor Gabriel Asfar, whose Arabic courses were so much more vibrant than linguistics alone; and Professors Nadje Al-Ali and Christine Allison, whose guidance and insight helped me to blend it all into a richly-flavored stew.

Barbara: would specifically like to thank Anthony Shay whose insight into the dance as a space of identity formation has been invaluable. Other influential people in the creation of this volume include Berri Leslie and Kimberly Sellers-Blais who throughout their lives have always been willing to attend a dance concert. A special thanks to my granddaughter, Kinsey Freeman, whose observations on life have caused me to rethink my own. I am very grateful to Angela Zhang and Carol Altilia who created the space and time for me to work on this project and to Jade Rosina McCutcheon who has challenged me to never be afraid to engage new ideas.

Introduction: The Interplay of Dance and the Imagined Possibilities of Identity

BARBARA SELLERS-YOUNG

> *Aesthetics are inherently social. The formal properties and presumptions intrinsic to the production and consumption of art are communicative currency developed by and circulating between artists, audiences, and critics, binding them together in interpretive communities, serving as bases for exchange in the public and private conversation that constitute art's relational and affective lives.* —Judith Hamera (2007, 3)
>
> *The imagination is now central to all forms of agency, is itself a social fact, and is the key component of the new global order.* —Appadurai (1996, 31)

When Gustave Flaubert (1996) wrote his account of visiting Egyptian dancer Kutchuk Hanem in 1877, he participated in the discourses of 19th century globalization to create an image of sensuality that would become the popular version of Arab women which would be replicated in paintings, postcards, performed at international fairs and festivals and integrated into films and television. Post-colonial theorist Edward Said coined the term "Orientalism" to reference this phenomenon. Said's review of the approach of Western writers, scholars, and artists to the Middle East formulated a theory of artistic imperialism and its relationship to power and the imagination. Since then, other scholars (MacKenzie 1995, Alloula 1986, Collingham 2001, Graham-Brown 1988, Lewis 2004) have expanded his original discussion to include visual arts, media and the performing arts. These scholars note the impact of "latent" and "manifest" Orientalism in the dances of Ruth St. Denis (Desmond 1991), dances associated with folklore companies and their goal to define a national identity (Shay 2001), the construction of the Arab as performative genre within American popular culture (Salem 1995, Jarmakani 2008), the ensuing dialogue between America and Egypt, primarily via the film industry, in which Orientalist constructions of the dancing female body are a primary image (Zuhur 1998, 2001), the almost complete erasure of the male body in global discourse (Karayanni 2004). The writing of these scholars in visual arts, film, and dance has delineated the synchronic and diachronic frames and related means, methods and people, paintings, photographs, writings, venues, media, and individuals who have contributed to the ongoing discourse of Orientalism and related issues of mimicry, hybridity and the status of the subaltern in a post-colonial world.

Today this global discourse from the perspective of the solo dance form most commonly referred to as belly dance takes place in three interactive locations. First the versions of the solo dance performed in rural and urban enclaves throughout North Africa and the Middle East at family celebrations, tourist venues and in films produced there. Second, there are the diasporic communities from North Africa and the Middle East throughout the world and the men and women who are participating in the dance from a standpoint of cultural retention of a community but through the lens of global popular culture. Third, there are women across the globe, from rural communities to urban environments, who integrate popular versions of Kutchuk Hanem and the Orient in a process of identity formation that reflects a passionate desire to (re)frame their identity and related subjective experience to stretch the boundaries of the gender roles of their community.[1]

Across the globe, these individual dancing communities have evolved a technical vocabulary and related aesthetics that may share some general characteristics such as hip articulations, shimmies and undulations; but their interpretation is specific to the individual community's shared social and cultural beliefs. Regardless each group is negotiating its performance within the global discourse of images and the imagination it engenders in an enactment of a performative self that Richard Schechner suggests "offers to both, individuals and groups, the chance to become what they never were but wish to have been or wish to become" (1985, 38). Individually and collectively, the dancers, professionals and amateurs, explore aspects of personal identity and power related to cultivating kinesthetic self-knowledge through the exploration of a general movement vocabulary and related music. In the end, this becomes an identity they perform publicly in dances for which they have created the choreography and costume and determined the music. Ultimately, Flaubert's 19th century version of Kutchuk Hanem is in ongoing dialogue with its global interpreters whose performances are shared via film and the cyber world.[2] The essays in this volume address the global discourses regarding belly dance in these communities to consider the following:

• The role of religious attitudes in the evolution and transmission of the solo dances of North Africa and the Middle East.
• The role of Egypt as the cultural center of North Africa and the Middle East and thus pivotal in the ongoing discourse and evolution of the dance.
• Orientalism as an ongoing frame which impacts the global discourse regarding North Africa and the Middle East as it defines the performance communities of dancers in North Africa and the Middle East, the related diasporic dance communities, and dancers who chose this dance form but who have no other cultural or economic connection to the Middle East/North Africa region.
• The ongoing evolution of the third wave of feminism as children of the second wave of feminism engage the dance form to discover the sensuality of their bodies and the related variant interpretations of the feminine globally.
• The discrete versions of belly dance which have evolved in relationship to an individual community's approach to Oriental imagery, social/cultural positioning of women, and the role dance plays within the cultural discourse of a social context; and therefore the forces of change and resistance.

Islamic Aesthetics and the Role of Improvisation

Lois Ibsen al-Farqui (1977) identified solo improvisational forms such as the Egyptian *raqs sharqi* that, along with combat, group and religious dances, managed to survive both medieval Islam and Christianity's discomfort with dance as a mode of expression.[3] Embedded in the tenets of Islam are concerns with human representation that Leona Wood and Anthony Shay (1976) note are part of Islamic attitudes toward the performing arts in general. It is an attitude that Shay labeled in his 1999 study on dance in Iran and its related diaspora as "choreophobia." This term encompasses a wide range of prohibitions on physical behaviors based on gender, age, social status, religiosity, context and individual personality traits which impact a dancer's reception in a particular context. Shay's model demonstrates the complex set of relationships that contribute to dance being a component of social celebrations and yet is also a mode of expression which needs careful regulation to prevent transgressions of accepted gender relations.

Al-Farqui (1977), And (1959), Monroe (1961) and Shay (1999) reveal the relationship between the movement vocabulary and related aesthetics of North Africa and the Middle East. Al-Farqui writes: "Aesthetic beauty was intuitively conceived as that which stylized and disguised nature, or avoided it completely in abstract designs" (1977, 7). Anthony Shay (1995) suggests that the movement vocabulary of the various solo improvisational dances tend to be patterned on abstraction and Islamic visual arts such as calligraphy. This is kinesthetically realized in a dance vocabulary that is inclined toward small intricate movements of the head, hands, torso or hips. The legs are used to augment the movement of the head and torso; the arms are used to frame the movement. In some versions of the dance, the dancer accents the movement of the hips and torso with the rapid fire accompaniment of brass finger cymbals. The dance's structure is based on improvised movements that evolve into a series of mini-crescendos which reflect the complexity of the music.

I have used the phrase "movement vocabulary" instead of the term "technique," as the dance in its traditional context does not have a named vocabulary that is transferred from teacher to student. Instead, belly dance's transmission process within North Africa and the Middle East and in the related diaspora is from one generation to another through improvised performances during celebrations most often related to such life cycle rituals as births and weddings. In these contexts, the role of the dance was an opportunity to express a shared joy in the continuity of the family. This improvisational mode creates the aesthetic frame for the dance. As Judith Hamera notes, an aesthetic construct of a dance form includes a dialogue between various social forces; "Aesthetics are inherently social. The formal properties and presumptions intrinsic to the production and consumption of art are communicative currency developed by and circulating between artists, audiences, and critics, binding them together in interpretive communities, serving as bases for exchange in the public and private conversation that constitute art's relational and affective lives" (2007, 3). The lack of named vocabulary has meant that the dance provided a boundary between the religious code which prohibited representation of the body and the innate desire to celebrate joyful events with expressive gestures of the body; an attitude that still exists. Regardless, the dance did engage in an improvisational aesthetic of abstraction, an aesthetic which in the absence of a named vocabulary ultimately allowed for a variety of interpretations by those outside of its original context who kinesthetically experienced the vocabulary as a mode of individual expressiveness. Thus, the "erasure" of dance as a legitimate expressive form within Islamic culture indirectly and ironically contributed to its interpretation by dancers who would in the 20th century adopt the movement vocabulary for their personal expressive desires, a set of desires unrelated to an Islamic ethos. In the final analysis, Islamic attitudes toward bodily representation combined with no named technical vocabulary and the abstract aesthetic noted by Shay provided an empty space for interpretation.

Global Transmission

Much of the global transmission of belly dance is guided through an act of mimesis both from the classes offered in dance studios and community centers to the media representation of belly dance via television, film, video and internet. As Michael Taussig points out, "Once the mimetic springs into being, a terrifically ambiguous power is established; there is born the power to represent the world, yet that same power is a power to falsify, mask and pose" (1992, 42–43). The act of mimesis often takes place within the framework of a global discourse that Arjun Appadurai notes is based on our imagination:

> The image, the imagined, the imaginary — these are all terms that direct us to something critical and new in global processes: the imagination as a social practice. No longer mere fantasy (opium for the masses whose real work is elsewhere), no longer simple escape (from a world defined principally by more concrete purposes and structures), no longer elite pastime (thus not relevant to the lives of ordinary people), and no longer mere contemplation (irrelevant for new forms of desire and subjectivity), the imagination has become an organized field of social practices, a form of work (in the sense of both labour and culturally organized practice), and a form of negotiation between sites of agency (individuals) and globally defined fields of possibility. This unleashing of the imagination links the play of pastiche (in some settings) to the terror and coercion of states and their competitors. The imagination is now central to all forms of agency, is itself a social fact, and is the key component of the new global order [Appadurai 1996, 31].

The various tropes of the Orient performed on the stage, projected on the screen, and carried over the internet as Taussig notes have power and have impacted the public perception and evolution of belly dance and its derivatives. Homi Bhabha (1994) and Marta Savigliano (1995) point out that these versions of the Orient often perpetuate within the transnational media an image of an exotic Oriental other that is highly sensual, mysterious and innately feminine. In their 1976 article "Danse du Ventre: A Fresh Appraisal," Anthony Shay and Leona Wood describe the history and persistence of a fascination with the Orient embedded in belly dance as both "durable and widespread, not only in literature and painting, but in music and dance as well" (1976, 19). Shay and Wood point to the difficulty in overcoming a stereotype once it has become part of the public imagination. As they further note, this is the case even when the public has been exposed to a more valid image. They demonstrate the truth of this statement by guiding us through the visual and performing arts of the 18th, 19th and 20th centuries and the representations of the Orient by Ingres, Delacroix, and Moreau, the exhibits of the Philadelphia and Chicago exhibitions in 1876 and 1893, the opera and ballets with Oriental themes by Mozart and Debussy, the numerous actresses, Collette, Maud Allen and others, who portrayed the character of Salome in Richard Strauss's version of Oscar Wilde's play, and finally the popular musicals such as *Kismet*. Thus, their 1976 essay foreshadowed Edward Said's theories and his theoretical framing of Orientalism; the totality of this discourse portrays the Orient as a site of sensuality, sexual promise, and unlimited desire.

This is an attitude that has placed the Arab female dancing body in juxtaposition to the Arab male body (who does not dance within the popular social imagination) and the consequence is an image of the Oriental dancing body as a myth that is unrelated to the ritual celebrations and dancing communities of North Africa and the Middle East. Amira Jarmakani in *Imaging Arab Womanhood: The Cultural Mythology of Veils, Harems, and Belly Dancers in the U.S.* (2008) further argues this point in terms of the power relationships in the commoditization of an Arab woman's body.

Arjun Appadurai (2001) and James Clifford (1997) have suggested that all cultural forms, including dance, are impacted by travelers, either as sojourners, immigrants or tourists, who have participated in the transference of culture. In some cases, this results in dance being transferred within the normative structure of its original location. For instance, there is the inclusion of solo dancing as part of Arab wedding celebrations in the large urban centers of the diaspora as an extension of similar celebrations in Egypt and elsewhere in North Africa and the Middle East. In other instances, the conception of the Orient, which belly dance represents, is part of a continuing Orientalist discourse and a process of creating and adjusting the image of the Orient through the input of a variety of dancers and contexts. More recently, the global positioning of the Orient has taken on an expanded visibility in the performances of the group Bellydance Superstars. The company, formed by rock promoter Miles Copeland, has performed across the globe a program that combines Egyptian style dance with variations such as American Tribal and choreographic fusions which feature India and Hawaii.

New Styles and New Identities

In the global transmission of the belly dance, dancers enact expressive identities that are outside of the framework associated with traditional performance of the form in North Africa and the Middle East. The American version of the form in the 1960s and 70s was associated with second wave of feminist ideals expressed by Betty Friedan (1976), Germaine Greer (1971), 2000), Robin Morgan (1984) and others that women needed to shed the patriarchal dominated image of the ideal body and discover the possibilities of an anatomy of freedom. Using the drum as a symbol of ritual invocation and the stage as am empty space of the imagination, female dancers of all ages, body types, personal histories, and occupational backgrounds renamed themselves Delilah, Jasmine, Scheherazade, and such to dance the erotic self through the kinesthetic embodiment of the power of the spirals, circles and shimmies and the external expression of an internal expressive desire. It is a power reminiscent of Audre Lorde's definition of the erotic. Audre Lorde draws her definition of erotic from the Greek word *eros*, "the personification of love in all its aspects — born of Chaos, and personifying creative power and harmony" (1993, 55). With this definition, Lorde removes the word from typical contexts of romance novels and adult movie theaters. Her definition of erotic is more closely allied with a similar word — sensual — in reference to the total experience of the corporeal body. This conception of erotic and its relationship to body/mind unites a deep matrix of thought and action that "binds together the scattered parts of the self and links a whole range of intense, creative experiences" (55). The erotic is released through the self as the individual discovers the inner layers of their being and sends this newly acquired energy throughout the body. This deeply felt connection colors the life of a person "with a kind of energy that heightens and sensitizes and strengthens" them (55). An experience of the erotic is not limited to belly dancing. It is a recognized mind/body connection that is part of many deeply felt experiences. The movements of this particular dance form seem to provide, however, a means for many women to become psycho-physically aware of this connection.

Belly dancers have also drawn inspiration from the early pioneers of modern dance Ruth St. Denis and Isadora Duncan; St. Denis for her inclusion of Oriental imagery of goddesses in her choreographic work and Isadora Duncan who used Greek myths in her desire to free the body from the physical and aesthetic confines of ballet. By extension of their ideas, the belly dance created a mythic association with the goddess cultures of the Middle East in an effort to provide a framework in which all social positions, body types and ages were incorporated in a dancing community. Examples of these belief systems are documented in books by Gioseffi (1980), Bonaventura (1998), Stewart (1990) and others.

While writing from specific socio-cultural contexts and within equally specific theoretical frameworks, previous essays on the evolution of global belly dance by authors from Turkey (Öykü Potuoğlu-Cook), Finland (Anu Laukkanen), Australia (Virginia Keft-Kennedy) and the United States (Donnalee Dox) note the paradoxical position of contemporary belly dance in local/global discourse regarding the role of dance in women's lives. Öykü Potuoğlu-Cook's 2006 article draws upon Pierre Bourdieu's (1984) conception of class and corporeal knowledge in a discussion of power and exoticism as suggested by Marta Savigliano (1995). It examines the complex relationship between the belly dance as part of the tourist industry and part of cultural life in Turkish urban environments. The study suggests the dance is a symbol of "chic" status among middle and upper class women in Istanbul associated with neo–Ottomania and its position in Turkish politics, as various facets of the government seek to become part of the European Union and still retain the support of Islamic conservatives. According to Potuoğlu-Cook, "before its gentrification, the public performance of belly dance denoted lower-class status" (644). However, Potuoğlu-Cook notes this position has changed as "belly dance itself has transformed from a participatory social form into a presentational" technique (644).

As belly dance increasingly participates in the global marketplace as a legitimate form of entertainment, Potuoğlu-Cook argues that belly dance comes to signify "cultural and economic proximity to cosmopolitan culture. It is a localized element in a redeveloped, gentrified, and thus, socially and economically more segregated Istanbul, in its aspirations for status as a global city" (644). Furthermore, she points out the political positioning of belly dance within the framework of new Islamic veiling or *tesettür* in which the complete head and forehead are covered; this practice that is also related to neo–Ottomania or the contemporary recreation of Ottoman aesthetics. Turkish belly dance is in Potuoğlu-Cook's analysis a site of neo–Ottomania and is in cultural dialogue with *tesettür* which is also a result of another component of neo–Ottomania. As she phrases it: "Thus *tesettür* and belly dance are fraternal twins — noble and nasty savage — of Islamic Turkey, delineating the contours of morally and materially acceptable female presence in public space. Engendered by neoliberalism, both *tesettür* and belly dance oscillate between abjection and sophistication" (649).

The paradoxical positioning of belly dance is not limited to countries of its historic origin. Anu Laukkanen researching Finnish dancers, Virginia Keft-Kennedy writing from Australia, and Donnalee Dox considering dancers in the United States all point out that dancers in these countries participate in fantasy images which appear contrary to contemporary feminist politics of identity, but is empowering to these dancers. Dox observes, "If European colonial gazes saw in the harem and the veil, repression, cultural backwardness, and frustrating secrecy, contemporary Western belly dancing transforms these same images into testaments to their own corporeality, the persistence of ancient wisdom in the modern world, and the uncontested value of open self-expression" (2007, 1).

Anu Laukkanen illustrates in her research on Finnish dancers (2003) that the exotification of self through the other is not without its psychological dilemmas in a global culture in which belly dancers move within and between different social/cultural groups and national boundaries. Finnish belly dancers through personal visits and media reports are very aware of the ambivalent status of professional dancers in North Africa and the Middle East, in particular in Cairo, as the center of the entertainment industry. The result of this ambivalence is a desire among many Finnish woman who study the dance to learn the movement vocabulary but not necessarily the dance form's cultural and social history.

Virginia Keft-Kennedy draws on the work of Mary Douglas' conceptions of "purity" and "danger" as reprised by Mary Russo to consider the belly dance's particular position for Australian women. Keft-Kennedy considers the women who initially performed belly dance in public venues in Australia as dangerous because they challenged "the social and symbolic system that would keep women adhering to the conventions of appropriate female behavior, and they are dangerous because they are vulnerable to derision for their transgression" (2005, 202). However, danger is not without its rewards and Keft-Kennedy argues that belly dance, as a transgressive performance, is both spectacle and masquerade, which makes visible the stereotype of the feminine. This is particularly true of the costume which accentuates the belly and the navel as a symbol of one's connection to the mother, birth and, as such, our individual mortality. The constant display of the navel as part of the performance of belly dance in restaurants, in the media and on the internet has made the navel as well as belly dancer a common sight and the dance's version of the feminine an extension of popular culture. In a global context, belly dance praxis is therefore located in a liminal space and therefore operates, as Keft-Kennedy suggests, "as a powerful yet unstable symbol of female empowerment" (2005, 280).

Communities in Movement

The desire for a transformation of body image among women has been well documented by Adair (1992), Bordo (1993), Grosz (1994) and others. As Christy Adair suggests, "there is an obsession with visual images and recording them. For women, this means being reduced to and equated with our bodies ... which result in women frequently feeling alienated from our bodies" (1992, 213). As suggested by Dox and Keft-Kennedy, the act of dancing through Orientalism's frame of the "other" in an act of self-exotification is an opportunity for the female dancer to unite an exploration of new identities through exploration of a desired other. These are acts which Helene Cixous refers to as "writing herself" (1981) or what Keft-Kennedy quoting Mary Russo refers to as "dilemmas of femininity" (291). A 1979 study by Judy Alves-Masters discovered that women who studied belly dance developed new levels of self-esteem related to an opportunity to explore the creative expressivity of their body.

This volume features a series of essays by dancer/scholars who further delineate the contradictions of a dance form that is a complex site of appropriation, liberation and community engagement. The essays incorporate new directions in dance studies which embrace the intersection between ethnographer and dancer and "literally dancing through and between ethnography and history" (O'Shea 2007, 146). This approach to ethnography derives from a convergence of anthropology, ethnography and the concept of the performative allied with cultural and performance studies. As such, it unites subjective experience with objective observation to reveal the intra-cultural discourses and related cultural flows (using Arjun Appadurai's conception of the forces of globalization related to technology, transportation, migration and the economy, 1996) that are integral to the intercultural adaptation of dance forms across social political boundaries.

Noha Roushdy and Candace Bordelon set the stage for the book in their separate essays which articulate the role the dance plays in the global hub of belly dance, Egypt, as a site of cultural identification through the community notion of *baladi* and aesthetic expressiveness through the concept of *tarab*. As Caitlin E. McDonald discusses in *Global Moves: Belly Dance as an Extra/Ordinary Space to Explore Social Paradigms in Egypt and Around the World* (2012), Egypt is the idealized center for dance. The famous 20th and 21st century dancers of Cairo, Samia Gamal, Tahia Carioca, Nagwa Fouad, and Aida Nour, are the models for dancers across the globe through attendance at festivals in Cairo or through constant review of video or YouTube performances. Egypt and its dancers and musicians are also the focus for members of the Arab diaspora.

Focusing next on Canada, Lynette Harper crafts a set of interviews which reveal the complex relationship women Canadian immigrants from North Africa and the Middle East have with belly dance as a popular staged form as opposed to the participation in the social form associated with family celebrations. The dancers of these interviews are struggling with finding an image of self that corresponds to their family experience with what Jarmakani (2008) in *Imaging Arab Womanhood* suggests is the marketing of the Orient.

Virginia Keft-Kennedy then reflects on the relationship between "how to" books on belly dance and the definition of the feminine that evolved in the 1970s and 80s. Other essays describe communities located in Australia (by Marion Cowper and Carolyn Michelle), the U.S. (Teresa Cutler-Broyles, Barbara Sellers-Young), New Zealand (Brigid Kelly), England (Siouxsie Cooper), and India (Smeeta Mishra) that integrate elements of local belief systems and aesthetics with Oriental imagery in a convergence with those images which have become part of the discursive framing of the dance.

In the age of the virtual, this community communicates across cultural and national boundaries via the social media sites on the internet — webpages, Facebook, blogs, tweeting — and face to face at international festivals held in cities across the globe from Singapore to San Francisco, São Paulo, Berlin, Istanbul and Cairo. The consequence is the development of new forms of belly dance that cross popular music and film. In her essay "The Use of Nostalgia in Tribal Fusion Dance," Catherine Mary Scheelar documents the intersections between present-day forms such as gothic belly dance and earlier forms which evolved out of San Francisco's artistic primitive movement of the 1980s.

Other dancers use the anonymity of Second Life as described by Caitlin E. McDonald in her essay "Digitizing *Raqs Sharqi*: Belly Dance in Second Life." In this focus on specific communities and dancers, this set of essays seeks to consider an individual dancer's engagement of a generalized vocabulary associated with North Africa and the Middle East in dialogue with the social imaginary of orientalism and framed within the processes of globalization and a specific community ethos.

Ultimately, the essays exist within the global dialogues of transnationalism, a discourse influenced by what Appadurai refers to as ethnoscapes, or the "landscape of persons who make up the shifting world in which we live, tourists, immigrants, refugees, exiles, guest workers, and other moving groups" (1996, 315–25). Thus, a solo improvised folk form to celebrate joyful events within the family and community has evolved through the possibilities of the stage as a space of the imagination. This stage is a liminoid space of the imagination that noted anthropologist Victor Turner (1982) has suggested is a secular space that is betwixt and between one mode of being and another. Primarily associated with rituals and the extra ordinary spaces, such as the stage, this liminoid imaginary provides an opportunity for the participant to explore the possibility of a new psycho-physical identity.

While Appadurai defines the imagination as social practice, Susan Bardo notes the dilemmas in intercultural communication created by a mediated social imaginary; "For one effect of this critique of the pervasive dualism and metaphors that animate representations of the body is to call into question the assumption that we ever know or encounter the body — not only the bodies of others but our own bodies — directly or simply. Rather, it seems, the body that we experience and conceptualize is always mediated" (1993, 30). The global evolution of belly dance is an example of mediation between desiring imagination, the global imaginary and the social/cultural forces of communities; and ultimately between the forces of the local community in relationship to the discursive structures of global economic and political power. The issues concerning belly dance's position within local community and global culture that these writers raise at the beginning of the 21st century share a concern with the continuation of Orientalism as a mode for interpreting the cultures of North Africa and the Middle East and associated diasporic communities throughout the world. At the same time, they are articulating how Orientalism's imagery has evolved in relationship to national cultures, as in the case of the neoliberal gentrification in Turkey, and has been used by women globally via a self-exotification and masquerade as a site of empowerment. A consequence of the discourse is that there is the solo improvisational form of North Africa and the Middle East and related diaspora often referred to as *raqs sharqi* that is part of family celebrations; and, there is a separate form, belly dance, that has evolved from the movement vocabulary of the North Africa and the Middle East, but which has evolved a performative mode that is distinct from its site of origin. As such, belly dance fits within the broad spectrum of invented traditions as articulated by Hobsbawm and Ranger (2012) with a social/cultural history that has evolved local traditions within a global discourse.

Notes

1. There are within the global belly dance community a group of male dancers both in North Africa and the Middle East as well as in North and South America, Europe and Australia. This group has expanded in the last fifteen years along with the global interest in belly dance. The best discussions of male dancers both historically and in the present are: Monroe Berger, "Curious and Wonderful Gymnastic," *Dance Perspectives* (New York, 1961), 4–43 (reprinted by Johnson Reprint Corp., 1970); Anthony Shay's "The Male Dancer" in *Belly Dance: Orientalism, Transnationalism & Harem Fantasy*, ed. Anthony Shay and Barbara Sellers-Young (California: Mazda Press, 2005), 85–113; and Stavros Stavrou Karayanni's *Dancing Fear and Desire* (Ontario, Canada: Wilfrid University Press, 2004).

2. Two films that represent the global discourse in dance are *Satin Rouge* from Tunisia and *My Mother Is a Belly Dancer* from Hong Kong. The primary theme of the narrative line in each of these films is the self-discovery of the main female character that learns to dance.

Works Cited

Adair, C. (1992). *Women and Dance: Sylphs and Sirens.* New York: New York University Press.

Al-Faruqi, L.I. (1977). "Dances of the Muslim Peoples." *Dance Scope* 11/1 (Fall/Winter), 43–51.

———. (1987). "Dance as an Expression of Islamic Culture." *Dance Research Journal* 10/2: 6–17.

Alloula, M. (1986). *The Colonial Harem.* Trans. Myrna Godzich and Wlad Godzich. Minneapolis: University of Minnesota Press.

Alves-Masters, J. (1979). *Changing Self-Esteem of Women Through Middle Eastern Dance.* Michigan: UMI Press.
Amin, A., and N. Thrift. (2002). *Cities: Reimaging the Urban.* United Kingdom: Polity Press.
And, M. (1959). "Dances of Anatolian Turkey." *Dance Perspectives* 3 (Summer).
_____. (1976). *Pictorial History of Turkish Dancing.* Ankara: Dost Yayinlari.
Appadurai, A. (1996). *Modernity at Large: Cultural Dimensions of Globalization.* Minneapolis: University of Minnesota Press.
Berger, M. (1970). "Curious and Wonderful Gymnastic." *Dance Perspectives* (New York, 1961): 4–43. (reprinted by Johnson Reprint Corp., 1970).
_____. (1996). "Belly Dance." *Horizons* 8/2; 41–49.
Bhabha, H. (2004). *Location of Culture.* New York: Routledge Press.
Bordo, S. (1993). *Unbearable Weight: Feminism, Western Culture and the Body.* Berkeley: University of California Press.
Bourdieu, P. (1984). *Distinction: A Social Critique of the Judgment of Taste.* Cambridge: MA: Harvard University Press.
Buonaventura, W. (1998). *Serpent of the Nile: Women and Dance in the Arab World.* New York: Interlink.
Cixous, H. (1981). *The Art of Innocence.* Paris: Editions des Femmes.
Clifford, J. (1997). *Routes: Travel and Translation in the Late Twentieth Century.* Cambridge, MA: Harvard University Press.
Collingham, E.M. (2001). *Imperial Bodies.* Cambridge, MA: Polity Press.
Decoret-Ahiha, A. (2004). *Les Dances Exotiques en France.* Paris: Centre National de la Danse, 2004.
Desmond, J. (1991). "Dancing out the Difference: Cultural Imperialism and Ruth St. Denis Radha of 1906." *Signs: Journal of Women in Culture and Society* 17/1 (Autumn): 28–49.
Dox, D. (2007). "Dancing Around Orientalism." *TDR* 10/1 (2007); 1–50.
Edwards, H., Ed. (2000). *Noble Dreams and Wicked Pleasures: Orientalism in America 1870–1930.* New Jersey: Princeton University Press.
Flaubert, G. (1961). *Three Tales.* [1877]. Robert Baldick, trans. Baltimore, MD: Penguin.
_____. (1972). *Flaubert in Egypt: A Sensibility on Tour.* Ed. Francis Steegmuller. London: The Bodley Head.
Friedan, B. (1976). *It Changes My Life: Writings on the Women Movement.* New York: Random House.
Gioseffi, D. (1980). *Earth Dancing: Mother Nature Oldest Rite.* Harrisburg, PA: Stackpole Books.
Graham-Brown, S. (1988). *Images of Women: The Portrayal of Women in Photography of the Middle East, 1860–1950.* New York: Columbia University Press.
Greer, G. (1971). *The Female Eunuch.* New York: Bantam Books.
_____. (2000). *The Whole Woman.* New York: Anchor, 2000.
Grosz, E. (1994). *Volatile Bodies: It Toward a Corporeal Feminism.* Indiana: Indiana University Press.
Hamera, J. (2007). *Dancing Communities: Performance, Difference and Connection in the Global City.* New York: Palgrave.
Hobsbawm, E., and T. Ranger. (2012). *The Invention of Tradition.* Cambridge, MA: Cambridge University Press.
Jarmakani, A. (2008). *Imaging Arab Womanhood.* New York: Palgrave Macmillan.
Jullian, P. (1977). *Orientalists: European Painters of Eastern Scenes.* Oxford: Phaidon.
Kabbani, R. (1986). *Europe Myths of Orient: Devise and Rule.* Hampshire, UK: MacMillan.

Keft-Kennedy, V. (2005). "How Does She Do That? Belly Dancing And the Horror of the Flexible Woman." *Women's Studies* 34/3–4 (April/June): 279–300.

Laukkanen, A. "Stranger Fetishism and Cultural Responsibility in Transnational Dance Forms. Case Oriental Dance in Finland." Gender and Power in the New Europe, the 5th European Feminist Research Conference, August 20–24, 2003, Lund University, Sweden.

Lewis, R. (2004). *Rethinking Orientalism: Women, Travel, and the Ottoman Harem.* New Jersey: Rutgers University Press.

Lorde, A. (1982). "The Uses of the Erotic: The Erotic as Power." *Zami, Sister Outsider and Undersong.* New York: Quality Paperback.

MacKenzie, J.M. (1995). *Orientalism: History, Theory and the arts.* Manchester: Manchester University Press.

McDonald, C. (2012). *Global Moves: Belly Dance as an Extra/Ordinary Space to Explore Social Paradigms in Egypt and Around the World.* LeanPub.

Morgan, R. (1984). *The Anatomy of Freedom.* New York: Doubleday.

Noland, C., and S.A. Ness. (2008). *Migrations of Gestures.* Minneapolis: University of Minnesota Press, 2008.

O'Shea, J. (2007). *At Home in the World.* Connecticut: Wesleyan Press, 2007.

Potuoğlu-Cook, Ö. (2006). "Beyond the Glitter: Belly Dance and the Neoliberal Gentrification of Istanbul." *Cultural Anthropology* 21/4; 633–660.

Said, E.W. (1978). *Orientalism.* New York: Pantheon Books.

Salem, L.A. (1995). "One of the Most Indecent Thing Imaginable: Sexuality, Race and the Image of Arabs in American Entertainment 1850–1999." Ph.D. Dissertation, Temple University.

_____. (1999). "Far-Off and Fascinating Things: Wadeeha Atiyeh and Images of Arabs in the American Popular Theatre, 1930–50." *Arabs in America: Building a New Future.* Ed. Michael Suleiman. Philadelphia: Temple University Press, 272–283.

Savigliano, M.E. (1995). *Tango and the Political Economy of Passion.* Boulder: Westview Press.

Schechner, R. (1985). *Between Theatre and Anthropoloy.* Philadelphia: University of Pennsylania Press.

Shay, A. (1995). "Dance and Non-Dance: Patterned Movement in Iran and Islam." *Journal of Iranian Studies* 28, 1–2 (Winter/Spring): 61–78.

_____. (1997). "In Search of Traces: Linkages of Dance and Performative Expression in the Iranian World." *Visual Anthropology* 10 (Fall): 335–360.

_____. (1999). *Choreophobia: Solo Improvised Dance in the Iranian World.* California: Mazda Publishers.

_____. (2002). *Choreographing Politics.* Connecticut: Wesleyan Press.

Stewart, I. (2000). *Sacred Women, Sacred Dance.* California: Inner Traditions.

Taussig, M. (1992). *Mimesis and Alterity: A Particular History of the Senses.* New York: Routledge.

Turner, V. (1982). *From Ritual to Theatre: The Human Seriousness of Play.* New York: Performing Arts Journal Press.

Wood, L., and A. Shay. (1976). "Danse du Ventre: A Fresh Appraisal." *Dance Research Journal* 8/2 (Spring/Summer): 18–30.

Zuhur, S. (1998). *Images of Enchantment: Visual and Performing Arts in the Middle East.* Cairo: American University Press.

_____. (2001). *Colors of Enchantment: Theatre, Dance, Music, and the Visual Arts of the Middle East.* Cairo: American Universtiy Press.

What Is *Baladi* about *al-Raqs al-Baladi*?
On the Survival of Belly Dance in Egypt

NOHA ROUSHDY

Prelude

It is Friday night. I accompany a group of friends to a recently opened night spot in downtown Cairo. I recognize the place. I had been there a few years back when it was still an old restaurant and bar. Now, it is completely transformed; obviously, new owners, new style. The Arabic name[1] of the place could not have prepared me for what I was about to see. As a number of restaurants opening up in the capital since the turn of the millennium, the interior design of the place spelled out neo–Oriental. A rustic wooden bar, arabesque wooden partitions, Arabic lanterns and huge chandeliers made of Egypt's traditional beer bottles give the place the aura of an old shabby bar. Black and white posters of famous belly dancers ornament the walls. The music, as expected, is the usual mix of hit tunes from the European and American music charts. A TV screen hanging on the wall shows a film on the life of Michael Jackson. Fancy-looking young men and women fill the place. The tables are covered with Oriental mezze; smoke fills the space and beer bottles are in everyone's hands. Everyone is dancing.

At midnight, the waiters collect stools and place them amidst the guests' tables. A large wooden board is balanced on the stools. Minutes later, a belly dancer enters the place. The DJ switches the music to the recently popular *sha'bi* song, *El-Dunya Zay el-Morgiha*.[2] Aided by the waiters, she takes her stand on top of the board and starts dancing surrounded by a crowd of guests.

El-dunia zayy el-murgiha yom taht we fo'
Fi khal' 'aysha we mertaha we nas mesh fo'
Wana mashi batmargah fiha men taht le fo'[3]

Besides the fact that the dancer is facing Michael Jackson throughout her performance, underneath the make-believe stage is a crowd of middle and upper class young men and women. Not only are they not seated in their chairs watching the performance from afar as is the customary attitude during a professional performance, they are instead engaged in their own fervent performances to the song. No one is throwing money at the dancer.[4] Besides the people who are seated around the spot where the dance board was placed, none of the other guests move closer to see the performance. Before the song has ended, only a dozen eyes are still gazing at the dancer. Everyone is dancing and singing along. Twenty minutes later, the dancer steps from the stage and leaves the place. The DJ tries to switch back to American music, but every once in a while a guest approaches him to ask that a favored Arabic song be played. Hours pass by and the crowd gets more hyped up as older and more *baladi* songs infiltrate their ears and move their bodies. By 2 A.M., it appears that it is only the playing of Western music that would stop the dancing and urge the guests to leave.

Baladi as Shared Sensibility

Volumes have been written about the contentious situation of belly dance in its native land. In his obituary of legendary Egyptian dancer and actress, Tahia Carioca, Edward Said (1999) wrote, "What she did was obviously performed inside an Arab and Islamic setting but was also quite at odds, even in a constant sort of tension with it" (160). This tension that Said, and most observers of *al-raqs al-baladi* in the Middle East, rightfully identify relates to the incongruity of the stylization of the female body in *al-raqs al-baladi* with societal emphasis on the value of *haya'* (commonly translated as sexual modesty) which is expected of women in their everyday comportment in public. In effect, while there is recognition of the artistic skills and cultural worth of figures the likes of Tahia Carioca or Samia Gamal, there is also widespread, and at times even official, stigmatization of professional female dancers as depraved women akin to sex workers and their subsequent moral marginalization in Egyptian society.

The contentious situation of professional female dancers in Middle Eastern societies has certainly been the subject of the limited but growing body of literature on belly dance. In Karin Van Nieuwkerk's (1996) unique ethnography on professional belly dancers from Mohamed Ali Street in Cairo, the unfavorable public perception of female dancers is associated with the sexual objectification of women in Egyptian society. "Female performers," according to Van Nieuwkerk (1998), "differ from 'decent' women because they use their bodies to make a living, instead of hiding them as much as possible" (34). However, this sexual underpinning of what Anthony Shay (1999) termed "choreophobia" to explicate the "negative and ambiguous reactions towards this dance tradition" (10) in the Middle East in general has its analytical limitations.

Not only does it disregard the incidentally remarkable survival of this dance culture in Egypt as a dynamic cultural form that can be observed in numerous public and private settings, it also fails to take into account its organic relationship to social and cultural transformations that these societies have experienced throughout the twentieth century. In his important critique of the modern Western conception of art, Clifford Geertz (1976) wrote:

> [T]he definition of art in any society is never wholly intra-aesthetic, and indeed but rarely more than marginally so. The chief problem presented by the sheer phenomenon of aesthetic force, in whatever form and in result of whatever skill it may come, is how to place it within the other modes of social activity, how to incorporate it into the texture of a particular pattern of life. And such placing, the giving to art objects a cultural significance, is always a local matter; what art is in classical China or classical Islam, what it is in the Pueblo southwest or highland New Guinea, is just not the same thing, no matter how universal the intrinsic qualities that actualize its emotional power (and I have no desire to deny them) may be [1475–76].

Instead, to understand the "aesthetic force" of objects, movements or sounds, Geertz maintained, is to "explore a sensibility, that such a sensibility is essentially a collective formation, and that the foundations of such a formation are as wide as social existence and as deep" (1478).

In this essay, I build on Clifford Geertz's understanding of aesthetic forms to attempt an explanation for the endurance of belly dance as a popular leisure activity among Egyptians. Going beyond the body of literature that addresses itself explicitly to the stigmatization and marginalization of professional performers in Egypt, I follow Geertz's approach in focusing on this shared sensibility that sustains the role of belly dance, as an aesthetic form that is Egyptian in identity, against the flow of global values and practices from the East and West of Egypt. The category of analysis upon which my discussion is based is the very descriptive category that defines this dance culture among Egyptians; namely *baladi*. My analysis is based on conversations I shared with 10 middle-class Egyptian professionals, both males and females, on the notion of *baladi* and its possible relation to the practice of *baladi* dance. Throughout this essay, I will be arguing for a consideration of *al-raqs al-baladi* as an embodied cultural form that materializes a particular experience of personhood for Egyptians in the twenty-first century.

Globalization and the "Artification" of Baladi

In defense of the widespread deprecation of professional *raqs baladi* in Egyptian society, many supportive public voices of the dance try to instate the local dance as an art form that relies on aesthetic principles and proper training. Part of the efforts to instate such an understanding are expressed in the terminology and codifications of *al-raqs al-baladi*[5] and in the attempts made by professional dancers to institutionalize the training of dancers in Egypt. Such concerns come in parallel to the growing presence of Western women in the dance scene of Egypt and the gradual disappearance of star Egyptian dancers as popular performers in wedding celebrations or in the media. Not only has it become growingly common for restaurants and night-

Musicians at Al-Fishawi Cafe, Khan el Khalili, Cairo (photograph by Caitlin E. McDonald).

clubs in five-star hotels to present professional performances by foreign women, but more recently specialized satellite channels have offered the Egyptian household around the clock *baladi* dance performed exclusively by non–Egyptians.

During the time I was conducting fieldwork research in 2009–2010 with the aim of understanding the culture of *al-raqs al-baladi* in Egypt I was overwhelmed by the parallel world, which the network of foreign dancers occupy in Cairo. From the Egyptian dance festivals, to the belly dance trips and finally to workshops and private lessons that cater primarily to non–Egyptian professional and amateur dancers. On the one hand, the registration fees for the festivals or for the private classes exclude the majority of aspiring Egyptian dancers from participation. On the other hand, and though amateur dancers are often the customers of these services, the dance culture of Egypt would largely conceive of these activities as not befitting women who are not planning on becoming professional dancers. Even though belly dance classes are becoming widespread in fitness centers in Cairo, they are presented as an alternative aerobic workout for Egyptian women and as an enjoyable way to lose weight.

As part of my ethnographic research, I participated in these activities and interviewed a number of these women, who proclaimed, in dismay, that Egyptians do not appreciate this dance. As a participant in these classes my experience, however, bore little resemblance to the familiar experience of dancing with friends or even on my own. When I asked one of the instructors why no Egyptians attended her classes, she complained to me that Egyptian participants usually attend her classes to have fun, thinking there is nothing for them to learn about *al-raqs al-baladi*. I tried to hold fast to her remarks as I followed her classes, though receiving formal instruction about the way to move my body in reaction to familiar Arabic music continued to impose an alienating experience on me. I enjoyed my practice, but something about it did not *feel* right to me. Still, I was impressed by the choreography and the ability of European women to master the physically challenging techniques of *al-raqs al-baladi*— an observation I shared with other Egyptians involved in the organization of such workshops. Indeed, many of the musicians expressed their frustration that *al-raqs al-baladi* was appreciated by foreigners, while it was attacked in Egypt. But is it true that Egyptians do not appreciate this dance?

Al-raqs al-baladi is an extremely popular leisure activity among Egyptians. In spite of its representation as a performance that entails an overt display of feminine sexuality, this never hindered its transmission and practice within Egyptian homes and in intimate contexts. For most of the 20th century — and until today — the wedding procession of the bride (known as the *zaffa*)[6] among the urban middle and upper classes was led by a professional *baladi* dancer and most wedding celebrations entailed a professional *baladi* dance performance. *Baladi* dance is also progressively growing as a public leisure activity in Cairo. There is no need any more to hire a professional dancer is a repeated sarcastic comment made by the older generations among Cairo's middle classes to criticize the growing practice of *baladi* dance in wedding parties by the bride, groom and their guests.[7] In effect, as described in the scene at the beginning of this essay, the public dancing of amateurs appears to be slowly undermining the need for professional performances. According to one professional dancer from Mansoura, the growing tendency among Egyptian families since the 1990s to hire DJs instead of live musical bands for their wedding parties is a reason for the slow marginalization of professional dancers from the center of entertainment in Egypt. In the following pages, I examine the relation between the notion of *baladi* and Egyptian belly dance with the aim of unraveling the "aesthetic force" that has allowed the dance to persist in Egyptian society despite its resistance from both conservative and modernist forces.

The Meaning of Baladi

The word *baladi* is an Arabic word that stems from the word *balad*, meaning country or land. As an Arabic word, it merely means "my land" or "my country," but as an Egyptian word, it means more: *Baladi*, as often used in speech in Egypt, is an adjective, a descriptive category of an array of goods, practices or even ideals. A person can be described as *baladi*, so can bread, a piece of furniture, or an item of clothing. A way of speech could be labeled *baladi*, a hairstyle or even a gesture. The word *baladi* as used among Egyptians has been associated with the term *awlad al-baladi* (literally sons of the land), which according to Sawsan El-Messiri's work (1978), *Ibn al-Balad: A Concept of Egyptian Identity*, is a fluid social categorization of the urban working classes in Egypt that pertains to an early nineteenth century administrative category of the native residents of Cairo (12).

Throughout the 20th century, the designation *awalad al-balad* and its *baladi* derivative has acquired a socio-economic, cultural and subjective signification that distinguishes between who and what is perceived as essentially Egyptian and what has been affected, shaped or introduced through foreign, mainly Western, cultural influences.[8] The multiple connotations to the word *baladi* as used by different people in different contexts leaves little space to determine with accuracy whether the designation implies a positive or a negative quality. In one sense, the concept of *baladi* denotes that which is not modernized, developed or refined. In another sense, it implies that which is authentic, pure and unadulterated.

Among the different dances that are practiced in Egypt,[9] only one form is classified as *baladi*. Though formally referred to as *al-raqs al-sharqi* (Oriental Dance), yet reference to this dance throughout the 20th century and until today has retained its *baladi* attribute. As opposed to the region-specific or ethnic dances performed throughout the country, *baladi* dance is not the prerogative of any particular social or ethnic group in Egypt. *Baladi* also refers to both the professional performance and non-professional social practice of Egyptian belly dance. As performed by urban Egyptians, *al-raqs al-baladi* is, however, visibly distinguishable from the version of belly dance performed in rural areas,[10] and it is the former to which this discussion is dedicated.

As I previously mentioned, the word *baladi* has multiple connotations in its various usages among Egyptians. It could be used in a neutral sense to distinguish between local and foreign goods, as in the case of *baladi* bread for instance. Yet generally, to describe something or someone as *baladi* commonly carries a derogatory tone. It implies lack of sophistication, lack of decorum or simply bad taste. At the same time, to refer to someone as *ibn balad* or (the feminine) *bint balad* is to praise a demonstration of venerated local values such as valor (*gad'ana*), generosity and a sense of justice and belonging to community. It also expresses an appreciation for spontaneity and sincerity. As employed in common usage, anyone, irrespective of wealth, religion, or gender, can exhibit *baladi* qualities in a given context.[11] In effect, it is sometimes admirable among middle and upper class Egyptians to express *baladi* qualities, but one would not be perceived with admiration if one were to be or act *baladi* all the time.

This paradoxical attitude towards what is perceived to be local[12] among Egyptians has its roots in Egypt's colonial experience. A significant body of literature has examined the impact of Orientalist representations over the course of the 19th and early 20th centuries on Egyptian intellectuals and the country's political elite (Mitchell 1988, Massad 2007). Most significantly, scholarship on gender and sexuality has addressed itself explicitly to the underlying sense of inferiority that buttressed the modernization projects of colonized societies (Chatterjee 1989, Masaad 2007, Ahmed 1992, Najmabadi 1998). Unfortunately, while the growing body of literature on belly dance has established the role that Orientalism played in shaping the performance of *al-raqs al-baladi* and the perception of which impacts its performance both at home and in the West (Sellers-Young and Shay 2003 and 2005, Karayanni 2005), such inferences have contained no discussions on the local practice of *al-raqs al-baladi* within the seemingly one-dimensional analytical category of "auto-exoticism" (Savigliano 1995, Shay and Sellers-Young 2003).

In literature on belly dance, Karin Van Nieuwkerk (1995, 1998) introduced the notion of *awlad al-balad* in her discussion of strategies adopted by professional dancers from Mohamed Ali Street to offset their representation as fallen women. Relying on El-Messiri's characterization of *bint al-balad* as well as her interlocutors' self-representation, Van Nieuwkerk limited her analysis of the relationship between the culture of *awlad al-balad* and the dance tradition's function in the lives of professional performers. In a different light, Cassandra Lorious (1996) has approached a more nuanced analysis of *baladi* culture in her examination of Fifi Abdou's performances.[13] For Lorious, however, *baladi* is "an 'imaginary' identity," (289) "a class appellation" (289) that Fifi Abdou adopts in her performances "to play with the ambiguities inherent in different notions of *baladi*." (290). As a "key concept" (289), however, Lorius's characterization — though comprehensive — fails to infer relations between that particular performance of Fifi Abdou, which she described in her article, and the larger cultural field, in which the dance is practiced. In effect, much like Van Nieuwkerk's, her analysis represents *baladi* as a compact and distinct concept (289) that perhaps adds an explicit and particular style to the performance, but not one that defines the very contours of the dance in this cultural sphere.

Lorius wrote:

> Like *sharqi*,[14] the term [*baladi*] has resonances of an assertion of ethnicity in the face of foreign domination. The meanings ascribed to *baladi* are largely context-specific. They invoke multiple references, implying values such as authenticity, ethnicity, nationalism, class affiliation, and codes of lifestyle, gender roles and sexual behaviour. According to Early, it is usually contrasted with the notion of *afrangi*, a pejorative term for modernity when used by the *baladi*. She notes that *baladi* self-ascriptions refer to authenticity, honour, pride and hospitality as against the privileged *afrangi* lifestyle that the *baladi* describe as amoral, superficial, insincere and inhospitable by contrast. This culture is stereotyped in popular culture as earthy and the women are characterized as sexually uninhibited [289–90].

Accordingly, the significance of Egypt's colonial experience with respect to the local dance that I wish to focus on in this article is its construction of the category *baladi* as an integral constituent of the Egyptian identity, as an alter ego against which the 20th-century Egyptian developed his/her modern identity.[15] Note that the word *afrangi*, used in Lorius's description as the opposite of *baladi*, means Western or literally Frankish. There is no other standing category for Egyptian in this schema than *baladi*. To illustrate my argument I invoke the responses of my interlocutors when asked to describe the notion of *baladi* and its relation to the dance.

On Being Baladi

For Omneya, a 32-year-old graphic designer, *baladi* essentially means *sha'bi* (i.e., pertaining to the urban working classes) and typically refers to something that is deeply-rooted in Egyptian culture.[16] Omneya was hesitant to explicate her understanding of *baladi* because she does not like to use the word for its classist usage among Egyptians. Yet, upon my insistence, she drew out a picture of the *baladi* woman:

> Her interactions with other people are not reserved; she is more open and unconstrained in her social behavior. She is more daring and impulsive as compared to a woman who is not *baladi*. She would, for instance, not be selective about her choice of words, and probably uses her hands frequently in conversations. A woman who is not *baladi* ... is more reserved and adopts different ways of dealing with people in different contexts [2012].

Omenya considers herself a mélange between *baladi* and modern—because she grew up in a lower middle class or *sha'bi* neighborhood—and because of her middle-class upbringing and education. As a great fan of *baladi* dance, Omneya thinks that *al-raqs al-baladi* is intimately connected to this model because it also relies on this unrefined or natural way of self-expression. According to Omneya, *al-raqs al-baladi* comes naturally to Egyptian women; it does not depend on instruction like *baladi* behavior. She adds that *al-raqs al-baladi* is not bashful; it is "an exposition of femininity" (2012). Like a *baladi* woman, who Omneya perceives as bold and unafraid of her femininity, she enjoys imagining an observer's gaze while she dances even when her eyes are closed or when she dances in the privacy of her home before a mirror. "I refuse to see anything obscene about that," she stated (2012). Antonius, a 35-year-old Egyptian writer and actor, defined his perception of *baladi* as that which is more instinctive and intuitive. As opposed to a modernized Egyptian man, the prototype of a *baladi* man as perceived by Antonius is uneducated or uncultured and is thereby incapable of expressing himself in a sophisticated manner. "Lack of sophistication is a central feature of a *baladi* person," he maintained (2012). Yet, commenting on such representations of *al-baladi*, Habib, a geographer and fervent opera fan, pointed out that this lack of sophistication has more to do with a very particular mode of expression typical of *baladi* culture than it does with lack of expressive capacity. Like Omneya, he relied on the generalized representation of a *baladi* woman to elucidate his opinion. As opposed to a Western woman, Habib thinks of the *baladi* woman as one who is always giving contradictory messages to a man she desires. "This is her appeal. She acts available to a man and then excuses herself, for instance because she needs to take care of something. She never says she is not interested, but is effectively never available" (2012).

Indeed, Hind, who is an aspiring singer, associates this stereotypical representation of a *baladi* woman to another commonly held assumption that, as opposed to a modernized Egyptian woman, the *baladi* woman is fearless and hard to fool.

> For instance, if I curse a man who [sexually] harasses me or flirts with me on the street, I am perceived as *baladi*. Likewise, it is commonly held to be true that a real *baladi* woman could never be fooled by a man. Even if she goes out with one or falls in love, she will not allow him to touch her before they are formally committed [2012].

The merger between the absence of boundaries, fearlessness and simplicity is best captured in Hoda's account. A 28-year-old psychologist and trained performer of modern dance, she described her relation to *al-raqs al-baladi* as follows:

> I feel that both this modern and this *baladi* woman are inside me ... but when I *baladi* dance, I lean heavier on my *baladi* side. I don't place boundaries between myself and others; I interact with other dancers more freely... Everything is less complicated, fluid ... just as we say "*bel baladi*"[17] [2012].

Rafik provided me with a different illustration of *baladi* modes of expression. As part of his work in an NGO, he was once in a meeting with a group of young men in one of Cairo's working-class neighborhoods.

> I lit a cigarette and everyone in this meeting was also smoking. Suddenly, one of them told me, "your smoke has blinded us." I didn't get it. He repeated this phrase a couple of times and every time I got more confused because smoke was being exhaled from everyone present. Eventually, one of them leaned over and told me that what was meant by that expression was that the person wanted him to offer them his brand of cigarettes.... I think this is typical *baladi*. To me, it is really about a mode of communication that it is not explicit.... I think this is why I don't get *al-raqs al-baladi*. It is primarily communicative ... and I don't have very good *baladi* communication skills [2012].

This relation that Rafik establishes between the notion of *baladi* and *al-raqs al-baladi* has been confirmed by my interlocutors through their different perceptions of the dance, whether as dancers or observers.

Nadia, a journalist, who is also passionate about *baladi* dance, thinks *al-raqs al-baladi* embodies the fluidity, metaphor and simplicity that represent Egyptian culture:

> I feel that when I dance I perform this vagueness typical of *baladi* way of speech. For instance, I am usually conscious that my movements accentuate my figure and expose my femininity, and I enjoy that, but when I perform, I always try to hide, or play around this eroticism. For example, girls in Egypt always pretend that they don't want to or can't dance even if they are dying to dance and think themselves excellent dancers. Sometimes I see a girl dance very well and is very involved in the dance and then suddenly she will stop, give an embarrassed face and act like she can't continue or that she can't dance. I know she is pretending but this is very typical. We are always alternating between taking the dance and its significations seriously and then taking it lightly and joking about it. I think this is very Egyptian [2012].

These descriptions offered by my interlocutors of *al-baladi* and its relation to *al-raqs al-baladi* suggest that *al-raqs al-baladi* for this group of Egyptians reflects what Arjun Appadurai (1996) termed "hard cultural forms" (90). As an embodied practice that Egyptians learn in childhood, *al-raqs al-baladi* is perceived to be intimately connected to a set of values and meanings preconfigured under this imagined sphere of *al-baladi*. As an aesthetic form, it invokes a sensibility pertaining to values deemed essential to an authentic Egyptian character, unaffected by modern values, practices and modes of behavior.

Take, for example, this exchange of opinions between Habib and Antonius with regards to *al-raqs al-baladi* as art:

> Antonius: I feel it is art because there is something very moving and aesthetically enchanting about *al-raqs al-baladi*. I think it is non-art because there is no tableau in it; no drama, no storyline, no message [2012].
>
> Habib: I think this understanding of art is problematic and not that *al-raqs al-baladi* is not art. You just said that a *baladi* attitude is instinctive and that *baladi* people are typically uneducated, or if educated, still retain uneducated, perhaps crude, ways of expressing themselves. Yet, your understanding of art presumes that art is a purposeful act. Of course, a popular leisure activity that any woman can perform like a professional without receiving any education like *al-raqs al-baladi* cannot fit in this limited conception of what art is. We have seen such attempts made by Samia Gamal and Farid al-Atrash, for instance, when they tried to present *al-raqs al-baladi* as part of an operetta. They had the theatrical stage, the narrative, and the music composed by a leading Arab musician, but it stopped being *baladi*. Who can mimic that at home! [2012].

Not surprisingly, when asked about their opinion of the performance of *al-raqs al-baladi* by foreign women, all of my interlocutors found them to be lacking. Since for most of them unpretentiousness and simplicity characterized *baladi* behavioral patterns, what they found to be imperfect about non–Egyptian belly dancers was that their performances exposed their training. When I asked Omneya, for instance, why she does not like foreign belly dancers, she answered: "Because they have *learned* the dance; they did not drink it. How can they carry this spirit of *baladi*" (2012). Amin, a 26-year-old engineer, likewise, thought the reason why foreign dancers don't appeal to him was that they "have not grown up with *al-raqs al-baladi*" (2012).

At the same time, none of my interlocutors identified themselves as *baladi*. In effect, most of them explicitly presented themselves as not *baladi*. Their descriptions of *baladi* women or men were also typically invoked by characters from Egyptian cinema, or by common representations of this culture, whether through sayings or images that they and I are familiar with. In effect, none of them used their own individual attitudes or behaviors to illustrate the notion of *baladi*. Though a number of them recounted contexts or incidences where they demonstrate *baladi* behavior, yet throughout their largely positive description of some *baladi* qualities (that was obvious in their sparkling eyes as they spoke) the negative connotation of *baladi* was hardly challenged. As Nadia remarked, "I think we are always pointing out when someone says something or behaves *baladi*. It is easier to say this is very *baladi*, even about a certain gesture, facial expression or body movement in *baladi* dance. It is much harder for me to think of instances where we point out the opposite. I don't think we do, we just know it is the opposite of *baladi* because it is not *baladi*" (2012).

Yet, reflecting on the ease with which the young generations among middle and upper class Egyptians perform *al-raqs al-baladi*, Shahira, a 28-year-old human rights activist, noted:

> I think there is a trend among Egyptians today that is more appreciative of practices that were typically regarded as *baladi* among my parents' generation. Not only are we now more familiar and enthusiastic about *sha'bi* music but we also hold *henna* parties,[18] smoke *shisha* (waterpipe) and dance *baladi* much more often. All of these practices our parents used to find repulsive when we were younger [2012].

In addition, and as opposed to the static representation common in Western scholarship, none of my interlocutors mentioned that they practiced the dance in familial settings, and when they did they deemed it an unfavorable context for *al-raqs al-baladi*. Instead, they expressed preference for dancing with friends and in public settings, such as parties or dance clubs, where everyone present would also be dancing. Such observations and the account of the nightclub provided previously, reflect a fundamental social transformation enjoyed by both my female and male interlocutors that pertains primarily to the permissibility of gender mixing and the strong presence of women in urban public spaces, such as nightclubs. This should not imply, however, that these transformations have only affected Egyptian society at the turn of the 21st century. Yet, as indicated in Shahira's comment, a liberal lifestyle in the 1960s or '70s explicitly sought to emulate Western mores that it deemed compatible with local values and customs. During that time, it was most common for the middle and upper classes to perform dances popular in the West in public. In addition to the professional *baladi* dance performance, entertainment at wedding celebrations and nightclubs typically have included a live band that played popular Western music, to which people could dance. It did not consider values and embodied practices that manifested *baladi* culture (or, in other words, expressed the culture of the working classes), as the ones referred to above, as compatible to its conception of a modern identity.

Conversely, and in spite of their stronger exposure and access to global cultural flows, from taste in clothing to modes of political participation, contemporary Egyptians in urban centers attest to feeling more comfortable around aspects of Egyptian culture that were deemed un-modern or backwards in mid-century. This observation is not only exclusive to Egyptians deemed liberal, but equally so with regards to the same class of Egyptians who profess to be more conservative or religious in their outlook and lifestyle.[19] Thus, unlike references to *baladi* made by Karin Van Nieuwkerk (1998) or Cassandra Lorius (1998), my interlocutors' conception of *baladi* culture was intimately associated with the configuration of the dance in the social imaginaire as part and parcel of an essentially Egyptian lifestyle and habitus that is resistant to modern values and practices. Accordingly, neither a *baladi* attitude nor the skills needed to perform the dance can be acquired. "You either can dance *baladi*, or you can't" (2012), Hind tells me.

Conclusion

In his quest to understand the stigmatization of professional dancers in Egyptian society, William Young (1998) has argued that the shift to commodity production and the ensuing commercialization of cultural practices and goods is the reason for the negative perception of professional dancers as depraved women in Egypt. Drawing from Young's hypothesis, I have shown through this essay how the very same economic process which, according to him, undergirded the stigmatization of professional performers, is currently challenging the de facto stigmatization of *al-raqs al-baladi* among categories of Egyptians that are commonly represented as Westernized or modern. From fitness centers, to private female beaches on coastal resorts, fancy nightclubs and wedding parties in five-star hotels, we see how in Egypt, such venues, essentially modeled to transport cosmopolitan culture and practices to the country's middle and upper classes, and keep them up-to-date, currently provides space for younger generations to negotiate their identity in global culture.

I have tried to argue that the practice of *al-raqs al-baladi* in Egypt materializes what Egyptian deem to be essentially embodied cultural values and practices that are sustained by the fluid ideal of *baladi*. Yet, not unlike the evolution of its professional practice from a street performance in the 19th century to a staged performance in cabarets in the early 20th century or in theatre halls in the '60s and '70s, the contemporary practice of *al-raqs al-baladi* continues to express local ideals (considered negative or positive) through the web of interlacing and seemingly inconsistent local and global cultural flows. As an array of *baladi* practices and ideals, it continues to offer Egyptians a betwixt and between experience of their subjectivity; betwixt and between the boundaries of what is local and what is global, what is fixed and what is changing.

As an experience during which boundaries of profession, class, religion, degree of religiosity or gender are dissolved, it primarily materializes collectivity. Likewise, through its associations with occasions of festivity — it materializes a shared aesthetic appreciation for *a socially mediated* expression of what is *baladi,* perhaps unrefined, uncivil or immodest, but also pleasurable, natural and unique.

Notes

1. Few Egyptian nightclubs, restaurants or even stores carry Arabic names, most especially those that cater to upper classes.
2. The song became popular in discotheques and dance clubs in Cairo in 2010. *Sha'bi* music typically reflects the musical taste and lyrics popular among the working classes in Egypt. It mostly speaks of the life of young working class men.
3. Rough translation of lyrics:

>Life is like a swing; one day down and one day up
>Some are living and having it easy and others are not up there
>Ana I am swinging with it from down to up

4. The practice is commonly referred to as *tan'it.* *Nuqta* or *nu'ta* in Egyptian dialect is also used to refer to a practice that takes place during wedding celebrations, which is a form of gift giving (of cash money) by the donor to the families of bride and groom. *Tan'it* is not particular to professional dancers and the tradition is fairly established in the wedding celebrations of the working classes.
5. Classifications such as *sharqi, baladi* and *sha'bi,* common among Western dancers I encountered during my fieldwork are, however, completely unknown to the Egyptian public. Egyptians typically do not recognize different genres of *baladi* dance, just as they do with popular Egyptian and Arabic music. Though recognition of different styles exists, these are relegated to the individual renditions of different dancers and the context within which the dance is performed.
6. Though *al-zaffa* is still a main feature of Egyptian weddings, it is more often led now by a troupe of male musicians and female dancers, similar to folkloric art troupes known as *zaffa dumiati.*
7. Note that it is traditionally frowned upon that the bride dances on her wedding night.
8. It now also pertains to a distinction between rural and urban goods, the former perceived to be more authentic. In effect, among the younger generations in Egypt *awlad al-balad* are thought to be rural Egyptians as opposed to the urban working classes as was the case for most of the 20th century.
9. Magda Saleh (1979) documented twenty distinct dance forms performed in Egypt at the time of her research. These included dances that are performed by men, dances performed by women and dances in which both men and women participate.
10. Urban belly dance in Egypt is visibly influenced by the so-called cabaret style that all Egyptians are exposed to through its depiction in the media. In effect, rural belly dance is more likely to be referred to as "*raqs al-fallahin*" (the dance of the peasants).
11. Even though the classification *baladi* is nominally the prerogative of the lower-middle and working classes of society, its subjective usage by different groups in society renders it a relative classification. It is, however, an attribute of non–Westernized practices and

can, accordingly, be used to describe upper-class Egyptians whose lifestyle is not adequately Westernized.

12. I would like to point out that even the word local in English but pronounced with an Egyptian accent is growingly common among all segments of Egyptian society to signify more or less the same attitude towards *baladi*.

13. Lorius (1996) posited that *baladi* culture is associated with rural migration to slum areas in urban centers. Her statement in that regard contradicts the findings of Sawsan al-Messiri's study. On the other hand, it confuses a standard distinction common among Egyptians between *'ashaw'iyyat* (slum areas) and *manati' sha'biyya*, where the latter are considered the locus of *awlad al-balad*. Al-Manati' al-Sha'biyya (or popular quarters) are old established urban neighborhoods that were formally inhabited by the working-classes *and* the class of artisans and tradesmen who businesses still dominate these areas, such as al-Hussein, al-Sayyeda Zeinab or al-Hilmiyya.

14. Though this author equals *baladi* with *sharqi,* it is important to note that in Egypt *baladi* refers to something Egyptian whereas *sharqi* refers to goods, practices and ideals of the Maghreb passing through the Levant and reaching Iran. *Sharqi* food is most typically Levantine or non–Egyptian Oriental food.

15. For more on the discursive formation of *al-raqs al-baladi* in Egypt see Noha Roushdy (2010), "Baladi as Performance: Gender and Dance in Modern Egypt" in *Surfacing: An Interdisciplinary Journal for Gender in the Global South* 3(1): 71–99.

16. Note that Omneya's conflation of the terms *baladi* and *sha'bi* problematizes the various usages of these words by the international community of belly dancers.

17. This expression that Hoda mentions is typically used among Egyptians when they wish to say something that they prefer to express in simple and unsophisticated words.

18. Henna party is the equivalent of a bachelorette party common in the West. It is a traditional practice throughout Egypt that takes place the night before the wedding. Though the practice had dwindled throughout the 20th century among the urban middle classes, since the 1990s the practice has gained in popularity among all segments of Egyptian society. It usually takes place in the bride-to-be's home and is attended by female friends and relatives. Typically, a *hannana* (typically a Sudanese *henna* artist) attends the party accompanied by a female DJ. Arabic dance music is played all night long and dancing *baladi* is the central feature of this event. Lately, it is also customary that the party planners (typically the *hannana* or female DJ) provide the bride-to-be with different *baladi* customs that she changes according to the different music played. For example, the traditional (*baladi*) customs of women from Lower Egypt (*banat bahari*) would be worn to a performance that the bride-to-be is expected to give to music, for instance, that praises the beauty of girls from Alexandria. A *galabiya baladi* (traditional long and wide garb of *banat al-balad*) would be worn to the *sha'bi* music (like Ahmed 'Adawiya). The guests typically attend the event without the two-piece belly dance costume or any revealing or sexy clothing.

19. Note that widespread religious forms of clothing and modes of comportment that are not expressive of *sha'bi* culture or are not common among young women and men in urban working classes in Cairo are unlikely to be perceived as *baladi*.

Works Cited

Amin. (2012). Interview, February 4, Cairo, Egypt.
Antonius. (2012). Interview, January 28, Cairo, Egypt.
Appadurai, A. (1996). *Modernity at Large: Cultural Dimension of Globalization.* Minnesota: University of Minnesota Press.
Chatterjee, P. (1989). "Colonialism, Nationalism, and Colonized Women: The Contest in India." *American Ethnologist* Vol. 16, No. 4; 622–633.
El-Messiri, S. (1978). *Ibn al-Balad: A Concept of Egyptian Identity.* New York: Brill.

Geertz, C. (1976). "Art as Cultural System." *Comparative Literature* Vol. 91, No. 6; 1473–1499.
Habib. (2012). Interview, January 28, Cairo, Egypt.
Hind. (2012). Interview, January 27, Cairo, Egypt.
Hoda. (2012). Interview, February 2, Cairo, Egypt.
Karayanni, S.S. (2004). *Dancing Fear and Desire: Race, Sexuality and Imperial Politics in Middle Eastern Dance*. Ontario: Wilfred Laurier University Press.
Lorius, C. (1996). "'Oh Boy, You Sault of the Earth': Outwitting Patriarchy in Raqs Baladi." *Popular Music* Vol.15, No. 3 (Middle East Issue): 285–298.
Masaad, J.A. (2007). *Desiring Arabs*. Chicago: The University of Chicago Press.
Mitchell, T. (1988). *Colonizing Egypt*. California: University of California Press.
Nadia. (2012). Interview, February 4, Cairo, Egypt.
Najmabadi, A. (1998). "Crafting an Educated Housewife in Iran." *Remaking Women: Feminism and Modernity in the Middle East*. Ed. Lila Abu-Lughod. Cairo: American University Press, 91–125.
Omneya. (2012). Interview, January 26, Cairo, Egypt.
Rafik. (2012). Interview. February 9, Cairo, Egypt.
Saleh, M.A.A.G. (1979). "Documentation of the Ethnic Dance Traditions of the Arab Republic of Egypt." Ph.D. Dissertation, New York University.
Savigliano, M. (1995). *Tango and the Political Economy of Passion*. Connecticut: Westview Press.
Shahira. (2012). Interview. February 4, Cairo, Egypt.
Shay, A., and B. Sellers-Young. (2003). "Belly Dance: Orientalism: Exoticism: Self-Exoticism." *Dance Research Journal*, Vol. 35, No. 1; 13–37.
_____ and _____. (2005). "Introduction" *Belly dance: Orientalism, Transnationalism, and Harem Fantasy*. California: Mazda Publishers, 1–27.
Young, W. (1998). "Women's Performance in Ritual Context: Weddings Among the Rashayda of Sudan." *Images of Enchantment: Visual and Performing Arts of the Middle East*. Ed. Sherifa Zuhur. Cairo: American University Press, 36–56.

Finding "the Feeling"
Oriental Dance, Musiqa al-Gadid, *and* Tarab

CANDACE BORDELON

Art has the power to generate reverie, fascination, and contemplative study. Poetry, painting, music, and dance can move us to elation, depression, laughter, and oftentimes tears. Although reactions, experiences, and meanings made are uniquely felt by each individual and may differ somewhat between artistic mediums, art has the potential to lure us away from our everyday lives and into a world of transcendence and transformation.

Musiqa al-gadid, or "modern" classical Arabic music, is particularly known for its transformational qualities in both performer and listener. *Tarab,* commonly translated as ecstasy, transcendence, or enchantment, is described by ethnomusicologist Ali Jihad Racy (2003) as a merger between music and emotional transformation. While scholars have begun to apply the term across artistic mediums, for most Egyptians, *tarab* has an inseparable connection with music, specifically regarding the lyrics of songs, the improvised tradition of the *mutrib* or *mutriba* (*tarab* singer), and the great Egyptian singer Umm Kulthūm.[1]

Oriental dance, or belly dance,[2] as it is performed in nightclubs and at weddings throughout the Middle East and Arab diaspora, is highly connected with *musiqa al-gadid.* In Cairo nightclubs in the 1930s and 1940s, belly dance developed as an artistic and theatrical dance form alongside *musiqa al-gadid.* These clubs employed Oriental dancers like Samia Gamal and Tahia Carioca as well as singers, musicians, and composers such as Farid al-Atrash, Muhammed Abd al-Wahhab, and Umm Kulthūm — now considered some of the greatest *tarab* musical artists of the twentieth century. Today, Oriental dancers recognize this genre of music as a necessary component of the dance form. In my own classes with Egyptian teachers, many of them remarked that the most important aspect of the dance form is that the dancer understands the music, because her role is to interpret the emotions in the music through her body within the Oriental dance movement vocabulary. These dancers acknowledge the music as the *single most important factor* which links dance with emotion and audience connection.

With the understanding that Oriental dance is inseparable from the deep emotive content of *musiqa al-gadid*, it is not surprising that dancers themselves as well as audience members have been known to undergo intensive emotional transformations during Oriental dance performances. Many Egyptians have stated to me that what makes a good dancer is her ability to express "the Feeling." Tamra-henna, an American dancer who performed in Egypt, explained in an interview in June 2010, "She [the dancer] has to have that "feeling." That's what everybody says, that's the first thing they say" (2010). During an interview in Cairo, Egyptian dancer Randa Kamel said that when she performs, "I affect people only by my feeling ... we are talking together by feelings" (2010). These statements sparked my curiosity. Was the Feeling merely another way of describing *tarab*? Was this a consideration in the choices dancers made in the performance process? What new understandings about the *tarab* phenomenon might we gain by exploring Oriental dance? And what new understandings might we gain about Oriental dance by studying *tarab*?

To better understand the relationship between *musiqa al-gadid*, *tarab*, and Oriental dance as it is performed in its indigenous region as an artistic and theatrical dance form, in 2010 I interviewed eight professional Oriental dancers: North American dancers Shareen El Safy, Yasmina Ramzy, Hadia, and Tamra-henna, who all performed extensively in the Middle East, and Egyptian dancers Nagwa Fouad, Aida Nour, Randa Kamel, and Lubna Emam. While each dancer's story reflects her own unique experiences as a performer, her personal style and music preferences, and the particular social environment during the years of her performance career, many commonalities emerged that lend insight into how these dancers guide the audience through the journey of the entire performance to create the deeply emotional state of *tarab*.

Enter the Rakassa: Mapping the Journey

During our interviews, dancers described the process of how they arranged their shows. A traditional Oriental dance performance is actually a progression of many sets, or dance numbers lasting an hour or longer, performed by the same solo dancer with several costume changes. The first song was simply referred to as the Oriental Introduction. This first song provides a time of transition for the audience, allowing them to visually and mentally become acquainted with the dancer. Egyptian dancer Randa Kamel (2010) described this part of the show as being on display. She divulged that during this transition the audience is free to talk about her, her body and shape, her looks, her style, her costume. While the Oriental Introduction allows time for the audience to become familiar with the dancer, it also offers time for the dancer to size up the audience. This song is not just about saying hello, as the information gathered will assist her in structuring the rest of the show. The dancer scans the horizon, looking at the crowd, noting the ages and ethnicity of the audience members and how they are dressed. Aida Nour, Tamrahenna, Nagwa Fouad, and Randa Kamel all spoke of looking for the audience's facial expressions, physical gestures, movements in connection with the music, and vocal utterances as affirmations of engagement. Tamra-henna (2010) would ask herself: Is this an Umm Kulthūm crowd (classic) or an Amr Diab crowd (pop)? The dancer will then communicate with the bandleader about the rest of the show. Aida Nour (2010) disclosed that the different components of the show can all be arranged to suit the audience, depending on the atmosphere of the place, the people, their faces, and their reactions. If there are people from the Gulf, Yasmina Ramzy (2010) revealed, she throws in a *kheleegy*, a traditional woman's dance from that region; if there are Lebanese, Yasmina includes a short *debkeh* section or she asks the band leader to play something with the *debkeh* rhythm. Tamra-henna conveyed that "you have to be able to adapt to the audience, play the song they want at a moment's notice and dance the dance they want — make the customers happy" (2010).

While the goal of the dancer is to please the audience, engage them in the performance, and lead them to a place of feeling within the parameters of the Oriental dance show, she must also navigate within her own frame of mind. Aida Nour (2010) explained that the mood of the dancer going into the show affects the performance, explaining that each performance is different because the dancer feels differently. Randa explained that while she chooses music for the audience, she also has to work within her own feelings at the time. "How can I dance to a song [if] my feelings are so far away from this song, and my body doesn't feel it?" she asked (2010). Randa elaborated:

> If you stay in Egypt for a week and you come to watch me dancing for the entire week, seven days, you will find me every day different than the day before on stage. This day [a friend] gave me a hard time, I'll dance a certain way. The other day I had a wonderful time, I'll dance a certain way. If my son is ill, I'll dance in a certain different way. Each time you'll find a uniquely different way of dancing, and different facial expression, and different feeling on my part [2010].

Barbara and Ali Jihad Racy (1998) claim, "It is [the] intense relationship between the dancers, singers, and musicians as well as the impact of an emotionally charged audience that imbues Arabic dance and music with its soul and vitality" (104). During the Oriental Introduction, the dancer is literally thinking on her feet — she must scan the horizon, chart the roadmap she will follow during the rest of the show, and guide this audience to a place of feeling emotionally charged.

The Light Song: Unifying the Audience

Many dancers referred to the music that immediately followed the Oriental Introduction as a Light Song. This can be a fairly new song or a song that is not too old but not too new — a well-known song that the Egyptians and other Arabs in the audience would recognize and bring smiles to their faces. To capture the attention of the audience, the song must be spirited with an energetic tempo. Randa explains her motives during this song:

> I want to make a song that comes directly after the [introduction] that has some ... effect on people.... I am telling you "laugh, come with me and forget all about the world around you so that we can be happy together." It is an invitation. I invite you to come with me using the words [of the song]. I don't make a big dance technique, I just make contact with the people ... forget all about everything else now, and just concentrate with me [2010].

If the Oriental Introduction was not enough to draw the audience away from the outside world, this Light Song encourages those audience members who are lagging behind to join the group. Tamra-henna refers to this as unifying the audience: "It's kind of like they're there and they are having fun and there's music and everything, but everyone is not on the same page, even among each other" (2010). The playfulness of the song creates a sense of fun — one that is lighthearted and not too heavy in content. Faster rhythms, higher tones, and uplifting lyrics distract the audience from the outside world and draw them into that place where, Tamra-henna describes, the dancer can take them away from their problems. The dancer playfully confronts individuals who are not yet fully engaged by making direct eye contact, smiling, and gesturing to them as if to say I'm dancing, pay attention! This song draws them deeper into the experience as more and more audience members surrender to the moment and begin to clap, move, and smile.

Aida Nour mentioned that she intentionally chooses a popular song that will "bring some memory for the people" (2010). When I probed her further, she explained that she wanted the people to remember something happy from their past. When audience members recognize this song, it conjures memories of when and where they heard that song before — perhaps a wedding or other celebration when that song was played. I have observed audience members at this stage, and as soon as they recognize the song, they smile broadly and nod, indicating approval. Often the dancer plays to those in the audience who are responding in an obviously positive way — and others naturally follow. Tamrahenna remarked, "I really think people can pass those ideas and it doesn't have to be verbally. It's in their reaction, and other people see that and respond to that" (2010). The individualism of each person begins to dissipate as each audience member appears to join the group. Thus the goal of the dancer during this Light Song is to not only further engage the audience, but also to unify them. As the show moves forward and the distractions of food, drink, and chatter fade into the background, the dancer becomes the focus in the foreground as the individuals in the audience slowly converge to form a cohesive community that will journey together.

Stopping in the Said: Memories and Physicality

Oriental dance shows usually include a folkloric dance or *beledi* (*baladi*) section, and often it is the *raks assaya* dance from the Said, a region in Upper (southern) Egypt viewed as an area that preserves true Egyptian culture, unsullied by the Westernization and corruption of Cairo and the northern part of the country (Armbrust 1996, 205). After a quick costume change, the dancer runs back onto the stage dressed in a man's *galabaya* or folkloric Saidi dress. This part of the performance makes a significant shift in the mood of the show, for not only is there a change in costume but also a change in musical mood with the use of folkloric instruments such as the *mizmar*, a whiney-toned reed instrument, and the *rababa*, grandfather of today's violin.

The *raqs assaya* conjures images of both the virile Saidi male and the innocent female. In her movements and attire, the dancer highlights gender differences while simultaneously blurring gender roles as she takes on characteristics of both the male and female. She is now covered in the long man's *galabaya*, yet uncovered as side slits display her smooth legs and the lower neckline displays her décolletage. Randa referred to this as being both strong and soft, man and woman, "Saidi comes from here" (2010). Randa then lifted her arm with strength and deliberateness and pointed to the front of this arm with her other hand. In a performance in Dallas in 2008, Fifi Abdo displayed her strength and prowess, whacking her stick against the floor, twirling it with speed and control. However, she interspersed these stereotypical masculine movements with hip movements and shoulder shimmies, the typical feminine movements of *raqs beledi* and Oriental dance. When I asked Tamrahenna about the significance of the Saidi section of an Oriental show, she thoughtfully responded:

The people who use the cane, the stick, in the *tahtiyb*[3] as far as Saidi is concerned, are the men. So when a woman is dancing with the cane, she is mixing some of that male energy into her dance ... the woman pushing the boundaries of sexuality, but not too far, still within the bounds of propriety.... I think anytime where the women is riding the edge of what is sexually appropriate and what is gender appropriate, it kind of titillates the audience and people like it. But if you do it within a certain boundary, people are going to have a good time and it's going to be seen as fun and people are going to enjoy it, but you have to be able to ride that line very well [2010].

Despite, or perhaps because of, the stereotypes of the Saidi people, it is one of the most cherished music and dance traditions in the country. Nagwa Fouad said that in her shows, "after one minute with Saidi music, after one minute, everybody is happy, everybody dance ... this is Egyptian dance" (2010). Tamra-henna mentioned that "I think it's necessary for a dancer to be able to do it.... Saidi is really important to the Egyptian people ... it's a part of their tradition and they see it as part of national pride" (2010). Lubna Emam, an Egyptian dancer revered for her Saidi dance style, says that above

A craftsman makes an Oud in the primary artistic area of Cairo Oud-makers Mohamed 'Ali Street. The Oud is one of the fundamental instruments of an Egyptian orchestra (photograph by Caitlin E. McDonald).

all, "Saidi means fun, this is not serious, and this is play, so the people want to play with you too" (2010). Part of this fun comes from the fact that, while blurring gender lines by embodying both male and female characteristics, the dancer is attempting to engage the audience deeper into her performance with humor and play.

The Saidi dance brings the audience to a different level of engagement — that which involves the movement of their own bodies. When I asked dancers about what they saw happening in the audience during the Saidi piece, all dancers responded that the audience participated through clapping and bouncing in their seats, or what some dancers referred to as dancing in their chairs. Tamra-henna remarked:

> Saidi serves to bring people into the dance a little bit more. I know that whenever I was dancing and there were older people in the crowd, particularly an older man would get up to dance. Anyone who had a cane would hand him a cane, to dance with a cane in his hand.... But I also think the cane is related to folklore and related to more of a *beledi* (*baladi*) aspect of the dance ... so that when you're dancing with the cane it brings the audience into it a little bit more.... There's a closer rapport, they're not so separated. One isn't a performer/Oriental dancer, but now you're all doing a dance that everybody does. It lightens the mood and makes people interact with the dance in a different way, and maybe have a closer rapport with the dancer [2010].

Nora Hamed, an American-born woman of Egyptian descent in her twenties, reinforces the views of these dancers. When I asked her to describe how she felt about the Saidi portion of an Oriental dance show, she responded:

> It brings very happy feelings of having my whole family around me ... celebrating. It is true that Egyptians go crazy when Saidi music is played. I suppose it is because everyone has their own special memories. It just makes us want to dance — even if it is while sitting in our chairs.... I think it is important in a dance show to have a Saidi piece to really engage the audience in the performance, either by clapping, smiling, dancing in their chairs, or just being happy and in a good mood. A Saidi piece is important because as an audience member, I may not be focusing on how good the dancer is, but how good she is at entertaining and putting on a show.... Saidi brings a feeling that the traditional Oriental piece doesn't carry [Email Communication, January 2011].

Saidi is a folkloric style dance, a dance of the people, and in the Arab world, folk dances are strongly connected with certain sentiments, moods, or images (B. Racy and A. J. Racy 1998). Arabic customers see movement they know and understand, recognize it as a part of their cultural heritage, and echo that movement in their own bodies. Tamra-henna commented that with Arabs, they have personal experience, a physical history with the movement they see, so they are compelled to move as well: "They are moving, they are raising their hands. They move, they dance, and with the Egyptians especially.

Some people will get up and dance onstage. It's like a sympathetic connection that we're having ... when somebody gets up and dances with you" (2010).

Shareen El Safy said that Egyptians "love to share their dance and their music, and it's a participatory kind of thing, the folk side of it" (2010). Tourists see the patrons around them reacting physically and are further influenced by the surrounding movement as they are pulled into this community. Tamrahenna remarked that tourists "were just fascinated with everything. I think when you balance the cane on different parts of your body they like it even if they don't understand the connotations of Saidi or that it's a folklore" (2010).

While tourists may not understand the nuances of meaning in the characters and culturally-specific gestures, the musicians, dancer, and indigenous audience members are generously sharing their traditions and including them in their public memories. There is a physical empathy in the room, with everyone now dancing to the same rhythm — the 4/4 rhythm of the Said. Even those individuals who are from other parts of the world experience their own kinesthetic empathy by seeing the extrovert expressions of feeling and joy on the faces of Egyptian and other Arabic patrons around them. In turn, this links them to a broader emotion that connects them with what is happening, even though it may not be in a way that is directly bound to the Egyptian or Arabic culture. This prepares them for the next phase of the performance in which the dancer will attempt to take the audience even farther — a place where the feeling resides, a place of emotional transcendence.

The Long Love Song: Memories and Umm Kulthūm

The Oriental Introduction, the Light Song, and the Saidi section serve as appetizers that stimulate and prepare the audience's palate for the love songs that follow. These songs, the emotional pinnacle of an Oriental dance performance, are part of the musical genre referred to as *musiqa al-gadid* or *tarab* music. More often than not, dancers perform to a song originally made famous by the great Egyptian singer Umm Kulthūm. In fact, when interviewing dancers, one question I always asked was: "If you had to choose only one piece of music, only one song to dance to for the rest of your life, what would it be?" Seven out of eight dancers[4] responded with anything Umm Kulthūm.

When performing to Umm Kulthūm, the dancer accumulates her potency through the emotions in the song, which are expressed through the *maqam*, or melodic mode, in which the song is written, the voices of the different instruments, the individual expression of the *taqasim* — an improvised section for a solo instrument — and the poetic meanings of the lyrics. However, while it is one thing to *say* that a feeling is reflected in movement, it is quite another to speak about the *physicality* of how that happens. When I asked Randa Kamel what was the difference between sad movement and happy movement, she stood up and said, "How you can do the movement with the sad music or the happy music? If the song is a sad one, it brings the sadness inside of me. When dancing something that is hurting me, you'll find my movement like *that*" (2010). Randa then executed a hip tuck, in which one hip was drawn deeply into her body by contracting the hip flexors and abdominal muscles on the side of that hip — it was almost a stabbing movement, as if a knife had been plunged into one side of her pelvis. Visually, the movement went *in* to her body. Randa continued, "If the feeling is a joyous one, you'll find my movement like *that*" (2010). Randa did another hip movement, but this time the movement came from her gluteus and hamstring in the back of the leg, giving it more of a lifted feeling and a completely different visual quality — this time, the movement went *out* of her body and resonated upwards. Randa also explained how her focus affects the quality of the movements she performs:

> For example, *Lessah Fakir* [*Do You Still Remember?*], the movement is deep, and strong, from my inside, because we have all felt sad at one time, all of us have been hurt. I bring my movement in[ward], I bring my eyes down. This brings the people into me, but also into themselves as they remember their sadness. We have all felt happy also at one time ... here I lift, I look out, it is open. My face is open, it is light, for the happiness [2010].

An important catalyst in the generation of *tarab*, or a deep emotional reaction in the audience, is the sensation of *memory*, and the songs of Umm Kulthūm play an important role in the invocation of both personal and collective memories in the dancer and her audience. Shareen El Safy (1996) remembered being an audience member at a performance by Egyptian dancer Mona El Said in Cairo in 1994. Shareen noted that Mona's performance to the Umm Kulthūm favorite *Lessah Fakir* was especially noteworthy:

> She dug deeply into herself, dramatizing the meaning of the words with exaggerated facial expressions and trembling hands. The raw emotional value was palpable, and the intensity may have made some audience members nervous. I have a personal memory for this [Mona said]. I used to be married to a man I love very much, and we had a problem together. And I still remember him when I dance [to] this song [31].

Through her interpretation of the song, the dancer is reaching surprising corners of memory associated with Umm Kulthūm. Biographer Virginia Danielson (1997) explains, "Part of listening to Umm Kulthūm was a long evening of tea and camaraderie. Listeners remember the entire experience along with the sound" (1). Tamra-henna revealed that those experiences, even though they may have occurred forty or fifty years ago,

... get carried on from generation to generation, because then the mother has that, and when her daughter is born or her son is born, she sings and they dance together. It's like that energy passes, and then they [the children] have that whole feeling. You know, if see my mother listening to Umm Kulthūm, singing it to me and crying, then you think "oh I remember when I first heard this." Then you grow up and remember, and it's going to pass along [2010].

Tamra-henna shared that her favorite Umm Kulthūm piece is *Inta Omri (You Are My Life),* and remarked upon the mixture of happiness and sadness in the song:

Umm Kulthūm's lyrics are very emotional and they are either about love and loss or both. They are very emotional and poetic, and then you mix those lyrics with rhythm and the sounds of the different instrumentation, it touches you viscerally, almost physically. You can't *not* be affected by this, because everyone has felt something like this, and the song brings those experiences out.... It's also collaborative, it's all the people in the room, and it's all the experiences that song embodies that allow people to go somewhere else [2010].

Dancers described repeatedly how songs were chosen to generate memory in the people as well as songs that have special memory for the dancer. Life experiences, culture, memories — both personal and collective — are stored deep in the corners of our minds. If the music and dancer can infer or suggest an image that brings forth a memory, the audience can then establish an emotional context for themselves. The images, ideas, and feelings associated with that memory give them access to feelings that are transcendent because they are not limited to a specific time and place. The songs of Umm Kulthūm refer back to a time of strong Egyptian nationalism and pan–Arabism — perhaps now, in this era of new revolution, these old memories of pan–Arabism associated with Umm Kulthūm reinforce the politics of the present.

Literary theorist Carol Bernstein (2007) defines cultural memory as "the ways in which different cultural groups — which may be national, religious, or ethnic — identify and describe their shared pasts" (2). Thus, dancing to an Umm Kulthūm piece is more than the conveyance of the emotional conditions of the song; the dancer is offering the song as a conduit for remembering and creating an environment where these memories can be lovingly savored. The dancer *evokes* feelings and emotions from the music and lyrics and *invokes* images and memories from the past. The feelings produced by those memories, are, in turn, transferred to the current performance environment, inching the dancer, the musicians, and the audience towards a state of *tarab.* As music and dance conjure emotions and memories in the dancer, the images and ideas that inspire an Oriental dancer's process emerge as movement. But while the movement flows from the body of the performer, that movement is actually a facsimile, with a bit of pixilation. Individuals who share in these experiences clarify these meanings for themselves and find their own connection to a memory, which in turn, propels them into a world that is meaningful. This meaningful world is not just one that waxes nostalgic. The current sensations are *presently* alive with meaning, because the memory and the images associated with that memory gradually evaporate, and what comes to the forefront is the residue, the *essence* of the emotion often associated with being Egyptian or Arabic. It is this essence that lingers, that transforms both the dancer and her audience.

The Art of Listening: The Dancer as Sammīʻa

In addition to the individual and collective memories generated by the songs of Umm Kulthūm, the dancers all described the importance of listening. Not just *hearing* the music, but really *listening* to the music — the individual voices of the instruments, the lyrics. It is the *depth* of the dancer's listening and how she hears that music that serves as her main impetus for generating movement and connecting to the audience. A dancer's ability to listen, and to listen with sensitivity and sophistication, affects not only her choices but also the progression of the musicians' choices. Yasmina Ramzy elaborated on the importance of listening in building a relationship with the musicians:

> When the musicians feel a dancer is actually listening, then things come out of the musicians beyond the music ... they start creating little nuances, decorations here and there. Dancers who do a lot of tricks and combos and ta-da! ta-da! are not listening to the music. They are just doing steps, and they are trying to make it about them, and the musicians feel that and they can't play for dancers like that.... I mean, they can put on a song if they have to, but when the dancer is actually listening and authentically expressing the music, then things come out of the musicians beyond the music, and this way you start getting close to *tarab* [2010].

Racy (2003) explains that the colloquial word *sammīʻa* (singular masculine, *sammīʻ*) refers to "diehard *tarab* listeners, or literally, those who listen well" (40). These individuals are believed to have a special talent for listening and "form the emotional and artistic lifeline of *tarab* artistry" (40). Racy claims that *sammīʻa* are "naturally predisposed to feeling and responding emotionally to the music" and, when they listen, "display distinct musical focus, genuinely feel the music, and express what is felt in ways that *enhance the creative flow of the performance*" [author's emphasis] (40–42). During her performance to the music of Umm Kulthūm, I position the dancer as not just someone who hears and responds to the music in her ensuing dance movements, but as a *sammīʻa*,[5] a sophisticated listener who feels the music and translates her feeling into movement that expresses her genuinely felt *tarab* sensations.

While an individual may listen to, enjoy, experience, and be moved by the music alone, the role of the dancer is to act as a mediator between the music and the audience. She is an interpreter, a connecting link, a translator. It is the dancer's skill at listening that enhances the creative flow of the performance and ultimately becomes integral to the entire experience. Her facial expressions paraphrase the emotions of the song while her movements—be they gentle or strong—augment, magnify, and amplify the music for the audience. The words of Nagwa Fouad capture the feelings expressed by all of the dancers interviewed in this study, explaining that when she is dancing, "my hands dance, my legs dance, my hips dance, my eyes dance, my face dance, my feelings dance for the audience" (2010).

Not all dancers are *sammī'a*—the ones who are there just to show off, to wow the audience with their tricks and skills, who are all about technique—they do not have that special talent for listening. Obviously, most dancers may know their music, meaning they have the music memorized, they understand what the lyrics mean, and they know the rhythms that come into play. But knowing the music is not the same as being able to physically express what is felt in a way that *enhances the creative flow of the performance.* While this dancer may be a talented entertainer, while she may give a good show, while she may impress the audience with her technique, she is not a *sammī'a*.

Enhancing the creative flow of the performance implies that the dancer must not just listen to the music, but also listen to the audience. Like Umm Kulthūm during her own concerts, the dancer must intuitively create the performance as she goes to suit the unique audience present, so that they, too, can be *sammī'ah*. As the dancer is nourished by the energy of her audience, she is listening and watching for those genuine responses. She is shaped by their reactions, and even the less elite listeners—the non-*sammī'ah*—respond and react as they are able to tap into their own lived experiences. While not all audience members will be *sammī'ah,* the ones who are able to communicate their own ecstasy through facial expressions, body language, gestures, and verbal expressions are the dancer's artistic lifeline within the performance.

The dancers interviewed all commented that the dance, the *movement*, created an experience that was different from just listening to the music. While all the dancers credited the music as the source of *tarab*, Hadia explained that it is the dancer's "physical interpretation of it that makes it all come together, because the energy keeps generating from your body, and then it is regenerating and regenerating even more, because you are working with the music. You are working with the songs and your body is within that" (2010).

The *sammī'a* allows the music to flow from her body, enabling the audience to also have an enhanced listening experience. The *sammīʿa* dancer does not impede *tarab*, she escalates it by giving the members of the audience a physical representation of the music into which they can imaginably insert themselves. The onlooker can become the music through the dancer because the dancer, as *sammīʿa*, has the ability to become the music herself. The audience members can identify with the dancer and thereby access the music in an entirely unique, physical fashion. During the emotionally charged love songs of Umm Kulthūm, the dancer's ability to listen and respond authentically to what she hears is paramount. If not, her performance could appear forced or contrived. Her listening must go beyond the music, though, and extend to the audience. The dancer listens to their reactions and in turn acknowledges the dominant tastes expressed, for they too are listeners. Thus, the dancer, as a listener, responds to the music, directs the energy it produces, and nurtures the relationship that continues to develop between herself, the music, and her audience. As the dancer listens, and then channels the energy and emotive content of the music through her body, it is the audience's positive reactions that encourage her to go deeper and deeper, giving more and more. Aida Nour explained in her interview that "This is very deep, deep relationship between the artist and the audience.... I give energy and you take, then you give energy and I take. Both have to happen for the lights to go on" (2010).

Al-Fann Ihsas: Art Is Feeling

One of the significant conclusions of this study is that Oriental dance, while somewhat dependent on the music to which it is performed, is not a slave to it. Although it may be the music itself that generates *tarab*, the movement and various levels of interaction that unfold over the course of an Oriental dance performance create the potential for an enhanced, or at least, differently-felt, *tarab* experience. The dancer is listening to, performing with, interpreting, and moving to this music as well as interacting with her audience. Likewise, the audience is listening to this music, watching the dancer move to this music, moving to this music themselves, and interacting with the dancer and one another. The dance, then, is not just an afterthought — it adds another dimension, another voice, another layer of richness and sensation. It is the complexity of the relationship that produces the nooks and crannies in which deep emotion can take root, grow, and then transform.

In Arabic there is a saying, *al-fann ihsas*— art is feeling. In an Oriental dance performance, the dancer has the feeling, the musicians have the feeling, and the audience has the feeling. All of this feeling is the Feeling which so many dancers and audience members describe as being the most important aspect of Oriental dance. The Feeling is not forced, though, as the dancer must possess an intuitive ability to affect the audience in relation to the myriad of variables that surround the performance process. It is the Feeling that continues to keep the dance form vital and relevant in the midst of hard economic times, religious conservatism, and decreased tourism amidst political unrest. As Nagwa Fouad, one of the most famous Oriental dancers of the 20th century, reminds us:

> Art is about creating something with meaning for other people, not for you. It is not enough to be a strong technician; that is more like sport. You can watch a dancer and think "this is a good dancer." She can do lots of steps; she entertains me with her skill. But then, when she is over, you forget. Because there was no meaning in what she did, nothing with feeling to remember, nothing from inside, except "look at me." When the dance is done, we don't think of steps. We only remember the Feeling [2010].

Notes

1. Various spellings include Om Koultoum, Om Kalthoum, Oumme Kalsoum and Umm or Um Kolthoum.

2. While interviewing dancers, observing master classes, and collecting other data in 2010, I realized that while dancers used the terms Oriental dance, belly dance, and *raqs sharki* interchangeably, the most common way of referring to the dance was indeed "Oriental dance." Consequently, here I embrace the name "Oriental dance," as it was the one most commonly used by the Egyptian dancers interviewed.

3. The *tahtiyb* is a combat-style of dance originally from the Said region performed by men using bamboo sticks or large staffs. The men beat the staff on the ground, hit their staffs against the staffs of other men, hit each other with the staffs, and twirl them in a way that demonstrates their combat skills with considerable panache.

4. Nagwa Fouad was the dancer who said she did not want to dance to the music of Umm Kulthūm. She mentioned that Muhammad Abd al Wahab, who composed several pieces for the great singer, asked her the same thing. Her response to him was, "Because you close your eyes, listen to the music, and you get happy without me. Give me music for me, and see what I do" (interview, June 2010). al Wahab then composed *Qamar Arba'-tashar (Full Moon of the Fourteenth)* for Nagwa in 1976, the only music he ever composed especially for a dancer.

5. To form a feminine noun from the masculine in Arabic, a *taa marbuta* (ة) is usually added to the end of the word. This gives a short "a" sound at the end of the word. Here, I have converted the word *sammī'* as used by Racy (2003), to apply specifically to the dancer, who is a woman, thus warranting this adaptation of the word.

Works Cited

Armbrust, W. (1996). *Mass Culture and Modernism in Egypt*. Cambridge: University of Cambridge Press.

Bernstein, C. (2007). "Beyond the Archive: Cultural Memory in Dance and Theater." *Journal of Research Practice* 3(2), Article M14. Retrieved January 2010 from http://jrp.icaap.org/index.php/jrp/article/view/110/98

Danielson, V. (1997). *The Voice of Egypt: Umm Kulthūm, Arabic Song, and Egyptian Society in the Twentieth Century.* Chicago: University of Chicago Press.
El Safy, S. (1996). "Mona El Said: Moving in Mysterious Ways." *Habibi: A Journal for Lovers of Middle Eastern Dance and Arts* 15(1); 2–5, 31.
El Safy, S. (2010). Interview, Dallas, Texas.
Emam, L. (2010). Interview, Cairo, Egypt.
Fouad, N. (2010). Interview, Cairo, Egypt.
Hadia. (2010). Interview, Toronto, Canada.
Kamel, R. (2010). Interview, Cairo, Egypt.
Nour, A. (2010). Interview, Cairo, Egypt.
Racy, A.J. (2003). *Making Music in the Arab Word: The Culture and Artistry of Tarab.* Cambridge: Cambridge University Press.
Racy, B. and Racy, A.J. (1998). "Music for Dance." *The International Encyclopedia of Dance*: (e-reference edition). Oxford University Press. Retrieved February 2010 from http://www.oxford-dance.com/entry?entry=t171.e1214.s0002.
Ramzy, Y. (2010). Interview, Toronto, Canada.
Tamra-henna. (2010). Interview, Dallas, Texas.

Performing Identity/ Diasporic Encounters

Lynette Harper

Veils of mystery and stereotyping obscure Arab women's lives outside the Middle East. Exotic representations of oppressed and subservient Arab women pervade North American media discourse, but have little to do with daily life of women in their home countries or in the diaspora (Abu-Lughod 1998, Saliba 2000). Currently, visual artists of the Arab diaspora are actively challenging those dominant discourses in high profile exhibits that subvert distorted assumptions (Bailey and Tawadros 2003, Buller 2007). But dance artists of the Arab diaspora are rarely noticed, their presence obscured by a highly visible belly dance community dominated by white middle-class dancers and Orientalist expectations (Dox 1997, Jarmakani 2008, Maira 2008). Belly dance itself is devalued in relation to classical dance forms, particularly those of European origin, and its performers are usually categorized as entertainers, rather than artists.

On Canada's west coast, the city of Vancouver is the centre of a large and active belly dance community. Though community members provide entertainment in ethnic Greek and Persian restaurants, special events, and festivals, the dancers themselves talk about their dance as a transnational art form and for this reason produce shows in mainstream theatrical venues. Dancers, teachers, and students in the community reflect the ethnic pluralism of the Vancouver region in which a majority of residents are of British and European origin as well as a strong presence of ethnic Chinese and Asian origins (Statistics Canada 2012). Residents of Arab origin comprise less than 1 percent of the population.

Belly dance performance and classes in Vancouver are dominated by what is called "Egyptian" dance and a proliferation of "fusion" genres that mix the belly dance movement vocabulary with different ethnic dance forms —

Bollywood, jazz, hip hop, flamenco, African and Celtic. National folkloric styles from the Middle East are seldom presented. A majority of dancers and students embrace forms of belly dance identified as American in origin, in particular "tribal" fusion styles. Belly dance, like most dance forms, tends to reproduce dominant notions of gender and identity (Alderson 1997, Rowe 2008). In both stage and studio spaces, belly dance comfortably coexists alongside Orientalist ideologies which reproduce notions of veiled, exotic and mysterious Arab women — despite the presence of some Arab Canadian dancers whose lives contradict the stereotypes.

Arab Canadian women take part in diverse Vancouver artistic communities. Some perform with companies of contemporary and flamenco dance, but most participate as independent artists or troupe members in the belly dance community. Like Arab women elsewhere in North America, they study and perform Middle Eastern belly dance and folkloric traditions as a means of connecting with their heritage, with pride and sometimes ambivalence (Maira 2008, Shay 2006).

I invited four Arab Canadian women[1] who live and dance in Vancouver to share their experiences and concerns.[2] Some were raised Muslim, some Christian. All are well-traveled and well-educated and each woman holds at least one university degree.[3] Rasha and Mira are immigrants to Canada who move back and forth between family in their home countries and in Canada. Their transnational lives are defined by a sense of mobility and cross-border networks, lived in complex geographies of community, identity and citizenship (Faist 2010, Harper 2001, Purkayastha 2012). Phedra and Rahma, like myself, are first and second generation Canadians, who have visited the homeland of our parents and grandparents.

We identify ourselves as Lebanese, Tunisian, or Egyptian, as well as Canadian. We also call ourselves Arabs, a choice made despite stereotypes perpetuated in contemporary media (Said 1979). Fluctuating levels of anti–Arab prejudice in North America, linked with national and international politics, mean that claiming an Arab Canadian identity can be socially compromised and compromising (Eid 2007). Yet the Arab world's rich cultural history supports a desire to raise awareness through artistic endeavors, while promoting Arabness as a positive cultural identity (Nagel and Staeheli 2010).

We are members of the Arab diaspora[4] and our stories challenge the narrow categories of Orientalism, Islam, nationalism, and feminism that have bound Arab women (Saliba 2000). All five narrators identify multiple belongings and have chosen flexible cultural identities that link the national and the transnational. In our creative work, we dance among contradictory discourses of multiculturalism and essentialism and exclusion, diversity and difference (Haw 2009).

Lynette: A Way to Connect with My Arab Heritage

I am a grandchild of immigrants who left Lebanon over a century ago. My Arab ethnicity is a symbolic one which has informed my research and dance activities throughout my life. I was born and raised in Vancouver, in a white middle-class neighborhood. I looked like I belonged with my fair skin and my father's Scottish Protestant heritage. But my personality and values were profoundly influenced by my mother's Lebanese family. It wasn't until I studied anthropology and journeyed to the Middle East as a young adult that I recognized that my character may be more Lebanese than Canadian.

Dance is my joy and my solace. Even though I knew my body didn't meet the western ideal of a dancer, I adored childhood dance classes in ballet, jazz, modern, and Highland dance. I returned from a year of travel in 1976 to find that belly dance fever had struck big in North America. I embraced belly dance as a way to connect with my Arab heritage and pursue my love of dance. When I wasn't working at my museum job I took classes and apprenticed in what we called belly dance, eventually becoming a part-time working performer and teacher. I've struggled to find a balance between my dance and my other academic life. I've also struggled to respect the cultural origins of the dance and music, while supporting personal creativity and thoughtful innovations. My early performances reproduced historical and folkloric forms. But I have come to think of myself as a contemporary Arab dance artist with a creative practice that explores Arab women's experiences, and relations between West and East.

My delight in belly dance has been tempered by growing concerns about the negative stereotyping of Arabs and Muslims that dominates public discourse in North America. Since 2001, the War on Terror and Islamophobia have magnified race, gender, and power relations implicated in the dance. These attitudes have not stopped the momentum of Orientalist fantasy or the swelling ranks of women and men, of various ethnicities though mostly northern European, who participate in Canadian belly dance communities. Therefore, I find, more then ever before, that I struggle with how and where to produce and perform my dance, and my Arabness.

Rasha: I'm a Belly Dancer, but on My Own Terms

I can't really say which year I started dancing because I grew up in Egypt. I just remember clearly that I would watch the black and white movies on television. We liked them because they were simple and had music and dance.

Lynette Harper and Rahma Haddad explored their shared Lebanese roots and Arab-Canadian identities through dance and storytelling in *Bekaa Valley Girls: A Lebanese Saga* at Vancouver's Dance Centre (photograph by Frank Julian Roberts).

I was fascinated by the dancers, especially how they used scarves and twirled them in the air. Of course, I didn't have scarves, so I would use a bed sheet as a scarf.

I loved to dance and as children we would dance at weddings and engagement parties, right before or after the hired belly dancer danced. This is how we learned how to dance by watching and imitating black and white movies, weddings, and hired belly dancers. In villages, a group of women at a party or gathering would play music and one woman would dance and then she'd grab another woman and they would dance, and so on. In the city, the same thing happened but usually in gatherings held before weddings or engagements.

I was in an all girl's school and at recess we would go to some secluded place with our Walkmans or recorders from home and dance. Even though belly dancing is still the national dance of Egyptians and everybody belly dances, they would not allow it in schools! But school parties always ended up in an attempt to belly dance in one way or another.

Not every girl or woman in the Middle East in my generation learned how to belly dance. First of all, it was frowned upon and still is. Second, when I grew up, I was born in the 1970s, there was a significant Western cultural influence. Girls were more interested in jazz dancing, hip hop and Western music. So, not everybody learned how to belly dance. Later many of these people became students of the dance.

So how did I get into teaching belly dance? After some time it was very clear that I liked belly dancing. I didn't do anything with it, except at parties and weddings. I would dance with my friends and people noticed that I danced better than others. After going to university and working for a while, I regularly attended a jazz club in Cairo which mainly focused on live music. Some of the people played fusion Arabic jazz. And I never had any inhibitions dancing in front of other people, also, I knew everyone, so I'd be on the bar or tables dancing. And some friends would actually call me, and say, "Are you going to be there? Because that would be an upper for the party!" A band asked me to join them, as a dancer. I said, "I don't know, like you I have a career [in computer science]. And I don't know what my dad is going to think of that." Honestly, that's what I would have loved to do, be a belly dancer with a band doing fusion. But I felt like I should do something with the dancing so I started giving classes.

I took a course about teaching with a dance center in Egypt. I was coming to Canada quite a lot at that time so I also went to a dance center in Toronto, just to see what they were doing there. I was really impressed by their movement skills. I wasn't impressed with their auras. After that, in Egypt, I started giving classes at a friend's house. After a while belly dancing came into the picture again, though it's still not the hippest thing to do in Egypt. People want to learn, to be able to fit in, basically at weddings. They wanted to be able to dance in weddings, whether they're brides or invited guests.

We've only been here [in Canada] about a year and a half, permanently. This last year, we're putting things into place. I have lots of ideas along the lines of teaching non–Arab women who are dancing about understanding the culture, the lyrics, where the dance is coming from. I would love to give little class sessions here and there about it. Not as my full-time career. I also love performing. But as much as I love it, I don't like to just perform anywhere, it has to mean something to me. I wouldn't mind performing, to show an example of an Arab woman dancing the dance. If it's a party, I wouldn't perform to be paid, full stop. I don't mind being paid, don't get me wrong, but it's not going to be my main purpose. Being paid or not, those are two different things. If I'm at the party on my own, I make the decision when, and where, and how I do it. But if I'm being paid, I have very little to say. I'm not afraid to perform, and I'm not afraid to say I'm a belly dancer, but on my own terms. And being on my own terms, means that I'm more in control of outcomes, the environment. I can decide if I can dance here or not. Based on my understanding of what's going on. I would have reservations about performing for Egyptians or Arabs. If you're a western woman doing the dance, they might think, "Oh yeah, she wants to be hip," because they know about belly dancing in the West. But if an Egyptian woman is performing, a common view of a dancer is equivalent to that of a prostitute. And I don't want to be approached this way.

It Is a Dance Related to Your Identity

I have thought differently about belly dance [over time]. When I was really young, I think it helped me to understand my anatomy. There are parts you don't really take note of, unless you're moving them. When I was a teenager, it was an art of seduction. As I grew a bit older, I thought of it as seduction, but with artistry blended in; seduction with grace. I think I still hold that thought. The dance is more of an exaggeration of what my normal movements would be in life. Even though I am in birth and blood completely Egyptian, I have been exposed to so many different cultures and my movements are affected by them. It is a dance related to your identity. So if you see me dance, you will see that it has everything to do with me, with what I was exposed to. It's not a step dance like salsa, or tango, or whatever. I still can move in a way that is typical Egyptian, and I can switch to that, when I dance.

When I'm dancing, it's important that I'm me, and have in mind what the dance is about. I'm Egyptian, not an Arab. Egyptians do distinguish themselves from Arabs. I'd say I'm Egyptian, like someone you've seen in museums. There are very few Egyptians in Vancouver. In Vancouver, I don't think people have seen many Egyptian women. I did not want to mix with the Egyptian community, at least initially. The thing is, even in Egypt there are differences. There are different classes of people, and different circles. And each circle has its own attributes, traits, and that's acceptable. When you come to a different culture, a different country, these circles are dissolved in relation to Canada, or the States, or the country you are in. So I might not get along with a person just because he's coming from a different circle, or different background, than I come from in Egypt. And we'd recognize that instantly. It is very classist, but that's how it is, because there's such a big difference between these circles. People might be a bit liberal, or very religious, or have financial difficulties; they might be very literate, or very political. There is such diversity; it's not easy to integrate all that in one person. However, meeting someone who is Egyptian here, we are both more open to accept each other. But we know there is a big possibility that we might not get along. Like cats, basically!

Preconceived Notions

I'm concerned about how people [in North America] see Arabs, in general. When they know that Egyptians are Arabs, I think they have preconceived notions. Because of everything that's happened, about Muslims, and terrorists, and about what they think and do. But now it's more positive. When I went to high school in the states, people knew nothing about that part of the world, nothing. Twenty years ago, people were completely oblivious. You'd tell them where you came from, and they'd think, "We don't know about this part of the world." Later on, with all the terrorist actions that happened in the world, they were very scared. In Canada now, it's a completely different story. For instance I'll hear, "Oh, I understand where you're coming from. You fast in Ramadan." Or, "Oh, you're a Muslim; you don't eat pork, right?" So even though limited, there is some familiarity. Not that I fast or don't eat pork! But I noticed that people do know a little bit more than before. In North America 20 years ago, nobody ever asked me, or thought there were any differences. There's much more awareness and much less fear now, than in the 1990s or 2000, at least in Canada. I wish I could say the same about the States, as it may be true that there is more awareness about the Middle East, but unfortunately there is much more fear, to the extent of paranoia. In terms of discrimination, I think that it's mostly the government that discriminates, and not so much the people, in any culture.

Rahma: I'm Very Much in Love with the Music

From as early as I can remember, I have had an interest in dance. When I was a kid [in Edmonton], I took ballet and tap. I was always begging my mom to give me more lessons, but she didn't. And of course we had the dabke parties when relatives came from Lebanon, but I was too shy to participate in them, I just watched. They would always encourage me, and I'd try to participate. But mostly I was doing Western dance, watching Eastern dance. As a teenager and young adult I was active, I was a skier and played on the school teams. My dad wanted me to be a lawyer, but I thought, "I can't sit, and read all those books." So I took my degree in physical education.

Lucky for me there were a lot of dance courses. There was modern, social, folk, and ballroom. I was also involved in gymnastics. For the folk dance course, we were supposed to teach an ethnic dance or bring somebody in. I brought Evelyn Farrah, who did belly dancing. She shocked us as the dance was so sensual. But it was really beautiful. And I guess that was when I started to think, I want to do that, even though I felt intimidated. However, I got really involved in modern dance at university. We did a big performance, I was so nervous I screwed up my performance entirely. It was the first time I'd performed since I was a child in recitals and such. Here I was on a big stage, all by myself. I just froze. It was a good experience though, because now I know how people feel when they do their first performance.

I always thought I would go back to university to do a master's in dance. They have a program at the University of California. Sometimes I regret not having done it. Then I think, would I be different if I did? Would my life be different? I don't know.

I moved to Vancouver to teach art and physical education in a high school. Someone took me to a great contemporary dance class. It was a pivotal moment. I worked with Evelyn Roth's Moving Sculpture Company and took Afro jazz classes. Ultimately, I did modern dance for a total of 10 years. Then one day I saw a picture of myself, in a leotard, with all the skinny girls. I was chunkier; I looked terrible in a leotard! I was never aware of it before, I was just enjoying myself.

My cousin was going to a belly dance class one day, so I said, "I want to come! I've always wanted to do that." That was in Vancouver, 1975, with Alexandra Dikeakos. I thought I was the worst one in the class. That's because I have trouble learning choreography. I'm more of a dancer who takes the principles of dance and internalizes them; dancing from inside out, rather than a technical dancer.

There was a lot of excitement around belly dance in the 1970s, and we were very creative. We weren't stuck in this style or that style. We were aware of different styles; we'd had lots of workshops with people like Aisha Ali and Masha Archer. Most of our influence at that time came from California, Jamila Salimpour, our own Delia, and the amazing Badawia from Portland. I was dancing with a troupe, sometimes dancing solo, in restaurants and other places. There was a Lebanese lady who danced for us, doing a lot of floor work. I still love floor work, and that loose, flexible, agile style. My first introduction to the real cabaret style was when I brought Gamila Asfour to Vancouver from Montreal in 1982. Her Egyptian style had a lot less movement and was more contained and subtle. That was an interesting contrast to what I had seen and was doing. I didn't consciously change my dance, but my style was expanded in response to that exposure.

Belly Dance Is an Ethnic Dance

To my way of thinking—and I could very well be wrong—belly dance means Oriental dance. Or it means, this is dance that comes from the Middle East. That's the meaning of it. Now, people dispute that, because they say it doesn't have to mean that. But, that *is* what it means! That's the definition of it to me. My feeling is that tribal fusion is not belly dance. Sometimes it's fabulous, there are some great dancers and great artists that do wonderful interesting things and sometimes cross over with belly dance. But belly dance is an ethnic dance. You wouldn't take Chinese dance, and take it way out there, and then call it Chinese dance. Or you wouldn't take flamenco, and take it way out there, and call it flamenco.

Tribal fusion, I call it belly dance confusion. People don't really know what belly dance is anymore. So that, I guess, makes me want to always make sure that people know this is an ethnic dance, it's not an American dance. Just because you bare your belly, doesn't mean it's belly dance. Or just because you use those movements that are used in a lot of other kinds of dance; for example in hip hop, in breakdancing, jazz, and reggae. It's the presentation, what it represents, not the movements themselves, which make a dance what it is. Yes, the movements are important. However, when you or I throw modern dance and ballet into belly dance, we do it with a Middle Eastern feeling to expand the boundaries of the dance, and still retain its essence.

There are lots of people [in Vancouver] who do good mainstream belly dance. There are not many people who are great, because they don't have an intense connection with the music. Someone can be a less technically proficient, but really appreciate the music, and be more enjoyable to watch. I saw one dancer who does all the moves perfectly to the music. It's a perfect imitation of an Oriental dance. But it's an imitation, because it's not coming from her soul.

I look at belly dance as three different things. There's Arabic dance as social dance, how people dance at parties. There's Middle Eastern dance as art (including folkloric), and there's belly dance or "Raqs Sharqi" or "Oriental Dance" as entertainment. They're not cut and dried categories, but they definitely are different ways it can be used and performed. Middle Eastern people themselves love to watch it. They consider it a low class thing to do as a public performer, but they love it. They love to do it at parties themselves. That's such an interesting hypocrisy, but it's part of the history. Everybody knew how to do it, they grew up dancing. So if you couldn't do anything else, if your husband died or you were kicked out of your home, then you became a dancer and/or a prostitute. Because that was the only way you could live.

An Accepted Racism

There's definitely racism, an accepted racism against Arabs, whereas racism would not be accepted against any other group in North America or in the world. It's condoned to be racist against Arabs. It's totally unfair; there are extremist groups which give Arabs, and particularly Muslims, a bad name. But there are extremist groups in every religious group, and it's still not accepted to be racist against them. It's definitely a concern. Although we were always told, "We're not Arab, we're Lebanese." We were always told that. Lebanese are not Arabs, but they speak the language, they have the music, the culture, the food, because the Arabs invaded the whole area, and North Africa, and everywhere in the Middle East.

How to address racism in dance? You just present the best face, or the best presentation that you can. I think the relationship is that people need to know that this dance they enjoy, doing or watching, is a part of that culture. That the reason there are wars going on there currently, is a result of Western colonization and interference. It's not because people are bad. That's the only way it relates to dance. I think sometimes people, some dancers included, want to dissociate Arabic dance with the Arab world. But you can't, that's where it comes from.

I'm No Longer a Performer in the Way That I Was

The style I teach, I call it *baladi*. It's not really a style you would see in a nightclub. It's an earlier style, it has folk influences. When I perform, I use improvisation and rarely choreography. I dance that style because of my early beginnings with dance. I don't see myself as a glamorous person, I see myself more as a dance artist and an entertainer. There's a huge component of sexuality, even in *baladi*. It's a big part of belly dance. But it's not overtly in your face. I'm not a nightclub dancer. I have done it, but I put my own style in it, funkier I guess. When I performed regularly, I was a good entertainer. That's what I did, dancing maybe 7 to 10 shows a week, for many years. I did belly grams for a long time; they were a good way to make money. I gave up doing other things, because I was raising kids. It influenced why I did it, and how I did it. Sometimes I'd have to take the kids with me. It relaxed people, because Canadians don't know what they're getting with a belly dancer. At that time, there was a very small Lebanese community in Vancouver. I danced sometimes for the Church, and occasionally parties. Though sometimes they preferred having somebody really white, it depended on the occasion. The Church liked me; they knew I was Lebanese, and that I wasn't going to intimidate people. That it would be more of an ethnic style of show, sensual and flirtatious rather than overtly sexual. When I danced for one Egyptian wedding I was told, "I hired someone to dance for a retirement at my work, and I was so embarrassed. She came wearing hardly anything."

There's room for everybody, all expressions of the genre, it's just that it has to be the right person for the place. I was often hired for Greek parties and nightclubs; they were very appreciative of my lively style. In those days, there was no local Persian community to speak of, but now that community has grown hugely. There were no Iraqis then, and there are lots now.

But what I do, and what I wanted to do even way back then, was to present Middle Eastern dance to the broader Canadian community. So in my bigger shows I present folk dance, as well as belly dance, and all the genres and combinations in between. I think that's always been important to me. When I teach now, I tell students that my background is Lebanese, and this dance and music is part of my background and that I have danced all my life, not only belly dance, but other styles; but this is the one that I love.

I dance because I can't help it. I'm very much in love with the music, that's the biggest part for me, the music. Not the specific movements themselves, but the music.

Phedra: It Felt Really Earthy

I did dance as a kid; my parents put me into things. I took ballet lessons; I don't think it was really my thing. I did jazz; I really wanted to do jazz dancing. I did Ukrainian dancing, the costumes were so wonderful. I got the boots and the flowers in the hair. I just loved being a Ukrainian dancer. It's pretty intense, good exercise too. But I was really discouraged from going into that. My father discouraged that, he was the patriarch.

I took my first belly dance class in the small town I grew up in, with a wonderful dancer called Karema. That was great, it felt really earthy. I was only 18, I didn't know anything. It just felt like something that was very good for the spirit. Then I graduated from high school, and I came here [to Vancouver]. I didn't take another class until maybe three years later.

I did an art history degree at university, with a lot of courses within fine arts for breadth. A few of them were contemporary dance, some with live drummers. It was good. I took belly dance classes on and off [outside university]. It's probably bad, but I think too much about all the issues in belly dance. I get very irritated with the romanticism, the lack of knowledge, and the lack of respect. I have a fit, and I stop, and then I do it again.

I was taking other kinds of dance, African, Afro-Brazilian. Then one day, my Afro-Brazilian class was canceled, and I thought, what am I going to do for exercise? So I went back to Rahma's class, and she needed someone to be in her group show. We did a folksy Egyptian thing. And it just happened from there, taking classes again, taking tons of yoga, practicing for two hours a day. I was very committed, for a while. It was 2005. I did some performing, and I danced with a group. We did a lot of summer festivals; we did Gay Pride that was really cool. We put on our own show and took part in other shows.

I'm not doing it at the moment. There isn't a place for me in belly dance. Part of that problem is that I'm not a self-promoter. But I see a lot of dancers doing that. And they're representing this dance, that's not really theirs. It just feels like you get pushed aside by girls who have no connection with the culture. All of a sudden everybody is a belly dancer. Of course, I don't have a problem with people trying things out from other cultures, but it's when they claim to represent it that I get very irritated. I don't see a lot of interest in the culture. I take other kinds of dance, like West African. And I don't know a whole lot about the culture. But then, I just go there for fun, and I'm not going to be a professional. But if I was to pursue it, I would probably go there [to Africa], and get to know the culture and the language.

I Didn't Find Out That I Was Arab until 2006

I was born here, of more than one ethnic heritage. Growing up, my childhood experience was feeling different but not being visibly different. I looked like a lot of my friends, but at home I had a different upbringing. My Ukrainian side, my mothers' side, was a wonderful thing to have in my life, so rich, such earthy gentle people. And I had a lot of experience with it as my grandparents were alive when I was growing up. On my father's side, the Greek-Arab heritage, he was very much the patriarch; he really controlled a lot of what happened in our house. So when I say feeling different, I mean not being allowed to do anything that other kids were allowed to do; eating different food, having different decor in my house. People knew my dad was from Egypt, but he made us think that we were just Greek-Egyptian. I got a lot of teasing around when mom dressed me up as Scheherazade for Halloween. Everyone else was Cinderella or Snow White. People would say stupid silly things, "What are you, an Arabian?" Then the Gulf War started, and someone said to me, "If we find out you're related to Saddam Hussein, we're going to kick the shit out of you." I'm serious, somebody said that. "You could be, because your dad is from Egypt."

I found out about my heritage when I was in Greece. I was with my great-aunt and great-uncle, we were having coffee at a little cafe, and she let it slip: My great-grandfather was told that he had to basically play Greek to marry my great-grandmother. Speak Greek, and be Greek Orthodox. I don't know if he was Muslim, we'll never know. In that part of the world, everybody was changing and switching in that period of time. She said, "Your last name is Lebanese." It turns out it's actually Syrian, not Lebanese, but they were the same people, before the area got carved up and colonized. So that was really shocking. Because then it clicked into place. Because I'd always feel, why do I feel this connection to this dance? Why am I getting so possessive about it? I didn't even know. That was when I was dancing a lot. I thought, that's why I feel like this is mine.

In some ways I feel very possessive about things like belly dance. And I get really upset and angry when I hear negative stuff, like stereotyping and racial profiling, and the abuses in Gaza. Then I think, but I was born here. And I look like any other Canadian. I could be any number of things. So do I really have a right to speak for this culture? I feel like maybe I should just hold back, and be careful. I do hold back. Because I don't even speak the language, but I really feel this is what I am. I also feel equally strongly about my Greek and Ukrainian heritages. I feel more Egyptian than Arab, because when I grew up I heard more about Egypt, I met more Egyptians. I don't know anything about Syria. I find that Arab Canadians and Arabs are very warm and accepting of me, because I have an Arab last name, and I look like I could be Middle Eastern. At the same time, I'm so Canadian. I have a struggle with that. I don't feel that I'm one thing, one solid blend of things. It's so interesting; I'm so glad that I found out this is part of me. At the same time, it's thrown my analytical frame into a hurricane!

When you first asked the question about identity, I was thinking ethnic identity, because we were talking about dancing. My identity first is as a mother. In being a mother, I know where I'm going, and what I would like to be. I'd like to be a teacher, that's what I'm on my way to doing. I'd like for that to be part of me, and what I give to the world. Definitely I think of gender a lot, but all that sits on top of this unrest, the ethnic identity stuff. I define myself as "mother," "teacher" and basically an ethnic mishmash, but not dancer. Even a year ago, I would have said dancer just after mother. However, I have been practicing yoga for the last couple of years and in that process have been learning to let go of some of the anxiety that comes with defining myself as a belly dancer. That is, anxiety around feeling left out of the community, pushed aside, annoyed by certain attitudes, pressured to promote myself, etc. In learning to let go of my ego a bit I have happily discovered that my path is more about helping people than defining myself as a dancer. That is partly why I am focusing on my studies and volunteering at the moment. I can say with confidence now that if I do belly dance again, it will be just for joy, so I don't really consider myself a professional dancer.

Sometimes I Just Want to Belly Dance

Before I had a baby, I had time to blog. I was on Live Journal, and I joined a few belly dance groups. I try not to get involved in that too much now, because it's really bad for me. I get angry, annoyed, and consumed. I don't even remember what one argument was about, I think it was tribal [dance]. I think I was saying something about pulling from flamenco, and Indian, and African and more, saying, "That's all fine, but isn't it a little disrespectful? What gives you the right to pluck whatever you want from these traditions that have deep roots, and just throw it together, to some American music? Can you not study it in more depth, give it some due respect?" Then I said, the reason I'm protecting this, is its part of my heritage. Nobody else was from any kind of Middle East background. And I remember an intense argument, and being charged with reverse racism. This was around 2005. It's discouraging. But what can you do, it's like a whole sea of ignorance. In an online forum, can you really change somebody's mind? I tried. I would write lengthy paragraphs. But it didn't really come to much.

When I was in the troupe, we had open discussions about it. We had a troupe member who had an Irish background so she'd use Celtic music. I really felt like she was bringing something of herself to it. She wasn't saying this was better than the other. She felt that I was concerned about things like that, so she would bring it up. It's unusual that people talk about these things, I find. I hate to say it, but unless you have some kind of academic background, it's not really something they teach you to do in public school. I learned to think critically by going to university, it's a real privilege to have that background and to be able to think that way. When I first went to university and these ideas came up, like colonialism and feminism, I remember being very thrown by it. So if it's the first time you're hearing a debate like that, I know that people can get touchy, because I've been there. But when you look at a forum online, when people bring up things like that, they tend to get shut down immediately. And people get very defensive. They say, "Are you telling me that I can't dance? Are you telling me that I can't belly dance because I'm _____?" They're very touchy, because they're not listening.

Sometimes it's not fun. Sometimes I just want to belly dance and not be so ethical about everything. I can't. I can't do it in any aspect of my life. I hold such high ethical standards for myself that it's a problem. In everyday life, I'm always weighing everything. I don't like the attitude that what is Arab is traditional, and therefore stagnant, and not very interesting. So that we here, we North American girls, we're going to make it interesting. We're going to make this something people want to see. I couldn't help but notice that when tribal dance exploded in popularity, that a lot of the Arabness was washed out. That's how I see it; I don't know how other people see it. We were in the middle of the Iraq war. Islamophobia and anti–Arab racism were at their peak, especially in America, where this tribal belly dance was flourishing. I'm not saying that people who were involved in tribal belly dance were racist, or anti–Arab. I always wondered if this white-washing of an Arab dance form had anything to do with what was happening in the Middle East. What America was doing in the Middle East at the time to say nothing of what it continues to do in Gaza! And these two things seemed to just happen, right at the same time. The attitude, "Well, American women want to belly dance, but it's really not very interesting, it's too weird, it's too exotic, it's too Arab. Let's set it to different music, and call it something else, and pull together this mishmash of costumes, from all over the place. Let's just not call it belly dance anymore." There was this rhetoric. That's what I think. When I say I get very angry and irritated, I'm thinking about that. People justify doing belly dance, because they say it was a birth ritual, or made up in a birthing temple, or something like that. Why can't you just do it, and admit what you're doing? It's an entertainment, and yes it's an entertainment for men too.

I would never say to anybody that they're not welcome to belly dance, or welcome to be interested in Middle Eastern culture. I would never say that to anyone. But there's a difference between pursuing an interest, and claiming it as your own and representing it to other people, who know nothing about that culture, as your own. I think it's wonderful that so many women want to belly dance. It's so much fun and has the potential to be a real community-building thing. It's great when troupes come up; they sort of mushroom up and perform. Even when they're not professional dancers, I think it has wonderful potential. My only wish is that if people are going to be serious about it, and be ambassadors for it, to know what you're talking about.

Mira: Arab Women — You Play the Drum and They Will Dance

I was never introduced to dance, I was born with it. When I was a little child, 9 or 10 years old, our neighbors used to come and knock on the door. They would ask my mom, "Can you let her come to dance?" In Tunisia, people get together after dinner, or any kind of gathering, they start singing and dancing. Some of the people don't even have drums, they just use pots. They would invite me because I loved dance, and I was good. But my father, he hated it.

Coming from a family of well-educated people, the focus of the family was study and education, to obtain degrees. Everyone had to have university degrees. I have an MA in French literature, and I worked in the family business. My father thought being a dancer was a sin. It was not done in public; he refused even to hear the idea. If you are dancing, you are the black sheep of the family. But I couldn't let go of my passion and I'm so glad that I didn't.

When I was 13 years old, my mother enrolled me in the National Conservatory of Dance in Tunisia. That was the hardest journey I had in my life, to go through seven years of study without my father knowing. It was thanks to my mom as she knew my passion for dance. She would take me with her, like I was going to her work, and I would go to my class. I danced with our national troupe, performing in Germany, Italy, and Cuba in the 1980s, without my dad's approval. I started teaching at the Conservatory and continue teaching today.

I first came to Canada just to visit and I have stayed. I could not survive without music and dance. I started my journey here working as a singer then I met dancers. I was encouraged by one belly dancer, who asked me to take on her classes when she traveled. Then I started teaching for myself, doing workshops on my own, and some performances. It's been a wonderful, wonderful journey, and now I am doing it with my girls, my daughters. I did a workshop in Victoria when I was 8 months pregnant! I will continue to perform and teach, though more slowly, with the girls and my full-time job.

Dance: It Always Has to Have Meaning

Tunisian folkloric dance is a different style, it's beautiful. Being from Tunisia, and a master instructor, I pass on this knowledge. I am in Canada, so I am trying to promote the dance here. I am doing workshops and promoting it in order to save the dance. It's very sad, because the style has a huge history. Traditional dance is disappearing right now, and I'm trying to bring it back. There are fewer folkloric dancers now and more modern and fusions.

I have seen some fusion performances with Tunisian. It's not what I would do, but I appreciate that they use the movements. So long as the music is good, and the dance is good, the style doesn't matter. If it's creative, has "weight," is well done. Not just a couple of movements here, a couple of movements there. As long as it's thought about, its meaning.

When people choose their dances, they have to have a meaning, a purpose, and be informative. In Tunisian dance, it always has to have meaning. Like the folkloric dance from the south of Tunisia, about girls. In the olden days, it was the girls' job to go to the source to get water. They gossiped, they talked about boys they had seen. And they would have special moments when singing and experiencing the joy of dance.

My principle is, don't do anything I cannot master, in dance and in daily life. I love other dances. I'll always be teaching Tunisian dance, the way it is and has been, as a cultural dance. Fusion is beautiful, but some kinds you cannot touch. And I am honored to teach Tunisian dance. I can belly dance, but I will not be a "belly dance teacher." I leave the expertise for the experts, and I have great respect for other styles. Performing is different. Yes, I will belly dance; I have no problems with performing. But in teaching, I teach Tunisian style. The response from the belly dance community and their feedback, is amazing. Everyone is enthusiastic. It brings tears to my eyes. Even people I don't remember will walk up and say things about my workshops. I have never heard negative feedback for me personally or for my dance.

For People Passing on the Street, I Could Be from Anywhere

Tunisia is a very small country. Tunisians are versatile, having been colonized by French, Greek, Turks, and Romans. We fit everywhere and anywhere. I speak seven Arabic dialects other than my own, as well as French and English. Around here, people think of me more as an Arab woman than Tunisian, because they see me as an Arab singer, more than a dancer. I see myself as an Arab woman, but it's such a wide word. Yes I am Arab, but I come from North Africa. It's not part of the Middle East. But we're similar;

I don't see any important difference. We speak the same language, we have the same spirits, we have a close culture, and it's basically the same.

Yes I am Tunisian, and feel Tunisian—but I am an Arab woman first, because there is this connection. There is bad press and people don't make the distinction between being Muslim and being Arab. It doesn't affect me in daily life; if people don't know me, they can't tell I'm an Arab woman, even by my name—though it is typical, it comes from a Berber tribe. I am sorry to say, but it is a result of certain ignorance about Islamic religion, and the Arab world. They don't understand and don't try to learn. It makes me sad to hear. I think you can't break a mountain with a hammer, but it is my duty to address it. I just go step by step to make people more aware. I definitely do that through my singing and dancing, it has to have a message to convey to get into people's hearts so they can be aware. My focus is to pass on my knowledge to dancers here. I am here and I will be here and I will still be the Arab woman and the Tunisian. Teaching Tunisian dance, and passing on my knowledge until the last day of my life.

Diasporic Encounters

Rasha, Rahma, Phedra and Mira are "invisible Arabs" with an ethnicity not readily identifiable to others—and in Phedra's case, not even to herself. This allows us creativity in presenting ourselves to the world. We mobilize personal and cultural identities strategically in different contexts. Sometimes we accommodate the social norms of Canadian or Arab society, and sometimes we resist them. Each one of us has constructed a different relationship with local Arab and belly dance communities. But we share a resolve to resist dominant social constructions of Arabness, and the dominant discourses of our families' homelands that castigate belly dancers. Each narrator has chosen to address discrimination, stereotyping, and systemic racism in their life and in their dance.

Dance offers a site for challenging and destabilizing assumptions about Arabness and Arab womanhood, for re-appropriating and transforming a socially marginalized dance into a source of pride. We sincerely believe that participating in dance has the potential to produce deeper, nuanced and meaningful understandings, and we actively contribute our knowledge of history, culture and music from countries of the Middle East and North Africa.

All of us believe that belly dance is an Arab cultural practice. The power relations that underlie North American presentations of Egyptian, Lebanese, Tunisian, and Arab culture are troubling, particularly American claims to ownership of the dance form. We experience varying degrees of discomfort, even anger, with belly dance discourses and practices that downplay, dismiss, or distort Arab associations with the dance, and marginalize the presence of Arab women.

These narratives argue for an ethical form of transnationalism in belly dance that respects the inevitable differences that emerge when crossing borders. Some of us hopefully envision a belly dance community that learns from a plurality of locations, while resisting the biases of appropriation and marginalization. Our dance and teaching encourages an aesthetic transnationalism that enriches and revitalizes dance through encounters and exchanges (Fluck 2011), just as the diversity and fluidity of our diasporic identities and transnational experiences have enriched our lives. When we belly dance, we perform our personal cultural identities. For Rasha, Rahma, Phedra, Mira, and I, each and every dance is an expression of self and joy, a demonstration of cultural pride, an educational tool — and an act of resistance.

Notes

1. Rasha Gadm Rahmma Haddad, Phedra, and Mira; Mira and Phedra are pseudonyms.

2. These narratives represent how we make sense of our lives and the world, at a particular point in time. Each one has been transformed from spoken word to text, and is simultaneously the product of two subjectivities: the narrator and myself as instigator, listener, and editor. The interviews with Rahma and Mira were shaped by our long-term relationships, while those with Rasha and Phedra took place during our first meetings. The dancers were generous in taking time from busy lives to explore notions of difference, authority, authenticity, appropriation and hybridity.

I interviewed each dancer individually, in their home or at a cafe, introducing broad topics and listening closely. Instead of dissecting the transcriptions with particular theoretical frameworks, I have chosen to present each unique voice in a coherent narrative. With the narrators' approval and sometimes their collaboration, I have organized and edited their words for this publication. The original transcripts were awkward and sometimes misleading without the accompanying vocal inflections, facial gestures and body language. So we have "smoothed" words so they can be read easily as text.

3. In recent decades Arab immigrants in Canada, like those in the U.S., have been relatively advantaged because of their high levels of education and professional qualifications (Nagel and Staheli, 2010).

4. Diasporan families are dispersed from their countries of origin, yet their beliefs and practices maintain collective dimensions that emphasize cultural distinctiveness through several generations (Faist, 2010). Diaspora is not defined by purity but by diversity and hybridity, and diasporic identities live with and through difference (Bhabha 1994, Braziel and Mannur, 2003).

Works Cited

Abu-Lughod, L. (1998). *Remaking Women: Feminism and Modernity in the Middle East.* Princeton: Princeton University Press.

Bailey, D.A., and G. Tawadros. (2003). *Veil: Veiling, Representation, and Contemporary Art.* Cambridge, MA: The MIT Press.

Bhabha, H.K. (1994). *The Location of Culture*. New York: Routledge.
Braziel, J.E., and A. Mannur. (2003). "Nation, Migration, Globalization: Points of Contention in Diaspora Studies." *Theorizing Diaspora* Ed. J.E. Braziel and A. Mannur. Malden, MA: Blackwell.
Buller, R.E. (2007). "Un/Veiled: Feminist Art from the Arab/Muslim Diaspora." *Al-Raida* 24: 16–20.
Dox, D. (1997). "Thinking Through Veils: Questions of Culture, Criticism and the Body." *Theatre Research International* 22; 150–161.
Eid, P. (2007). *Being Arab*. Montreal: McGill-Queen's University Press.
Faist, T. (2010). "Introduction: Diaspora and Transnationalism: What Kind of Dance Partners?" *Diaspora and Transnationalism: Concepts, Theories and Methods*. Ed. R. Baubock and T. Faist. Amsterdam: Amsterdam University Press.
Fluck, W. (2011). "A New Beginning? Transnationalisms." *New Literary History*, 42, 365–384.
Gad, R. (2010). Interview, March 25, Vancouver.
Haddad, R. (2010). Interview, March 24, Vancouver.
Harper, L. (2001). "By My Own Eyes: A Story of Learning and Culture." *Making Space*. Ed. V. Sheared and P.A. Sissel. Westport, CT: Berin & Garvey.
Haw, K. (2009). "From Hijab to Jilbab and the 'Myth' of British Identity: Being Muslim in Contemporary Britain a Half-Generation On." *Race Ethnicity and Education* 12; 363–378.
Jarmakani, A. (2008). *Imagining Arab Womanhood: The Cultural Mythology of Veils, Harems, and Belly Dancers in the U.S.* New York: Palgrave Macmillan.
Maira, S. (2008). "Belly Dancing: Arab-face, Orientalist Feminism, and U.S. Empire." *American Quarterly* 60; 317–345.
Mira. (2010). Interview, April 16, Vancouver.
Nagel, C.R., and L.A. Staeheli. (2010). "Citizenship, Identity and Transnational Migration: Arab Immigrants to the United States." *Space and Polity* 8; 3–23.
Phedra. (2010). Interview, April 10, Vancouver.
Purkayastha, B. (2012). "Intersectionality in a Transnational World." *Gender & Society* 26; 55–66.
Rowe, N. (2008). "Dance Education in the Occupied Palestinian Territories: Hegemony, Counter-Hegemony and Anti-Hegemony." *Research in Dance Education* 9; 3–20.
Said. E. (1979). *Orientalism*. New York: Vintage Books.
Saliba, T. (2000). "Arab Feminism at the Millennium." *Signs: Journal of Women in Culture and Society* 25; 1087–1092.
Shay, A. (2006). *Choreographing Identities: Folk Dance, Ethnicity and Festival in the United States and Canada*. Jefferson, NC: McFarland.
_____. (2008). *Dancing Across Borders*. Jefferson, NC: McFarland.
Statistics Canada. (2012). *Profile of Ethnic Origin and Visible Minorities for Census Metropolitan Areas, Tracted Census Agglomerations and Census Tracts, 2006 Census*. Accessed 17 March 2012. http://www.statcan.gc.ca/bsolc/olc-cel/olc-cel?catno=94-580-XCB2006005&lang=eng.

1970s Belly Dance and the "How-To" Phenomenon
Feminism, Fitness and Orientalism

Virginia Keft-Kennedy

Since the mid-nineteenth century the popularity of belly dance in the West has steadily increased. In particular the mid– to late 1970s witnessed a massive increase in the popularity of the dance form; particularly in the United States but also in the major cities of Europe and Australia. Belly dance classes sprang up in community centers and town halls, and the American nightclub scene boomed with nightly shows by belly dancers who entertained a growing international clientele. By 1979 the American Broadcasting Company television news program *20/20* reported that more than one million women in the United States alone were taking belly dancing classes (Sellers-Young 1992, 143). In addition to this developing sense of a global belly dance community, the dance was also becoming a highly marketable commodity. The late 1970s saw a steady flow of belly dance-related cultural products appear, such as instructional belly dance manuals, popular fiction in which the dance featured thematically, television series featuring belly dancers, as well as countless films produced in Egypt and in the United States. The variety of media products that sprang up during this time were pivotal in contributing to the collective cultural formation of belly dance as a social practice, or what Arjun Appadurai has usefully understood as a kind of imaginative social force resulting in "an organized field of social practices" (1996, 31). This chapter explores the emergence of popular belly dance instructional manuals published in the late 1970s and examines the ways in which they heralded the synthesis of a newly Westernized discursive feminist construction of belly dance within the growing global belly dance community.[1]

Prominent dancers in the United States, in particular, were prolific producers of popular instructional dance manuals and books that helped both popularize and codify the dance form. The key publications of this kind include *The Serena Technique of Belly Dancing: The Fun Way to a Trim Shape* (1972) by Serena and Alan Wilson; *The Compleat Belly Dancer* (1973) by Julie Mishkin and Marta Schill; *The New Art of Belly Dancing* (1974) by Adela Vergara, Roman Balladine, and Sula; *The Art of Belly Dancing* (1975) by Dahlena and Dona Z. Meilach; *The Belly Dancer in You* (1976) by Özel Turkbas; and *A Belly Dancer's Slim-Down and Shape-Up Secrets* (1979) by Lebwa.[2] This group of books — which I will collectively call the "how-to" books — were influential in the development of a belly dance subculture in the United States and subsequently throughout Europe, Australasia, South America, and Asia (Shay and Sellers-Young 2003, 17). It is my contention that the authors of the how-to books traversed an often difficult cultural terrain in their attempts to endorse and reinvigorate a dance form that continued to be tainted by the negative stereotypes it had garnered through colonialist encounters with Middle Eastern dance in the 18th and 19th centuries. Drawing on feminist discourse, along with emerging discourses on fitness culture, I argue that these books reveal an attempt by the authors to redefine the female body in belly dance as something other than a fetishized object, always-already appropriated for male pleasure. Rather, the how-to books position belly dance as a desirable activity for women; one that is healthy, artistic, and above all, liberating.

The how-to books, aimed at the dance's new devotees, attempted to challenge the dominant stereotypes about belly dance by reintroducing it as a respectable dance form, one that had long been subject to misinterpretation through ignorance and conservatism. In this way the mass-market belly dance publications of the 1970s had several pedagogical functions: to teach the dance with all its health and fitness benefits, to revise its degraded history, to challenge dominant perceptions and stereotypes about belly dance, and for the first time, to formulate a popular discourse on the dance that established not only its conventions as an empowering art form, but also suggested what it might mean for women to be part of an increasingly globalized belly dance community. These books were also intimately connected with two other significant cultural phenomena of the 1970s in the West: the burgeoning fitness industry (as the subtitles of the how-to books suggest), and the emergence of a strain of feminist thought that has come to be known as "goddess feminism" or "goddess religion." These two seemingly unrelated areas of 1970s cultural activity converged in the textual discourse on belly dance during this period.

While I maintain that the how-to books make explicit the possibilities of belly dance for a sense of female empowerment, I also wish to highlight the limitations of their discursive positioning of the dance within certain hegemonic socio-cultural structures of the late 70s and early 80s. The irony at work in the representations is that while the producers of these texts clearly aimed to generate a construction of belly dance as a liberating practice for women, they also tended to engage with the dominant ideologies of consumer culture which variously figured women and women's bodies as passive, domesticated, and ultimately, as sexual commodities. Moreover, they also incorporate, and are implicated in, other socio-cultural factors such as Orientalism and ethnocentrism. The instabilities, impartialities, and slippages contained within these books, however, make them no less potent as revisionist narratives but rather reinforce the complexities that have surrounded the practice of belly dance and highlight its potential for diverse meanings. In arguing this I examine the degree to which these texts achieve their feminist renegotiation of belly dance via an Orientalist discursive strategy. Interestingly, despite the large wave of Arab immigrants who settled in the United States during the 1960s and 1970s and the subsequent development of an Arab-American identity, the how-to books conspicuously presume their readers to be white, Western, and female. This subject positioning of the reader as necessarily female and white, further complicates and problematizes the development of multivalent femininities. Nevertheless, points of productive transformation are complexly and precariously achieved through the construction of Eastern otherness as Western feminist liberation. In *The Power of the Image: Essays on Representation and Sexuality,* Annette Kuhn offers a critical manifesto for feminist scholars to think about gender and representation by arguing that "in order to challenge dominant representations, it is necessary first of all to understand how they work, and thus where to seek points of possible productive transformation" (1985, 10). It was essential, then, that belly dance is simultaneously domesticated and transgressive in order to consolidate an audience within the socio-political climate of the 1970s. Thus, it is my argument that the three broadly connecting cultural interests — feminism, fitness, and Orientalism — converge, and compete, in the production and consumption of belly dancing products during the 1970s to facilitate a revolutionary, albeit ambiguous and contradictory, feminine empowerment.

In his book *The Field of Cultural Production* (1993) Pierre Bourdieu explores the critical concept of the cultural field. According to Bourdieu the cultural field describes the complex network of sites, products, practices, producers, and consumers surrounding a designated cultural activity. Central to the production of a cultural field is the institutionalization of certain discourses, resources, bodies of knowledge, as well as hierarchies of authority, and values which function to legitimate the field. As instruments of the field's capacity to educate consumers, the belly dance how-to books — products of the cultural field of belly dance — functioned to broadcast the field's practices and values, as well as to present an exchange of views, and to debate or confirm common assumptions about the field (Ferguson 1998, 600). The success with which the field's values and practices are transmitted is evidenced by the continued citation of the 1970s how-to books as significant texts in the literary history of belly dance. Indeed, these books have been so successful in transmitting the cultural values attached to belly dance that the global market is now brimming with newer how-to books and other products which reflect a clear parallel with work begun by their predecessors of the 1970s. This success, I would suggest, is in part due to the commodification and marketing of belly dance to a mainstream popular audience. Part of the belly dance field's project was to promote female empowerment via the endorsement of the dance as an alternative to the increasingly rigorous disciplining praxis of the mainstream fitness industry. In order to manufacture such a field for belly dance and simultaneously make it attractive both to mainstream hegemonic discourse and to women attempting to work against the grain of social expectations, the proponents of the field needed to work both inside and outside dominant structures of femininity, feminism, and fitness. In other words, in order to be transgressive they also had to be complicit.

Shifting Cultural Prescriptions of Beauty, Fitness, and Fashion

Since the mid-19th century, Western cultural conceptions of female beauty have undergone a massive transition. As Susan Bordo and others have shown, one of the most pervasive social constructions of ideal beauty for women is centered on ideas of what constitutes appropriate or inappropriate body size and shape. Bordo notes "corpulence went out of middle-class vogue at the end of the [nineteenth] century" and "excess body weight came to be seen as reflecting moral or personal inadequacy, or lack of will" (1993, 192). This was a trend that prevailed throughout the 20th century. The dominant cultural conception of ideal beauty and femininity in the first decade of the 20th century was epitomized by the iconic image of the Gibson girl. With her tightly corseted figure and soft mass of hair always arranged high on her head in buoyant curls, the Gibson girl was the symbol of consummate beauty, demonstrating all that was respectable about women of her time (Fangman et al. 2004, 213). The iconic Gibson girl was not only imagined to be beautiful but was, according to Kenneth Yellis, "maternal and wifely" (1969, 44). She was the embodiment of stability and the guardian of moral codes.

In stark contrast to the Gibson girl, the 1920s saw another icon of womanhood emerge in the form of the vigorous, youthful, and willowy "flapper." This symbolic image of the modern woman was controversial for her apparently skimpy dress, her boyish lean figure, bobbed hair, and hedonistic lifestyle which included drinking, smoking, and dancing (Yellis 1969). According to Yellis, the archetypal flapper was the "utter repudiation of the Gibson girl" and the traditional conceptions of "morality and femininity" that she embodied (1969, 44).

Although the 1930s saw the abandonment of the androgynous image of the flapper in favor of a softer, fuller bust-line and slender waist, the Great Depression signaled the need for cheaper fabrics and simple, straight skirts that were easy to make at home. The 1940s and 1950s saw the return to the diminutive waists and spreading skirts fashionable in mid-19th century dress (Mendes et al. 1999, 79, 128). In the

The Flapper generally had a willowy lean figure.

late 1950s and early 1960s, it was Marilyn Monroe, with her full curves yet small waist, who was often described as "femininity incarnate" (Bordo 1993, 141). At the same time, however, the iconic sophistication of the slender actress Audrey Hepburn presaged the ultra-slim look to come in the 1960s. The dominance of the hourglass shape made fashionable by Monroe gave way once more in the late 1960s to an ultra-slender and androgynous ideal body shape embodied by fashion models such as Twiggy and Jean Shrimpton. With their emerging emphasis on youth culture and bodily self-management through weight-loss and diet, the post–1960s decades saw the ascendancy of the standard of female perfection as a slender, toned, and tightly managed body. The rapidly changing social, economic, and political roles of women in the late 1960s, and specifically their large-scale entrance into the labor market, meant that women constituted a new brand of consumers. These changes, along with women's greater participation in consumer practices, were felt strongly in the fitness industry, especially with the development of aerobics in the late 1960s.[3] During the 1970s this emphasis on diet and weight management was joined by the fitness and exercise movement that had been gaining momentum throughout the decade and that would culminate in the 1980s as a veritable boom in exercise and "physical culture."

The strong, albeit ambivalent, relationship between exercise cultures and belly dance was forged during the 1970s and early 1980s. It was during this time that the cultural interactions between belly dance communities and the feminist movement developed a contrapuntal relationship to the burgeoning aerobics movement. This parallel between belly dance and aerobics, with their similarly aligned emphases on the physical health benefits of bodily strength and agility on the one hand, and the aesthetic appeal of external appearances and socio-cultural expectations of feminine beauty on the other, highlights the conflicts and struggles at work in discourses of fitness, exercised bodies, and bodily display.

The extent to which women have participated in recreational sports and exercise has varied over time, but it was not until the first half of the 19th century that substantial changes in attitudes towards the place of women in society assisted in broadening the scope for women's involvement in physical cultures (Costa et al. 1994; Marks 1990). By the late nineteenth century the persistent lobbying by female activists and health reformers had helped set in motion the machinery of social change that would allow women of today to engage more fully in sports, exercise, and fitness practices previously denied them. Historically, the exclusion of women from exercise and sporting activities has been profoundly shaped by sexual and gender assumptions that have pronounced women (and women's bodies) unfit for vigorous physical movement. Indeed, as Roberta Park has noted, the term fitness itself has ideological implications beyond simplistic notions of health or condition of the body, also incorporating, especially since the late 19th century, the construction of difference along the lines of gender, mental health, biology, class, and race (Park 1994, 62). According to Park, "Victorians tended to think of fitness in terms of biological adaptiveness," and "[a]thletes," she writes, "were often depicted as biologically superior males" (1994, 62).

In the 20th century societal attitudes concerning the importance of health and fitness for both women and men changed dramatically. Physical strength, stamina, and muscularity became, as early as the 1920s and especially since the second wave of feminism in the late 1960s and early 1970s, a sign of empowerment for women (Bordo 1993, Theberge et al. 1994). In their preface to *The Art of Belly Dancing* (1975), Dahlena and Meilach pointedly make the following statement to their readers:

> [A] politician, on a recent visit abroad, was photographed at a belly dancing exhibition. He looked delighted. His wife just looked. Maybe she didn't realise that belly dancing is no longer a spectator sport. Don't *you* stay on the sidelines. Join in the fun [Dahlena and Meilach 1975, preface].

Dahlena and Meilach evoke the notion of sport and physical activity — which had previously been the domain of men — and call women to take up belly dance as their own sport and warn against remaining on the sidelines. At the same time however, their reference to belly dance as a spectator sport also refers to the Orientalist constructions of belly dance as a source of scopophilic pleasure for men. In the statement above, the politician is actively delighted by the belly dancer, his wife however is passive; she just looks. His wife has been sidelined by the belly dancer who has drawn the attentions of her husband — or to borrow the Orientalist terminology of the how-to books — the belly dancer has hooked the "Sultan." Additionally, the word sport also conjures the notion of playfulness and sexual banter, the belly dancer's *active* sensuality suggested in her movements sets her apart from his supposedly *inactive* wife.

The multiplicity of meanings in the Dahlena and Meilach's preface is evident in the slippages surrounding the meanings of belly dance as a practice. The how-to books collectively strive to present belly dance as a form which has the possibility to allow women an alternative to mainstream fitness regimes and thus to achieve not only a sense of "embodied freedom" (Dahlena and Meilach 1975, 9) gained through the pleasure of physical exercise for its own sake, but also hints at the sexual freedom that might be gained by learning this dance. However, the books also revert to narratives which objectify the female body and suggest that by increasing physical fitness and, more importantly, learning the art of sensuality through belly dance, women might ensure their desirability to men. Dahlena and Meilach's book claims "you could be a bigger attraction [...] than Playboy magazine or Monday night football" (Dahlena and Meilach 1975, cover). Vergara also reveals this slippage toward condescension to male desire when she writes that through belly dance a woman "becomes more sexually appealing" and furthermore that men will be "charmed by her self-discipline" (1974, 13). Vergara's emphasis on self-discipline is in keeping with the rising socio-cultural push for women to engage with diet, exercise, and other forms of body management.

One of the contradictions within the second-wave feminist movement was that although the 1970s saw important advances for women with regard to new opportunities for the pursuit of health and exercise, the rapidly increasing emphasis on fitness placed new pressures on women to lose weight and maintain a thin and slender body (Bordo 1993, 140). As political debates over women's rights about corporeal empowerment and other biomedical issues intensified, culturally constructed ideas about what constitutes a healthy, empowered, and fit female body became more complex. On the one hand, women's rights to engage in exercise, sports, and fitness became valorized through the rhetoric of choice, in which women enjoyed their newly found freedom to use or transform their own bodies in any way they wished. Lebwa's how-to book, *A Belly Dancer's Slim-Down and Shape-Up Secrets*, espouses this notion of self-determination when she states "your physical condition can be controlled by your own personal wishes and desires. If you can control your psyche, you can control your physical well-being" (1979, 81). On the other hand, these ideologies of self-determination helped to naturalize women's complicity with disciplining their bodies in ways that conformed to normalized notions of femininity as necessarily thin and toned.

One of the telling ways in which the how-to books enacted their complicity with cultural values of slenderness was through the marketing technique of the book subtitle. For example, the subtitle of Özel's book *The Belly Dancer in You* claims that belly dancing is "The joyous way to a youthful figure and a more vibrant personality" (Özel 1976). Dahlena's and Meilach's *The Art of Belly Dancing* boasts the by-line, "The sexy exercise: Thousands of women have already discovered it. Now an expert demonstrates the sensuous way to a more beautiful you" (Dahlena and Meilach 1975). Similarly, *The Serena Technique of Belly Dancing* proclaims belly dancing "The fun way to a trim shape" (Serena 1972), while Mishkin and Schill's *The Compleat Belly Dancer* is subtitled "For everyone who wants to be healthy and slim and have fun getting there" (Mishkin and Schill 1973). These subtitles appeared prominently on the front covers of each book and indicated to consumers that belly dance was a healthy weight-loss activity that was positioned firmly within the growing consumer market for fitness products. Significantly, though the book subtitles reveal a divergence from the mainstream fitness trends by advocating belly dance as an exercise that is uniquely feminine, fun and sexy. Following the lead of the 1970s authors, a number of contemporary how-to books utilize remarkably similar marketing techniques. Tamalyn Dallal's 2004 book *Belly Dancing for Fitness*, for example, is subtitled "The ultimate dance workout to unleash your creative spirit." Similarly Dolphina published her 2005 book *Belly Dance* with the tagline "Get fit and feel fabulous with this unique workout for the mind and body." These newer books, although written over three decades later, undeniably draw on, and contribute to, the work begun by the authors of the 1970s how-to books.

The 1970s how-to books, just like their newer counterparts, encourage a sense of self-acceptance through the practice of belly dance. Serena's book states that through belly dance the "spirit is enlarged, fears of inadequacy ... are overcome; inhibitions are dispelled ... she is desirable not only to men, but to herself" (1972, 13). Özel's book claims: "there is a great and permanent need for women to express themselves — as women. Belly dancing is one non-exploitative way to connect with that need" (1976, 15). Serena advises, "Be a little selfish. As you learn the steps and practice them, spend time getting to know yourself" (1972, 24). Although the books encouraged their readers to slim down and keep fit, these texts also worked against ideas of pushing the body to extremes. Serena points out that many belly dancers are "fat" (1972, 27) and warns the reader: "Your body type, and the distribution of fat, depend on many factors, not the least of which is heredity. Starvation diets, overwork or excessive exercise ... in order to produce a dream body that you were never intended to have in the first place can be extremely dangerous" (1972, 27). Many of the how-to books discussed here simultaneously advocate the production of slim bodies but with the disclaimer that women's biology determines the body's appearance. Despite the attempt by the authors of the how-to books to negotiate the oppositions between approaching the female body as a biological given, and regarding it as a locus of self-determination and choice, slenderness is, nevertheless, constructed as a critical component of women's social and cultural success.

Changing cultural conceptions about ideal female bodies brought about another important shift in the late 1960s: to be slim and fit was not enough; one had to also be young. This emphasis on youth culture accelerated during the 1970s, so that by the 1980s both medical and popular discourse constructed mature figures as symbols of self-indulgence and irresponsibility (Dinnerstein and Weitz 1994, 7). The late 1970s' mass media message promoted a youth culture based on self-mastery, and, ignoring the realities of aging, said that with hard work, diligence, and willpower, dominance over the body was possible (Bordo 1993, 152, Dinnerstein and Weitz 1994, 7). Conversely, the how-to books presented a challenge to mainstream trends in fitness by embracing the realities of aging, and thereby resisting cultural dictates that perceived attractiveness to be the province of young, slim women. One of the key ways in which they navigated a feminist discursive position and achieved this resistance was through the belly dance movement's firm commitment to inclusiveness.

Belly dance is constructed in the how-to manuals as a form of dance open to women of all ages, backgrounds, body shapes and sizes. Serena claims that her students range from "7 to 75, and come from every walk of life" (1972, 5). Serena states that "there is no need to abandon all of the charms and pleasures of childhood because of the number of years you have lived. An active, interested, enthusiastic, flexible woman is *young*" (1972, 24). It is noteworthy that Serena evokes childhood rather than young womanhood in a negotiation of youth fetishism. Lebwa writes that belly dance is not a dance just for "young, shapely women" and has "no limits to age or sex" (1979, 36). In this sense, belly dance's apparent inclusivity is presented as a positive alternative to the rigid and often unattainable body ideals exemplified by the consumer culture's increasing emphasis on a slender, perhaps prepubescent, "hard body" type. The belly dance how-to books (and the increasing community of women who took up the dance) advocated a holistic approach to fitness where the benefits of the belly dance functioned equally to improve not only physical health, but also emotional and mental well-being, and fostered creativity and self-expression. The practice of belly dance ran counter to the popular ethos of what Brabazon has called the "tough fitness" of the seventies with its "no pain no gain" mantra (2000, 102).

Pressures on women to be thin are compounded in part by the ways in which, as Nicky Diamond explains, "fat" and "thin" are socially constructed as natural opposites (1985, 54). Diamond argues that where "thin" is seen as the natural state of the body, "fat" is imagined as "pathological and a problem" (1985, 47). She explains that seeing fatness as transgression works to reproduce "those cultural ideals of femininity which define 'thin' as ideal" (1985, 47). Moreover, there is a striking contradiction inherent in the process of simultaneously naturalizing thinness as "normal," while also suggesting that thinness needs to be achieved through hard work and disciplined body practices.

In the 1970s, with the resurgence of interest in belly dance, authors and performers of the dance addressed these issues by challenging the supposed naturalness of this ideology. Paradoxically, however, they did so by exploiting the very same health and fitness consumer market which helped to create these ideologies in the first place — they produced belly dance instructional texts which claimed to help women to keep fit and/or lose weight. Furthermore, rather than exposing the social constructedness of the idea that thin is natural; they somewhat contradictorily attempted instead to rewrite this opposition, such that a soft/fat body is constructed as a natural body. Turkish dancer and author Özel writes for example in the section on movements of the belly: "you're going to learn some incredible things to do with that stomach of yours. But first, you've got to get rid of any shame you feel about yours — it's an asset, whatever shape it's in" (1976, 101). Mishkin and Schill suggest that when women throw away their "confining elastic girdles" and "replace them with jingly coin belts" their "belly-roll workouts and rib lifts" will give them "a new outlook on the midriff scene" (1973, 9). Mishkin and Schill are saying two things here: firstly, that the exercise value gained through belly rolls and rib lifts will mean that women will not need the restrictive girdles meant to hide and suppress the belly, and secondly, they promote a discourse about self-acceptance and pride in women's bodies, their appearances, and especially, in their belly.

This notion of "honoring the belly" as the locus of female reproductive power was a prevalent concept in 1970s cultural discourse and manifested under a movement known as "goddess feminism" or "ecofeminism." Indeed, so powerful has this concept become for many writers and practitioners of belly dance that it continues to be a constitutive force in the transmission of information in the global processes which inform belly dance as a field of social practice. Newer books — such as *Grandmother's Secrets: The Ancient Rituals and Healing Power of Belly Dancing* (1999) by Rosina-Fawzia Al-Rawi — work within the generic conventions of the 1970s how-to book. Al-Rawi draws heavily on notions of the eternal feminine while blending personal memoir with popular myth and history of belly dancing along with step-by-step instruction on the dance. She recounts her earliest memories of learning the art of belly dancing from her grandmother in their family home in Baghdad and describes the "ancestral call" when her grandmother begins to teach her the "ancient craft" of Arabic women's dance (1999, 5). Al-Rawi recalls her grandmother's instruction to "draw a dot and concentrate all your energy into this one dot. It is the beginning and the end, the navel of the world" (1999, 5). Her grandmother continues, "when you circle your pelvis, you are drawing the dot, the origins. From this shape all other movements are born — they all stem from this dot, from the navel in your belly" (1999, 7). Al-Rawi's book, along with other more recent books such as Iris J. Stewart's *Sacred Woman, Sacred Dance* (2000), Tina Hobin's two books *Belly Dancing for Health and Relaxation* (1998) and *Belly Dance: The Dance of Mother Earth* (2003), Pina Coluccia, Anette Paffrath and Jean Pütz's book *Belly Dancing: The Sensual Art of Energy and Spirit* (2005) and Neena & Veena's *The Way of the Belly* (2006), can be seen as contemporary manifestations of the genre of the "how-to" belly dance book. Specifically, all of these books develop and explore the concept of belly-dancer-as-goddess. In keeping with their 1970s counterparts, these books utilize archetypal constructs of woman as sacred life giver and belly dance as "the dance of mother earth" (Hobin 2003, 170) to explore the spiritual meanings of the dance for the women who practice it.

Ecofeminism, Goddess Religion, and Belly Dance

The term "ecofeminism" describes a diverse social movement that emerged in the 1970s and which combined the agenda of the ecology movement (environmentalism) with those of feminism (1999, 10). As several critics have pointed out, along with its philosophical and political aspects, ecofeminism contains a strong spiritual dimension often referred to as goddess feminism. The notion of goddess feminism was an important and integral aspect of ecofeminist ideology in the 1970s. As Karen Warren notes, like feminism and ecofeminism generally, "there is no one version of 'spiritual ecofeminism'" (1996, 31). Nevertheless, spiritual ecofeminists such as Starhawk (1979, 1988), Charlene Spretnak (1978), Mary Daly (1973, 1978), Merlin Stone (1976), and Carol Christ (1979) agree that matriarchal symbols and spiritualities, such as those relating to Gaia and Goddess, are essential to ecofeminist thought (Warren 1996, 31). These authors, among others, explore the notion of goddess feminism and the idea that women's oppression came about when modern industrial societies split from ancient matriarchal cultures. The result of this split was understood as a division between "male culture and female nature" (Sandilands 1999, 11). The basic premise of ecofeminism is that underlying capitalism is a fundamental disdain for nature and, by extension, for women, due to their link with nature and the cycles of life (Sandilands 1999, 11).

Contrary to patriarchal traditions,[4] spiritually-oriented ecofeminists sought to celebrate women's reproductive capabilities and their supposed sacred association with nature as a source of strength, power, and virtue (Plumwood 1993, 9). However, as Plumwood writes, "[T]he ecofeminist vision" that appears "so sane and so attractive, seems to raise many problems and questions" (1993, 7). One such question that continually arises in relation to this vision, she argues, is whether "ecofeminism [is] inevitably based in gynocentric essentialism?" (1993, 8). Elizabeth Grosz elaborates on this notion of "women's essence" which she argues "is assumed to be given and universal and is usually, though not necessarily, identified with women's biology and 'natural' characteristics" (1989, 47). While more current feminist work, such as Judith Butler's theories on performative identity in her book *Bodies That Matter* (1993), as well as poststructuralist and postmodern approaches to ideas of difference, have challenged reductivist conceptions of women's identity by claiming that female subjectivity is not only diverse but dependent on innumerable social and cultural factors, the supposition that there is a definable universal woman's essence was taken up vigorously by the belly dance cultures of the 1970s (240).

In particular, it is expressly the notion that women's reproductive capacities (where the female "belly" is a potent symbol of fertility) sets women apart from (and above) the material and dominating concerns of men. Alluding to 1960s popular media icon Marshall McLuhan, Mishkin and Schill proclaim: "The Belly as Media. The Belly as Message" (1973, 17). This relationship between the belly, reproduction, and belly dance is illuminated when Mishkin and Schill explain that "belly dance was performed by helpful village women as another sister was giving birth to a child. The dance served as a rhythmic, soothing reminder to the woman in labor to use her abdominal muscles to aide [*sic*] the birth process" (18). Mishkin and Schill demonstrate a pervasive component of the imagined reconstructions of the histories and origins of belly dance. In such constructions the past is imagined as a pre-industrialized matriarchal society, elusively distanced to a time and place where the female body held social and spiritual power that is now assumed to be lacking in postmodern industrialized societies.

The collection of how-to books actively construct the female body as the locus of women's strength and in doing so reveals the essentialist discourses that are central to the understanding of belly dance as an expression of female empowerment. For Serena the experience of belly dance is akin to "searching for the natural and ultimate truth of woman" (1972, 20). Likewise, Özel claims that "belly dancing is exotic and erotic, it speaks of deep sexual knowledge.... It's deep. Profound. Eternal" (1976, 27). Likewise, Özel writes "the stomach is the real centre of your body. Vulnerable and unarmoured, it is where you really receive 'vibrations'" (1976, 26). The consistent emphasis on the expression of innate feminine modes of thought, feeling, and sensuality in all of the how-to books, for instance, is an example of such essentialist discourse. However, a meaningful slippage is discernible; one which problematizes the model of essentialist gender discourse in the how-to books. The notion that belly dance draws out an *a priori* feminine mode that taps into a sense of universal female identity is ultimately disrupted through the didactic nature of the how-to genre: belly dance must be learned, and practiced. Özel, for example, states that belly dancing is "human engineering, applied at a very high level. It's a marriage of mind and body" (1976, 12). Tellingly though, Özel informs the reader that she herself could belly dance from the age of five years old "without any formal training" (1976, 10). Serena tells her reader that "it takes time to develop the power, stamina, and skill required to do the steps properly" (1972, 40). Likewise, Dahlena and Meilach argue that belly dancing "must be approached in the same way as every other art form [and] can be accomplished on many different levels" (1975, 5). Belly dance, they write, "is the result of a discipline that demands a perfect concentration and coordination between mind and body" (Dahlena and Meilach 1975, 5). While there is no doubt that the authors of the how-to books unanimously invest these books with essentialist constructions of gender, they are nevertheless simultaneously both resistant to, and complicit with, those constructions. The very premise of the instruction manual — to teach — negates the basis of essentialist understandings of the belly dance as a natural, unlearned, and innate feminine dance form. Yet there is also the implication that (white) women, under Western capitalism, have become estranged from their femininity, and that belly dance provides the vehicle through which they might be reacquainted with their womanhood, bodies, and sexuality. Mishkin and Schill — in their section amusingly titled "Creaking Westerners"— declare, "Western man and woman have done a good job of separating themselves from their bodies, or denying much of the body in self-expression" (1973, 19), the Westerner, they submit, rarely expresses "ecstasy or longing" and has "sadly atrophied; separated from the body soul" (19).

Authenticity

Up until the 1970s critical discourse on the ramifications and meanings of Western women's adoption of Middle Eastern dancing was limited (Shay and Sellers-Young 2003). The publication of the many instructional manuals on belly dance in the 1970s marked the first time that popular texts attempted — however cursorily or inadequately — to raise the issues of appropriation, hybridity, "authenticity," and the politics of cultural ownership. Serena, for example, in *The Serena Technique*, writes that "women danced the belly dance thousands of years before I came along, but what I have done with the steps is *new*" (1972, 4). Serena also adamantly criticizes "artists [that] simply use the steps without giving credit where it's due" (18). Contradictorily though, earlier in her book she makes the assertion:

> Some people cling to the foolish logic that since much of the dance comes from Turkey, it must be true that the only authentic dancers are Turkish. Nothing could be further from the truth. All of the Turkish dancers I know learned the dance right here in the U.S.A. As a matter of fact, a very prominent dancer told me the she seldom heard Turkish music until she came to this country she listened to American jazz on her radio in Turkey! [1972, 4].

Serena's paternalistic implication that the U.S.A. has taken on the role of educator to the Turkish expatriate dancers in America, presents the reader with the dominant paradigms of colonialist and Orientalist discourse. Indeed Serena's suggestion that American belly dancers are more Turkish than the Turkish represents a patent usurpation of the very Eastern dance traditions that she claims to authentically represent. The problem, I suggest, does not lie with Serena's failure to present an authentic representation of traditional Eastern dance, which, as Said has argued, is an unattainable exercise: "We need not look for correspondence between the language used to depict the Orient and the Orient itself, not so much because the language is inaccurate but because it is not even trying to be accurate" (Said 1978, 71). Rather, the problem lies in the paradox that Serena's supposedly authentic representation of belly dance enacts an erasure of the East from her conception of the dance and instead views the dance through the lens of white American knowledge. Gayatri Spivak's (1985) notion of the epistemic violence of imperialism might usefully be employed here, wherein Serena enacts not only the severance of belly dance from its cultural heritage, but also the appropriation and assimilation of the dance into the American tradition. In an interesting reversal of Serena's figuration of America as teacher and Turkey as student, Özel proclaims: "If a Turkish mother could teach her five year-old child how to bellydance, I can do the same for a literate, intelligent American adult" (1976, 11). Özel self-reflexively reformulates and decenters the dualistic Western hegemonic construction of colonial dominator as tutelage and Eastern "other" as the perpetual child by reversing the paradigm.

Serena's Westernization (or de-Orientalization) of belly dance presents a quandary from a critical perspective: is it more culturally insensitive to (mis)represent the East, or to not represent the East at all? These notions of cultural appropriation and Orientalist misrepresentation of belly dance are difficult and complex. Indeed, all of the authors of the how-to books discuss the dance's tradition or derivation, some with greater cultural sensitivity than others. While Mishkin and Schill acknowledge the diversity of the cultural origins of belly dance as it is known in North America, they nevertheless problematically suggest that "when Islam unified the Middle East in the seventh century, the culture became homogenous" (1973, 17). By contrast, Lebwa not only acknowledges the Middle East as the cultural foundation of belly dance but also dedicates a section on the "Regional Variations" (1979, 151). Similarly Özel writes that the "ancient art of belly dance" (1976, 11) originates in various forms in Central Africa, Greece, Egypt, and Turkey (1976, 12). This kind of acknowledgement of the cultural traditions of belly dance, however basic they may be, reveals an attempt to speak to issues of cultural appropriation and to revise the epistemic violence that is central to many Orientalist narratives.

Orientalism as Female Empowerment

Joyce Zonana first used the term "feminist Orientalist" in her analysis of *Jane Eyre*, in which she argued that the use of Orientalist imagery by early British feminist writers functioned to displace "patriarchal oppression onto an 'Oriental,' 'Mahometan' society" (1993, 593). In particular, the institution of the harem and the image of the Islamic veiled woman has often epitomized Orientalist constructions of the "oppressive" and "barbaric" Middle East. In chastizing the Orient, Zonana argues, the "speaker or writer neutralizes the threat inherent in feminist demands and makes them palatable to an audience that wishes to affirm its occidental superiority" (1993, 594). The implication here, as Charlotte Weber explains, is that "patriarchy was an 'Eastern' element to be purged from the West" (2001, 125). My reading of 1970s representations of belly dance presupposes feminism to have a far less antagonistic relationship to the Orient than Zonana's original formulation implies. Liberal feminism of the 1970s was by no means free from ethnocentric assumptions about Western cultural superiority, but neither was it as hostile to the East or Islam as some critics might suppose (2001, 137). As Reina Lewis has suggested in relation to her work on women's literary and artistic contributions to Orientalism in the late nineteenth century, "there is room within the discourse [of Orientalism] for a feminine, and perhaps less virulently xenophobic, version of Orientalism" (1996, 171). My concern is with how this "feminine" version of Orientalism came to be articulated as a specifically feminist one. I submit that there is a complicated tension between the two constituents of feminism and Orientalism in the literary representations of belly dance in the 1970s. Specifically, I argue that ecofeminist discourses that link women and nature act as the axis at which Orientalism and feminism are harnessed into a construction of the liberated belly-dancing body. Orientalist discourse is seamlessly woven into the construction and marketing of belly dance as an expression of female power.

The belly dance movement of the 1970s utilized discourses of Eastern exotic femininity to explore ideas of social and sexual freedom supposedly denied to Western women. Edward Said has argued that "[t]he Orient was overvalued for its pantheism, its spirituality, its longevity, its primitivity, and so forth" (1978, 150). Repeatedly, the how-to books refer to belly dance as mysterious, exotic, and enriching, and in so doing utilize the familiar tropes of romantic Orientalist discourse. The ideological construction of the East as a source of spiritual fulfillment was an integral aspect of the how-to books, and belly dancing functioned as the key way through which women could access such heightened spirituality. In their book *The Art of Belly Dancing*, Dahlena and Meilach write, for instance:

> Middle Eastern dance is a marvellous physical and emotional experience. It frees you from your everyday, mundane routine. It may set your mind to dreaming of faraway places, of cultures that have much to offer. It gives you an opportunity to acquaint yourself with your body, to achieve a new sense of freedom [9].

Underlying this notion of spiritual transformation through belly dance is the assumption that the Orient holds a greater degree of corporeal and spiritual freedom than does the West, an idea that is closely aligned with Said's version of Orientalism. Orientalism, in this sense, becomes a discursive strategy of feminism whereby learning belly dance promises women access to the exoticism and mystery of the East as well as the chance to achieve a sense of embodied liberation. Mishkin and Schill explain what they call "Inter-Oriental magic": "In these lands, the passions of birth and life and love are woven into every facet of the culture with a special earthy quality that transcends morality in the Western sense" (18). As Mishkin and Schill and Dahlena and Meilach's statements reveal, despite the possibilities that belly dance presents to second-wave feminism, these books perpetuate prevailing cultural ideologies that equate the East with the exotic, and thus are imbricated within larger patterns of neo-colonialist consumption of "foreign cultures."

One way in which the consumption of the East is literalized in the how-to books is through the inclusion of recipes for Middle Eastern cuisine. All of the how-to books include a section dedicated to the discussion of food and most incorporate this section into a broader notion of "putting on a show" (Serena 1972, 194). In this section the how-to books give detailed descriptions of how to prepare Middle Eastern food, as well as tips on music choice, and interior decorating in order to set an "enchanting, dreamlike atmosphere" for an "Arabian Night's party" (Lebwa 1979, 242). The representation of recipes and food descriptions functions in part to authenticate Orientalist representations of cultural otherness. Alice P. Julier, in her discussion on discourses of race and gender in food consumption, argues that "ethnic food, like ethnic culture, is assumed to be static, such that any change is viewed as assimilationist or a loss of tradition" (2005, 178). Özel, in her section entitled "Cooking like a Turk," suggests "Turks have a fetish for traditional cookery, so much so that many of the recipes that delighted the Sultans of the 12th and 13th century have been passed down to us without much alteration" (1976, 181). Özel's divulgence of Turkish culinary history is akin to sharing a secret with her readers — a kinky one at that, suggested by her use of the word fetish. The inclusion of Middle Eastern food in such a way symbolically reinforces the reader/participant's access to the East and renders it a knowable entity. Ghassan Hage has argued that the "multicultural valorisation of ethnic food which stresses its enriching qualities in everyday discourse is often contrasted with the supposed poverty of the Anglo-Celtic culinary tradition" (2000, 120). Lebwa's book, for example, suggests that "the Middle Eastern kitchen is full of variety. I can think of at least 50 ways that the Turks cook chopped meat. Compare that with the American one-track mind, wherein chopped meat means 'hamburger'" (1979, 100). The construction of food in this way operates through a discourse of what Graham Huggan has called "depoliticised 'ethnic sampling'" (2001, 60).

It is also relevant to observe that while most of the texts either include recipes, or discuss Middle Eastern foods, they tend to elide eating. Specifically, women's roles in the how-to books are limited to the preparation and serving of food, as well as dancing — in the case of several of the how-to books — for your "Sultan" (Özel 1976, 179). The emphasis on the preparation of food rather than eating it acts to both domesticate and exoticize the belly-dancing woman. For example, Mishkin and Schill write:

> You've kept your practice sessions all between you and the mirror. Now you want to surprise your man. Serve him an exotic meal: shish kebab, rice pilaf ... followed by a baklava and Turkish coffee for desert ... bid your audience of one to make himself comfortable ... while you change into your costume ... make your entrance [153].

The food merely adds to the Orientalist atmosphere of the scene and authenticates the harem fantasy of the dancing woman for a masculine objectifying gaze.

Using a different but interconnected fantasy, some of the how-to authors attempted to explore the notion of sexual freedom. However, tensions are evident in their discussions of sexuality. There seems, for these authors, to be a fine line between discussing the possibility of sexual liberation whilst avoiding the specter of the female sex object. Özel for example writes: "you're not a sex toy but a thinking feeling woman" (1976, 27). While none of the 1970s belly dance instructional texts deny the sexuality of the dance, most prefer to identify "sensuality" as a more suitable description. Dahlena and Meilach pronounce, "Yes, the belly dance, or Middle Eastern or oriental dance — whatever you want to call it — has become virtuous and respectable" (1975, 9). Serena argues "the belly dance isn't sexy — it is *sensual*" (1972, 24), and Dahlena and Meilach make the same distinction (despite the subtitle of their book — "The Sexy Exercise") (1975, 5). Vergara firmly warns would-be performers of the dance "no winking ever" (1974, 76), a directive also reiterated by Özel (1976, 114). By emphasizing the spirituality of the dance, the potentially unruly sexuality associated with belly dance could be alleviated. The question arises: how does one downplay the sexualized stereotypes that have dogged the dance while also suggesting that this same dance might offer women a way in which to experience their bodies and sexuality in a positive way? The answer, for some it seems, lies in the overtly Orientalist topos of the Harem and the image of the hypersexual Eastern dancer. Lebwa writes, "When you do the Oriental dance you are transported to another world — sensuous and abundantly rich with delicious intrigue" (1979, 155). She goes on: "I have often used the dance to transport me in my imagination to an ancient Middle Eastern or Turkish palace where I become the Sultan's favourite dancing girl. It makes me feel like a woman all over. Try it, you'll like it!" (155). In Lebwa's exaggerated fantasy of herself as the "Sultan's favourite," the concept of dancer coalesces with a heightened sense of freedom made possible by the erotic promise of the romanticized East. Yet, this sense of sexualized freedom is further co-opted when sexual liberation is dedicated to the sexual satisfaction of her male partner — the Sultan: "Why don't you try making your husband or loved one the Sultan? ... Smother him with the riches only a sultan can afford. You'll maintain a svelte figure keeping him busy" (Lebwa 1979, 155). In this figuration Lebwa encourages her readers to engage freely with fantasy (an issue that was hotly discussed in the 1970s pornography debates), and to safely act it out under the guise of Eastern sexuality. Interestingly, Lebwa also returns to notions of maintaining an ideal svelte body might be achieved as a result of this sexual role-play. Dahlena and Meilach produce a strikingly similar argument when they write: "Whether you need exercise to get back in to shape after having a baby, or you want to create an Arabian nights atmosphere for one favourite sultan, you'll discover that belly dancing is the magical, aphrodisiacal answer to most women's dreams of keeping their bodies in trim" (1975, 2). The authors continually zigzag — at times they acquiesce to the notion of a tightly controlled body which sits wholesomely within 1970s normative paradigms of appropriate female behavior, while they simultaneously revel in a belly-dancing body that seems to suggest the subversive pleasure of the unruly female body as a site of potential excess.

"Let her strut and wiggle": The Grotesque Belly-Dancing Body

Mary Russo has argued that feminism has "stood increasingly for and with the normal" (1994, vii) which has "led to a cultural and political disarticulation of feminism from the strange, the risky, the excessive, the outlawed, and the alien" (vii). While images of the domesticated female body (as sensual, nurturing, and maternal) are employed in many of the how-to books' constructions of belly dance, the moving body they describe and advocate is, nevertheless, a body that seems undisciplined and disruptive to normative constructions of femininity: shoulders are "shimmied," hips are "thrust" and "rotated," pelvises are "tilted" and "twisted," and bellies are "rolled," "fluttered," and "popped." The descriptors of the belly-dancing body in motion might be read through the critical concept of the grotesque to designate a rupture both in conventional standards of female propriety and in normalized notions of beauty.[5]

In his famous study of carnival and the carnivalesque in *Rabelais and His World*, Bakhtin makes a distinction between the "classical" and the "grotesque" body (1984, 19–25). According to his analysis, the upper body is the classical body; it is predominantly secure and intellectual, and maintains its integrity. The lower bodily stratum, on the other hand, is the site of the grotesque body, which has orifices, genitals, and protuberances. The classical body emphasizes the impenetrable, the ideal, and the spiritual; the grotesque body foregrounds its penetrability and excrescences, sexuality, and bodily excess. Furthermore, in grotesque imagery there is a tendency to "efface the confines between the body and surrounding objects, between the body and world, and to accentuate one grotesque part, stomach, buttocks, or the mouth" (Bakhtin, 1984, 354). The representations of belly dance in the how-to books consistently emphasize the lower bodily strata — these are bodies that refuse to stay in their proper place; they twist, undulate, and transgress the boundaries of the closed, smooth, and harmless classical body. In a particularly potent example of grotesque imagery Mishkin and Schill maintain that belly dance will "set your body moving in an entirely new way — every part of you will move on its own, rotating or wiggling as though detached from the rest. The hands, legs, breasts, and, of course, the belly will say things you never even heard before" (1973, 21). Not only does the grotesque belly-dancing body "transgress its own limits" (Bakhtin 1984, 320) through its ability to disarticulate, but also, significantly, the body parts will speak. I am not suggesting here that belly-dancing bodies are actually grotesque but rather that the visual and verbal language used to describe them renders them as such in the Bakhtinian sense. The grotesque body, according to Bakhtin, is always in the process of "becoming" (1984, 317), and like both Russo and Bakhtin I view the element of the grotesque as having deeply positive (Bakhtin 1984, 19) dimensions.

In an articulation of women's power through bodily movement Özel assures the reader that there is "a belly dancer in you" and directs that "this is the time to unleash her, to let her strut and wiggle, to let her feel the special pride that can only be felt by an active woman ... in action" (1976, 10). Özel raises the grotesque image of the dangerous woman/feminist as animal "unleashed." Her reference to pride as well as the call to action and her directive to strut are also telling indicators that Özel was drawing on the feminist idioms of the time. Moreover she subverts the Western dualistic paradigm of mind/body which, as Bordo explains, views the "male as active, striving, conscious subject and female as passive, vegetative, primitive matter" (1993, 12), and instead figures the animalistic "wiggling" female body as the locus of woman's power. In this way the grotesque belly-dancing body presents the possibility for the valorization and re-connection of feminism with the conception of the body as multiple, protruding, and changing.

Iris Marion Young, in her book *Throwing Like a Girl*, argues that women and men use and regard their bodies in space in markedly different ways. Women are inhibited, she argues, from making use of a "body's spatial and lateral potentialities" (1990, 145). Furthermore, she argues, "[t]here is no inherent, mysterious connection between these sorts of typical comportments and being a female person" (147). Rather, the "timidity, uncertainty, and hesitancy" (146) with which women often approach physical engagements is the direct result of the complex social and cultural forces enacted upon the "lived body" (149). The how-to manuals encourage women to use their bodies in a variety of different ways, extending themselves into the space around them. Indeed, not only do they give women permission to move their arms and legs into the space around them, but significantly, encourage them to project their pelvises, breasts, buttocks, and belly into space. Mishkin and Schill for instance describe the belly dance movement called the shimmy, and advise their readers that they need to learn to "let it all hang out and flap around like a bowlful of jelly being gently jiggled" (1973, 83). The image of the female body as jelly is simultaneously both grotesque and domestic. Significantly the emphasis on allowing the belly hang out and flap around presents a blatant rupture from the increasing demands of the fitness industry on women to view the female abdomen as a site of excess and shame. As such the how-to books constitute a celebration of the unruly female body through dance as a site of strength and sensuality; and above all, they promote a sense of feminine power through an acceptance of women's corporeality.

Conclusions

The main task of the 1970s belly dance how-to book, then, despite its complicity with cultural pressures about women's vigilance in monitoring the body's contours or appearance, was to explore the pleasures of the belly-dancing body in motion. While I have shown the attempts by these authors to reinvigorate the practice of belly dance through discourses of feminism, Orientalism and fitness culture were not always consistent or unified, the importance, nevertheless, of these books as benchmark texts in the cultural field of belly dance cannot be disputed. They unanimously encouraged women to reconfigure the repressive conceptions of womanhood that had been a dominating force in gender politics during the first part of the century with a more liberating approach to women's bodies and bodily movement through belly dance.

The how-to books' construction of belly dance as an inclusive and open-ended practice meant that more nuanced notions of the multiplicity of sexuality, sensuality, femininity, and body politics could be developed. They not only demonstrated the ways in which belly dance provided a vehicle through which women actively challenged prescriptive ideologies surrounding their bodies, especially in relation to the fitness industry, but also encouraged a sense of personhood, where sensuality, otherness, femininity, and sexuality were also sites of self-empowerment. The redefinitions of femininity being mobilized in this context established a new vision of belly dance outside of its previous Orientalist connotations of erotic display in the service of men's desires, and instead constituted a response to the changing desires of women for a practice that encapsulated the pleasures of the female body in motion whilst also providing physical exercise. Taken together as integral components of the cultural field of belly dance, the how-to books are united in their attempts to establish oppositional discourses through belly dance as well as to delineate the difficulties of resistance, and underscore the struggle to negotiate competing social practices and ideologies.

The current myriad of social practices surrounding belly dance — and its equally complex consumer products — show the extent to which the work begun by the belly dance practitioners and authors of the 1970s continues to be a site of constant negotiation for global belly dance communities. The global market for belly dance products not only endures but is stronger than ever with the publication of new how-to literatures along with instructional DVDs, films, and online manuals using a plethora of ever changing technologies and platforms such as YouTube, Expert Village, Apps, just to name a few. As Tamalyn Dallal has aptly claimed: "belly dance is contagious" (2004, 33). The internet, for instance, has become a globalized space for feminist political demands by women who have created coalitions surrounding belly dance, its practices, and its philosophies. These newer how-to texts are as complex as the 1970s how-to books which preceded them and offer new spaces through which women might negotiate the politics of feminism and embodiment in belly dance, as well as present a productive site for further scholarship in the field.

Notes

1. It was been well established by researchers and critics that belly dance as a form of cultural expression is not exclusively practiced by women but is a genre "danced by everyone in a variety of performances, amateur and professional, by boys and girls, women and men" (Shay 2005, 52). However, my research focuses specifically on the relationship between belly dance and the 1970s liberal feminist movement and, as such, the topic of male belly dance is outside the scope of this essay. See also Karayanni (2005).

2. I refer to several of the authors of the instruction manuals by their first names only. I do so in accordance with the convention that belly dance performers/authors are frequently identified by a single stage name or by their first name, as well as in keeping with how the author's name appears in the book.

3. Dr. Kenneth Cooper published his highly successful book *Aerobics* (1968), and Jackie Sorenson and Judi Sheppard Missett, inspired by Cooper's aerobic system, are each credited with having invented aerobic dance separately around 1970 (Kagan et al. 1998, 166). It is interesting to note that Sheppard Missett also co-authored her popular book *Jazzercise* (1978) with Dona Z. Meilach, the co-author of *The Art of Belly Dancing* (1975).

4. The idea of a generalized "patriarchy" has been criticized as a mark of cultural universalism (Plumwood 1993, 11). However, I am using the term here because of the currency of its use in the 1970s, and in the texts I am discussing.

5. For an extended discussion on the grotesque belly-dancing body see V. Keft-Kennedy (2005), *Representing the Belly Dancing Body: Feminism, Orientalism and the Grotesque* (Doctoral Thesis), University of Wollongong. For an analysis of the grotesque in relation to 19th century representations of belly-dancing dancing bodies see V. Keft-Kennedy (2005), "'How does she do that?' Belly Dancing and the Horror of a Flexible Woman," in *Women's Studies* 34 (3–4): 279–300.

Works Cited

Al-Rawi, R.-F. (1999). *Grandmother's Secrets: The Ancient Rituals and Healing Power of Belly Dancing*. Massachusetts: Interlink Books.
Appadurai, A. (1996). *Modernity at Large: Cultural Dimensions of Globalisation*. Minneapolis: University of Minnesota Press.
Bakhtin, M. (1984). *Rabelais and His World*. Bloomington: Indiana University Press.
Bordo, S. (1993). *Unbearable Weight: Feminism, Western Culture, and the Body*. Berkeley: University of California Press.
Bourdieu, P. (1993). *The Field of Cultural Production: Essays on Art and Literature*. Cambridge, England: Polity Press.
Brabazon, T. (2000). "Time for a Change or More of the Same? Les Mills and the Masculinisation of Aerobics." *Sporting Traditions* 17(1): 97–112.
Butler, J. (1993). *Bodies That Matter: On the Discursive Limits of "Sex."* New York: Routledge.
Collucia, P.P., A. Paffrath, and Jean Pütz. (2005). *Belly Dancing: The Sensual Art of Energy and Spirit*. Rochester, VT: Park Street Press.
Cooper, K.D. (1968). *Aerobics*. New York: Bantam.
Costa, D.M., and S.R. Guthrie. (1994). *Women and Aport: Interdisciplinary Perspectives*. Champaign, IL: Human Kinetics Publishers.
Dahlena and D.Z. Meilach (1975). *The Art of Belly Dancing*. New York: Bantam.
Dallal, T. (2004). *Belly Dancing for Fitness: The Ultimate Dance Workout That Unleashes Your Creative Spirit*. Berkeley, CA: Ulysses Press.
Daly, A. (1978). *Gyn/Ecology: The Metaethics of Radical Feminism*. Boston: Beacon Press.
Diamond, N. (1985). "Thin Is the Feminist Issue." *Feminist Review* 19: 46–64.
Dinnerstein, M., and R. Weitz. (1994). "Jane Fonda, Barbara Bush and Other Aging Bodies: Femininity and the Limits of Resistance." *Feminist Issues* 14 (2): 3–24.
Dolphina (2005). *Belly Dance*. New York: Doring Kindersley.
Fangman, T.D., J. Paff Ogle, et al. (2004). "Promoting Female Weight Management in 1920s Print Media: An Analysis of *Ladies' Home Journal* and *Vogue* Magazines." *Family and Consumer Sciences Research Journal* 32 (3): 213–253.
Ferguson, P.P. (1998). "A Cultural Field in the Making: Gastronomy in 19th-Century France." *American Journal of Sociology* 104: 597–641.
Garland Thompson, R. (1997). *Extraordinary Bodies: Figuring Physical Disability in American Culture and Literature*. New York: Columbia University Press.
Grosz, E. (1989). *Sexual Subversions: Three French Feminists*. St. Leonards: Allen & Unwin.
Hage, G. (2000). *White Nation: Fantasies of White Supremacy in a Multicultural Society*. New York: Routledge.
Hobin, T. (1998). *Belly Dancing: For Health and Relaxation*. London: Gerald Duckworth.
_____. (2003). *Belly Dance: The Dance of Mother Earth*. London: Marion Boyars.
Huggan, G. (2001). *The Postcolonial Exotic: Marketing the Margins*. London: Routledge.
Julier, A.P. (2005). "Hiding Gender and Race in the Discourse of Commercial Food Consumption." *From Betty Crocker to Feminist Food Studies*. Ed. A. Voski Avakian and B. Haber. Massachusetts: University of Massachusetts Press.
Kagan, E., and M. Morse. (1998). "The Body Electronic: Aerobic Exercise on Video: Women's Search for Empowerment and Self-Transformation." *TDR* 32 (4): 164–180.
Karayanni, S.S. (2005). *Dancing Fear and Desire: Race, Sexuality, and Imperial Politics in Middle Eastern Dance*. Ontario, Canada: Wilfred Laurier University Press.
Keft-Kennedy, V. (2005). "'How does she do that?' Belly Dancing and the Horror of a Flexible Woman." *Women's Studies: An Interdisciplinary Journal* 34 (3–4): 279–300.
_____. (2005). *Representing the Belly-Dancing Body: Feminism, Orientalism, and the*

Grotesque, PhD thesis, School of English Literatures, Philosophy, and Languages, University of Wollongong. http://ro.uow.edu.au/theses/843.
Kuhn, A. (1985). *The Power of the Image: Essays on Representation and Sexuality.* London: Routledge & Kegan Paul.
Lebwa (1979). *A Belly Dancer's Slim-Down and Shape-Up Secrets.* West Nyack, NY: Parker Publishing Company.
Lewis, R. (1996). *Gendering Orientalism: Race, Femininity and Representation.* London: Routledge.
Marks, P. (1990). *Bicycles, Bangs, and Bloomers: The New Woman in the Popular Press.* Kentucky: University of Kentucky.
Mendes, V., and A. De La Haye. (1999). *20th Century Fashion.* New York: Thames & Hudson.
Mishkin, J.R., and M. Schill. (1973). *The Compleat Belly Dancer.* New York: Doubleday.
Neena, Veena, with N. Bruning. (2006). *The Way of the Belly: 8 Essential Secrets of Beauty, Sensuality, Health, Happiness, and Outrageous Fun.* Carlsbad, CA: Hay House.
Park, R.J. (1994). "A Decade of the Body: Researching and Writing About the History of Health, Fitness, Exercise and Sport, 1983–1993." *Journal of Sport History* 21 (1): 59–82.
Plumwood, V. (1993). *Feminism and the Mastery of Nature.* London: Routledge.
Russo, M. (1994). *The Female Grotesque: Risk, Excess and Modernity.* London: Routledge.
Said, E.W. (1995). *Orientalism.* London: Penguin.
Sandilands, C. (1999). *The Good-Natured Feminist: Ecofeminism and the Quest for Democracy.* Minneapolis: University of Minnesota Press.
Sellers-Young, B. (1992). "Raks El Sharki: Transculturation of a Folk Form." *Journal of Popular Culture* 26 (2): 141–152.
Shay, A. (2005). "The Male Dancer in the Middle East and Central Asia." *Belly Dance: Orientalism, Transnationalism, and Harem Fantasy.* Ed. A. Shay and B. Sellers-Young. Costa Mesa, CA: Mazda Publishers, 51–84.
Shay, A., and B. Sellers-Young. (2003). "Belly Dance: Orientalism — Exoticism — Self-Exoticism." *Dance Research Journal* 35 (1): 13–37.
Sheppard Missett, J., and D.Z. Meilach. (1978). *Jazzercise.* Toronto: Bantam.
Spivak, G.C. (1985). "Three Women's Texts and a Critique of Imperialism." *Critical Inquiry* 12 (Autumn): 243–61.
Spretnak, C. (1978). *Lost Goddesses of Early Greece : A Collection of Pre-Hellenic Myths.* Boston: Beacon Press.
Starhawk. (1979). *The Spiral Dance: A Rebirth of the Ancient Religion of the Great Goddess.* San Francisco: HarperSanFrancisco.
_____. (1988). *Dreaming the Dark: Magic, Sex and Politics.* Boston: Beacon Press.
Stewart, I.J. (2000). *Sacred Woman, Sacred Dance.* Rochester, VT: Inner Traditions.
Stone, M. (1976). *When God Was a Woman.* New York: Barnes and Noble.
Theberge, N., and S. Birrell. (1994). "Structural Constraints Facing Women in Sport." *Women and Sport: Interdisciplinary Perspectives.* Ed. D. M. Costa and S. R. Guthrie. Long Beach: California State University.
Turkbas, Ö. (1976). *The Belly Dancer in You.* New York: Fireside.
Vergara, A., R. Balladine, et al. (1974). *The New Art of Belly Dancing.* Millbrae, CA: Celestial Arts.
Warren, K. (1996). *Ecological Feminist Philosophies.* Bloomington: Indiana University Press.
Weber, C. (2001). "Unveiling Scheherazade: Feminist Orientalism in the International Alliance of Women, 1911–1950." *Feminist Studies* 27 (1): 125.
Wilson, S., and A. Wilson. (1972). *The Serena Technique of Belly Dancing: The Fun Way to a Trim Shape.* New York: Drake Publishers.

Yellis, K.A. (1969). "Prosperity's Child: Some Thoughts on the Flapper." *American Quarterly* 21 (1): 44–64.
Young, I.M. (1990). *Throwing Like a Girl and Other Essays in Feminist Philosophy and Social Theory*. Bloomington and Indianapolis: Indiana University Press.
Zonana, J. (1993). "The Sultan and the Slave: Feminist Orientalism and the Structure of *Jane Eyre*." *Signs* 18 (3): 592–617.

Dancing with Inspiration in New Zealand and Australian Dance Communities

Marion Cowper and Carolyn Michelle

Despite their geographical isolation from regions where belly dancing has its historical roots, Aotearoa New Zealand and Australia have become home to many and varied belly dance communities. Recent research comprising interviews with 26 belly dance practitioners suggests that dancers within these communities have adopted a variety of dance styles which they classify in general terms as belly dancing and attribute with having origins in the ancient Middle East (Cowper 2011). In this chapter, we consider the impetus behind the increasing adoption and adaptation of this dance form in geopolitical contexts that are far removed from its Eastern origins. What is the appeal of this form of dance "Down Under," and what understandings do women formulate of significant experiences encountered during their dance practice?

Although a broad range of material about belly dancing is now accessible online, women in Australasian belly dance communities are more commonly introduced to the activity of belly dancing through social events and interactions and via the regulative discursive interface of film and television media. Yet, while highly stereotypical, eroticized depictions of belly dancing have regularly featured in film over the last 100 years and more recently television, this research suggests that belly dancers from New Zealand and Australia do not necessarily identify strongly, if at all, with the imagined exotic belly dancing "Other" that is most frequently depicted within contemporary media (Cowper 2011). Indeed, they express some degree of resistance to dominant Orientalist constructions of belly dancing, while simultaneously reframing their own dance practice as offering access to profound embodied experiences that many described as transcendent or spiritual in nature.

We suggest such experiences can best be understood in terms of Mihaly Csikszentmihalyi's (1990) concept of "flow" and Abraham Maslow's (1968, 1970) notion of "peak experiences," and in this essay seek to illustrate how women's "flow" experiences were frequently ascribed spiritual, sacred, and inspirational meanings that had significance and influence beyond the immediate context of belly dance performance. Describing their experiences of belly dancing from a position of subjective centrality, many respondents articulated uniquely personal understandings of their dance practice, suggesting that while dualistic essentialist and Orientalist constructions of belly dance continue to pervade the wider public sphere, individual dancers are actively creating alternative and deeply personal meanings of this increasingly globalized feminine dance form. Further, several participants described how their involvement in belly dance had enabled them to construct new understandings of themselves, their bodies, their capabilities, and their roles as women, while a few were able to utilize the personal shift in perspective stimulated by belly dancing to devise novel strategies that transformed their personal interactions within a wider public context.

The research discussed here, then, offers insights that suggest the global dissemination of belly dance culture is linked not merely to the generation of locally relevant meanings and practices, but also to the deeply personal and interior subjective realities of individual dancers. While other essays in this volume delineate specific local expressions of belly dance in different geopolitical contexts, this one suggests that the global transference, evolution and transformation of belly dance and its evident appeal to women across diverse cultures may be linked to this dance form's capacity to offer women access to personally meaningful modes of self-expression, while simultaneously generating inspirational and transcendent experiences that many perceive has connected them to what they consider a "divine" or "universal" element. Their descriptions thus appear to reflect a common human tendency to ascribe religious or spiritual significance to profound experiences that surpass our mundane everyday existence.

As various scholars have noted, colonialist and Imperialist rhetoric of earlier periods attributed the Orient with the stereotypical feminine characteristics of mystery, sensuality, sexuality, lack of sophistication, and chaos, among others (Bock 2005, Desmond 1991, Dox 2006, Keft-Kennedy 2005, Sellers-Young 1992). Within this context, the belly dancer was represented as reconstructing the East in her image, resulting in Western commoditization of hybrid sexuality, further degrading the discursively constructed colonized East, and allowing for the commoditization of the belly dancing subject through film and television media for the male gaze (Cowper 2011). Subsequently, the gendering of the Orient and the essential positioning of the belly dancing subject has been sustained within many film representations, which has served to continuously re-inscribe the Oriental/Occidental dichotomy to present day — as witnessed most recently in Michael Patrick King's 2010 comedy feature, *Sex in the City 2*.

As part of the preliminary research for this project, a selection of 16 scenes depicting belly dancing and dancers drawn from film and television media were analyzed to reveal which aspects of this dance form (imagined and real) were rendered visible within the wider public domain and which remained absent, with a focus on exposing the contradictions and internal oppositions evident in contemporary media depictions. This approach presumed that media serve as primary cultural sites for public expressions of belly dance culture in the Australasian context, and hence that film and television representations should offer insight into the dominant discursive frames available to those who subsequently became involved in this cultural form, particularly since belly dance has not featured within the traditional cultural practices of Australians or New Zealanders, except perhaps within relatively small immigrant settler communities from the Middle East and North Africa.

Marion Cowper with veil during a choreographic section of the beginning of a belly dance solo.

This media analysis revealed that representations of belly dancing within film and television media have consistently operated to contain the belly dancer as the "subject of" and "subject to" dominant historical, Orientalist and essentialist discourses. The belly dancing subject has repeatedly been constituted via imaginary landscapes of the exotic East, revealing and elaborately adorned "Middle Eastern" costuming, and somewhat unbelievable story lines, and in alignment with embedded patriarchal social and cultural assumptions about the inherent sensuality and availability of (specifically, uncovered) Eastern women. Orientalist and essentialist discourses were routinely deployed in early depictions of the belly dancing subject, as seen in film classics such as Nazimova's (1923) *Salome*, and Broccoli and Saltzman's (1963) *From Russia with Love*. Such representations were also found to be underpinned by the male/female and subject/object dualisms affirmed within Western binary logic. The appropriation and resulting positioning of the subject belly dancer as a performer within the Western context aligned the subject closer to the Western ideal, and as therefore hierarchically superior to the more primitive Other — the Oriental woman. Yet, in these early film representations, the belly dancing subject was herself consistently positioned as Other to the Western characters, and was furthermore typically constructed as subservient to other characters, be they Oriental men or Western women. This subjugation of the dancer diametrically positioned the male as superior, and the Occident/Orient and male/female dichotomies were reinstated. Also significant to note is that in early film footage and in film and television through to the present day, the belly dancing subject has been depicted in performance, and is delimited by her relationship to an audience. The dancer has been costumed as a sexualized and fetishized object, and constrained within boundaries of performance which have enmeshed the belly dancing subject in a relational dependence on the male gaze. Under the male gaze, the passive female object appears to be surveyed, compliant and mute, while the active male gaze is assumed to be constant, watching, and assesses her performance according to pre-determined masculine standards of feminine desirability (Mulvey 1975).

With the introduction of the Motion Picture Production Code (also known as the Hays Code) in 1930, depictions of costumes exposing the navel or suggestive movements which were, in some cases, intended to signify the mystical and magical East in eroticized terms became subject to the authority of the censor (British Film Institute), and this further inscribed Western control over and regulation of the belly dancing subject. Nonetheless, the belly dancing subject continued to be heavily invested with fantasy and imaginary elements via costuming and film settings, and hence the Western colonization of the belly dancing subject persisted. Indeed, it could be argued that the continued reconstruction of a sexualized and compliant belly dancing subject disguised the censorship mechanism by fostering an impression of dancers' willingness, as representatives of the East, to comply with processes of appropriation by the West (Cowper 2011).

As anticipated, respondents did at times draw from these dominant discourses, which in some cases clearly framed their initial understandings of belly dancing. For example, Michelle's reflections on her earlier perceptions of belly dance can be seen to articulate key elements of the Orientalist discourse: "I thought it was feminine, exotic, a little sexy. I know it was from some generic Middle Easterny Indiany place ... when I think about it now I tend to visualise beaded curtains and incense sticks and cushions ... very harem fantasy type stuff" (2010). However, while objectifying post–Colonial constructions of belly dancing have prevailed within the wider public domain, the respondents' narratives more often indicated their ability to reject and even deconstruct the meta-narratives circulating within the public sphere, along with their access to alternative and highly individualized ways of seeing and understanding this dance form, which were clearly more personally salient and thus influential. As Csikszentmihalyi and Hunter (2000) suggest, "The blind spot of Cartesian dualism is its inability to consider the importance of first person quality of experience" (23), and it appears that in this case, understanding the nature and importance of the first person quality of the practice of belly dance may be fundamental to understanding the global transfer and evolution of this particular dance form.

For example, when considered in light of feminist theories of the male gaze (Mulvey 1975, Berger 1977), the belly dancing subject can be presumed to be simultaneously aware that she is an object that is surveyed, assessed, and possessed by the male gaze, and a surveyor of herself via the internalization of the masculine perspective (Berger 1977). Women's descriptions did suggest instances of subjecting themselves to their own gaze during their performances. However, their responses also began to elucidate a developing boundary between the construction of the belly dancer as an object of the gaze within the public sphere, and how they experienced themselves and others as performers. Some of their responses implicitly countered the antagonistic and disempowering voyeuristic assumptions of the male gaze, as is evident in Juliet's comments:

> I can still recall the first time I saw a belly dancer perform, it was like there was an aura surrounding her, she was shining and beautiful like a rainbow. A warmth and excitement and feeling of wellbeing welled up in me and I forgot about everything else outside of watching her dance. I loved the opportunity to see other teachers and dancers perform at concerts and just enjoy experiencing being swept away to another place while watching [2010].

In the following example, Jane acknowledges a connection to the audience which accommodates her position as the object of gaze; however, her explanation is articulated from a subjective standpoint inhabiting a position of centrality "within" the experience of belly dancing:

> I like to perform and I feel I am connecting to the audience and perhaps feeling the power the dancer has over the situation/scene/audience for that short while. You can share so much of an aspect of yourself or of a character you are being for that short moment: it is like being able to manipulate them but in a nice way; taking them with you on a little magical journey and sensing that they are feeling that they are with you is extremely rewarding and uplifting [2010].

Here, Jane's interpretation suggests that rather than the performer being dependent on the audience's evaluation and appreciation of her as the fetishized object of gaze, the audience is dependent on her presence as a performer; a reading in which she ascribes herself the power to determine and even manipulate the nature of her audience's engagement and response. This description indicates fluid movement between the construction of the dancer as the object of the gaze and the dancer as a Subject in performance, who is interpreting and expressing the embodiment of belly dancing from a position of centrality. This position of centrality, we suggest, illustrates the horizon of a developing personal sphere of belly dancing characterized by individual and relatively idiosyncratic meanings and understandings. By recognizing herself as a distinct subject, Jane is able to recognize the equally distinct Other and is arguably released, perhaps momentarily, from the prescriptions and limitations of the dominant discourses. The subsequent impact and dissolution of the boundary between performance and performer comes, we suggest, as a result of the dancer seeing herself *in* the Other, while subsequently recognizing that she is distinct *from* the other.

At other moments, women's responses appeared to be marked by some degree of resistance to established constructions of the belly dancing subject as compliant, passive and sexualized within the dominant discourses of the public sphere. In the following excerpt, Sarah describes a relationship to performance that appears to resist or refuse the objectifying male gaze, while also seeming to dispense with any notion of an internalized male spectator "within"; indeed, what is noteworthy about this response is its rendering of the spectator as entirely irrelevant in the face of women's individual engagements with the dance, even in the context of public performance:

> The fun is just getting up there, enjoying yourself and forgetting about everyone else and you don't have to worry at all or think about anybody else is up there or whatever, you know ... because you're just focusing on the music ... you're not really paying attention to who else is around you ... you're just out there for yourself and to enjoy your own company [2010].

As these responses highlight, women's interpretations of their experiences reveal a significant disjuncture between the discursive assumptions and prescriptions that continue to define the concrete site of public belly dance performance (and much academic theorizing), and their own individual conceptual understandings of the experiences that occur within those same spaces.

Berger (1986) suggests that "meaning grows out of creative interpretation, within one's active and creative imagination, perceived as an intermediary world between that which is a source of knowledge and that which, at the same time, remains unknown" (148). What became clear during this research is that many of the women had experiences during their dance which they considered highly significant and personally meaningful, but which were difficult to articulate or adequately describe, evidently because those experiences remain on the horizon of what is as yet discursively known, or explicitly recognized, within public constructions of belly dance. For example, when asked to "describe any emotions, thoughts and experiences that were most often evoked whilst dancing," Sarah said, with a considerable degree of hesitancy, "Well it's hard to describe. You can try and describe the emotions, you can feel it for yourself, what really does it for you the most, what gives you the most sense of well-being ... or I don't know what you want to call it" (2010). Ruby also found it difficult to put into words the nature of certain experiences encountered while belly dancing, which she nonetheless considered deeply significant:

> Um, your mind sort of goes elsewhere ... I don't quite know how to explain it, um.... Kind of a special feeling ... sort of puts you on a high.... Yeah and not quite sure what it is.... You sort of feel like you can do anything. Yeah it puts you there and it ... only like visits me every now and then, that's sort of more of a primitive feeling ... kind of thing, I don't want to use the word ancient but um ... and I don't wanna use the word ritual but along those lines [2010].

However, other participants did formulate their own idiosyncratic understandings of what appeared to be a shared set of experiences generated through their dance practice. These dancers frequently imaginatively deployed imagery, metaphor and allegory in an attempt to more adequately describe such experiences, which were consistently characterized as extra-ordinary, and transcendent, and often deeply profound; even spiritual. These experiences, we suggest, bear all the hallmarks of both psychologist Mihaly Csikszentmihalyi's (1990) concept of flow, and Abraham Maslow's (1968, 1970) concept of peak experiences.

For Csikszentmihalyi (1990, 1996, 1997), flow is a very positive and highly energized mental state experienced where a person is single-mindedly immersed in an activity, with her emotions, concentration and physical capacities all being channeled to and aligned with the activity in question, such that she experiences a loss of self-consciousness. Flow is characterized by feelings of spontaneous joy or even ecstasy while engaged in a task (Goleman 2006), and a sense of getting lost in the activity, with one's perception of time being shrunk to the present moment. Individuals experiencing flow feel intensely present in the "now," rather than being plagued by concerns about the past or future. Engaging in activities that stimulate or provoke flow experiences, Csikszentmihalyi suggests, provides access to feeling the essential "being" of oneself. Flow experiences are frequently cited by elite athletes (who often speak of being "in the zone"), artists, and religious mystics (1997, 29).

Most of our participants described their experiences of belly dance in terms that are consistent with this concept of flow. Some women explicitly employed the descriptors "zone" or "flow"; "in the zone" being a commonly used colloquialism for flow. Here, for example, Sarah describes flow in terms of an altered state of awareness: "You're just concentrating listening to the music ... you're just not thinking ... you can just go with the flow ... you've gone into that no thinking zone where you're not worried about everything else that's going on.... You're just going with the flow, you're just like the water, running with the water and it's going to take you where it's going to take you" (2010). Margaret similarly articulates a shift outside of her everyday experience and into a different state of consciousness while dancing: "I feel whole when I am dancing, channelling some energy with the focus of lifting the atmosphere and making people happy. I am in a different zone.... I am almost stepping into a different world. I feel free. I feel beautiful. I have experienced those feelings etc., at other times, but with dancing I can access them immediately. It's so easy" (2010).

Belly dance performance can thus be seen as a site where dancers are able to experience and understand their bodies and selves differently, not as objects to be appreciated and judged on solely aesthetic terms, but as vehicles for transportation to another realm defined in terms of personal meanings relating to self and other, rather than public constructions of the dance form *per se*. Juliet similarly expressed her personal connection to the dance in terms that clearly mirror key themes of joy, spontaneity, and creativity associated with the concept of flow: "I experience happiness, warmth, relaxation, stimulation, creativity, excitement, feeling a sense of enjoyment, sense of freedom, peace — a great feeling of peace while at the same time great energy — a moving meditation — like yoga. However, it's a creative meditation, as though you were creating shapes and new worlds with your movements" (2010).

For several of the women, belly dance was also a site which made it possible to access and subjectively experience what they termed their "true selves" or the "real me," and some expressed feeling a sense of self-acceptance in the face of external judgments and constraints. As Emily noted, "In those moments of belly dancing I get glimpses of how powerful I really am, like when I was giving birth, or living a completely organic lifestyle ... a self-love and acceptance that I have never felt at any other time" (2010). It is an experience that resonated with Ruby, "A bit of enlightenment on yourself and being a woman, not just a mother, you're not just working, you're not just whatever else — there's something special about you and this dance kind of brings it out. It's like reaching down into yourself and pulling that woman out that's been lying there dormant — like she could be quite wild if you let her be. It's a freedom kind of thing and you just feel re-energised" (2010). Occurrences of flow can also be understood in terms of Maslow's (1968, 1970) concept of "peak experiences," described as moments when the individual shifts outside their ordinary state of consciousness to feel a sense of harmonious connection between physical and spiritual realities. For Maslow, peak experiences uplift the individual and stimulate their creativity, conveying power and purpose. Particularly powerful peak experiences dissolve an individual's sense of self, promoting feelings of unity with a higher consciousness or connection with the wider universe. These ecstatic moments of flow, transcendence, and loss of self-consciousness are often ascribed mystical and sacred meanings by individuals experiencing them, or are perceived as having a sacred quality or essence (Maslow 1970). This is particularly relevant here, since many of the dancers in this study ascribed spiritual and inspirational meaning and significance to their experiences of flow, and spoke about their dance practice in ways that explicitly referred to the sacred, spirituality, and the divine, with some describing dance as a meditative practice that allowed them to connect with a higher power or universal energy, however conceived. For example, Helen expressed her experiences of flow in the following way:

> Every now and then I am totally captured by the moment, everything falls into place and I feel balanced and peaceful.... Belly dancing or any sport/dance has moments like this.... I think it is when we are so immersed in what we are doing and outside considerations disappear and we reach a state of "grace," a moment of balance, of revelation which is a personal spiritual experience — not religious but I am sure religion followers experience this moment of "grace" too [2010].

Margaret similarly elaborated on her experiences of belly dancing in spiritual terms: "I believe that I am channelling energy from 'above'; at the same time I reveal my inner soul. Sounds very spiritual, and that's a big part. Belly dance helps to connect to this very primal urge to express yourself" (2010).

As these comments suggest, several of the belly dancers involved in this study ascribed their peak experiences of flow with transcendental or spiritual meaning. We suggest that aspects of the practice of belly dance — rhythmic, repetitive and highly stylized movements specific to this genre of dance, elaborate and exotic costuming — may facilitate such interpretations, since they emphasize the ritualistic as well as non-mundane nature of belly dance as a cultural form, thereby elevating it to a position of transcending women's everyday or ordinary existence.

Furthermore, while this study was relatively small in scale, the frequency with which the women made references to flow, spirituality, connectedness and loss of awareness of time and space suggests that this may be a more widely-felt experience, one that perhaps offers a partial rationale for belly dancing's growing popularity globally. Indeed, while the research focused on Australasian women's experiences of flow, Rachel Kraus (2009) recently examined the creation of spiritual experiences by 77 belly dancers in the U.S., many of whom reported very similar moments when "(1) dancers can let go, lose themselves in the dance, get into a zone, be more introspective, and (2) develop deeper connections with a Higher Power, other people, or a deeper part of themselves" (612). Other studies have also delineated Western women's experiences of flow in relation to ballet (Kleiner 2009), and erotic dance (Barton & Hardesty 2010, see also Bond & Stinson 2000). Furthermore, Maslow's (1970) contention that peak experience is a universal phenomenon with certain elements being recognizable across cultural contexts, while critiqued in some quarters, is supported by cross-cultural studies in the area of sport and youth studies (for example see Privette, Hwang, & Bundrick 1997; Hoffman & Ortiz 2009). There are thus grounds to suggest that women in non–Western contexts may also have peak experiences or an experience of flow while belly dancing, although their descriptions are likely to reflect culturally — as well as personally — specific interpretations of such experiences. It thus seems reasonable to suppose that the burgeoning appeal of belly dance and the apparent ease with which it has been transported and assimilated cross-culturally may be linked, at least in part, to this dance form's capacity to generate peak experiences of flow that are experienced by some, and perhaps many, women as deeply meaningful, self-actualizing, and fundamentally transformative.

As we have illustrated, as a result of our participants inhabiting a position of centrality within the experience of belly dancing, the dancers' descriptions were characterized by uniquely subjective meanings and relatively idiosyncratic personal perceptions, while nonetheless appearing to attest to a common or shared experience of flow. Furthermore, women's subjective understandings were often articulated using examples which indicate how imagination and inspirational experiences informed the women's perceptions of themselves in relationship to their environment. At times, the women articulated examples whereby their new understandings had influenced how they saw their roles as women within the public sphere, and how they defined alternatives to those established gender roles. Lilly, for example, described inhabiting a different space that was removed from her gender role as a wife and mother, and also from the male gaze. Her remarks suggest a capacity to construct and inhabit a space within which the dancer is in control and retains full ownership of herself and her activities, independent of public roles or concerns. Here, she describes how she took ownership of her experiences of belly dancing: "I guess a lot of my life I've been doing things for other people ... but this is mine, this is my space and I do it ... not for anyone else, I do it for me and I like that aspect of it because I feel like I'm giving something back that's just for me, that's not for sharing or because somebody thinks I should or I think I should. It's my space" (2010).

Importantly, some of the respondents also suggested that, as a result of the unique experiences encountered during belly dancing, they had developed different perceptions of themselves, their bodies, and capabilities. In some cases, these new understandings were transposed beyond the realms of performance in order to influence other areas of their lives, marking a shift in their experiences from the conceptual to the concrete, and from the imaginary to the real. For example, Sarah said:

> You have a dance persona and your normal every day persona so once you really get into the dance you have a whole other side of you seems to come forward.... She's happy with who she is and doesn't care what the others think, it's just "this is me, this is who I am, take me as you see me" sort of thing and "if you don't like it that's just too bad 'cause I don't care".../.... She does come out at work sometimes, it's that whole confidence thing if I've had a really bad day and I have to go into a meeting, if necessary she might pop out and go "yeah, I'm here now, I'll take care of this for you." She can come out and do that, whereas I'm a lot more cautious—a lot more cautious [2010].

It thus appears that for a few participants, inspirational experiences stimulated through their belly dance practice helped transform their perceptions of themselves and their environments, which in Sarah's case had wider repercussions in terms of bolstering her ability to assert herself within the public domain.

In conclusion, we note that contemporary academic discussions of belly dancing reflect a developing trend in terms of focusing on the belly dancing subject, rather than the activity of belly dancing as a cultural *and* personal construct. Recent empirical research has delineated a more post-modern belly dancing subject, one conceived as a relatively active and "autonomous" agent in the process of appropriating belly dancing as a hybrid or fusion of cultural styles and identity. Consequently, the universalizing discourses around belly dance have become destabilized and space has been created for localized narratives to emerge. However, our research with belly dancers from New Zealand and Australian belly dance communities indicates that dancers do not necessarily strongly identify with either a standardized local understanding, or dominant global constructions of the belly dancing subject. In the latter case, this is perhaps due to the geographical isolation of these communities and the lack of a cultural tradition of belly dancing within the wider public domain. With reference to the former, this dislocation of belly dancing from its Eastern origins may open up space for the creation of locally and also *individually* specific meanings and variations on this global dance form. Thus, for these practitioners, watching other belly dancers in performance or describing their own performance and practice yielded interpretations which often did not entirely align with the prevailing discursive constructions of belly dance within the wider public domain. Rather, women's attempts to articulate the nature of their own experiences of the dance were frequently marked by hesitancy, resistance, negotiation and elaboration, suggesting that these experiences could not be easily expressed in terms of established frameworks, but required new ways of talking about and understanding women's embodied realities which have yet to become crystallized.

Some of these emerging understandings were expressed as women tried to describe significant spiritual and inspirational experiences which had occurred during their practice of belly dancing. Their explanations of these experiences indicated that they defined belly dance from a position of centrality "within" this cultural practice, rather than from the position of an external or internalized other/spectator. Their imaginative attempts to make sense of significant inspirational and transcendent experiences of flow encountered while dancing illustrate the necessity of moving beyond existing conceptualizations of this topic, in order to better understand the embodied realities of belly dance performance as simultaneously a cultural/public and deeply individual/private practice, one that may be marked by a common core of shared, but nonetheless subjectively interpreted, experience.

Works Cited

Akkach, S. (1997). The world of imagination in Ibn 'Arabi's Ontology.'" *British Journal of Middle Eastern Studies*, 24(1): 97–113.

Barton, B., and C. Hardesty. (2010). "Spirituality and Stripping: Exotic Dancers Narrate the Body Ekstasis." *Symbolic Interaction*, 33(2): 280–296. DOI: 10.1525/si.2010.33.2.280.

Berger, A. (1986). "Cultural Hermeneutics: The Concept of Imagination in the Phenomenological Approaches of Henry Corbin and Mircea Eliade." *The Journal of Religion*, 66(2): 141–156.

Berger, J. (1977). *Ways of Seeing*. London: Penguin.

Bond, K., and S. Stinson. (2000). "'I feel like I'm going to take off!': Young People's Experiences of the Superordinary in Dance." *Dance Research Journal*, 32(2): 52–87.

Bock, S.M. (2005). "From Harem Fantasy to Female Empowerment: Rhetorical Strategies and Dynamics of Style in American Belly Dance." Unpublished master's thesis. The Ohio State University, Ohio, USA. Retrieved from http://etd.ohiolink.edu/view.cgi/Bock%20Sheila.pdf?osu1144685165.

British Film Institute. [Screen Online]. Retrieved from http://www.screenonline.org.uk/feedback.html.

Carol. (2010). Personal interview: The experience of belly dancing. M. Cowper. Hamilton, New Zealand.

Cowper, M. (2011). "Negotiating the Discursive Constructions of Belly Dancing in New Zealand and Australian Dance Communities." Unpublished master's thesis. University of Waikato, Hamilton, New Zealand. http://hdl.handle.net/10289/5610.

Csikszentmihalyi, M. (1990). *Flow: The Psychology of Optimal Experience*. New York: Harper and Row.

_____. (1996). *Creativity, Flow and the Psychology of Discovery and Invention*. New York: Harper Collins.

_____. (1997). *Finding Flow: The Psychology of Engagement with Everyday Life*. New York: Basic Books.

_____, and J.C. Hunter. (2000). "The Phenomenology of Body-Mind: The Contrasting Cases of Flow in Sports and Contemplation." *Anthropology of Consciousness*, 11(3–4): 5–24.

Desmond, J. (1991). "Dancing Out the Difference: Cultural Imperialism and Ruth St. Denis's 'Radha' of 1906." *Signs: Journal of Women in Culture and Society*, 17(1): 52–71.

Dox, D. (2006). "Dancing around Orientalism." *The Drama Review*, 50 (4): 52–71.

Emily. (2010). Personal interview: The experience of belly dancing. M. Cowper. Taumarunui, New Zealand.

Goleman, D. (2006). *Emotional Intelligence.* New York: Bantam Books.

Helen. (2010). Personal interview: The experience of belly dancing. M. Cowper. Adelaide, South Australia.

Hoffman, E., and F. Ortiz. (2009). "Youthful Peak-Experiences in Cross-Cultural Perspective: Implications for Educators and Counselors." In L. Francis, D. Scott, M. de Souza, and J. Norman (Eds.). *The International Handbook of Education for Spirituality, Care & Well-Being* (pp. 469–490). New York: Springer.

Jane. (2010). Personal interview: The experience of belly dancing. M. Cowper. Taupo, New Zealand.

Juliet. (2010). Personal interview: The experience of belly dancing. M. Cowper. Adelaide, South Australia.

Keft-Kennedy, V. (2005). "Representing the Belly-Dancing Body: Feminism, Orientalism and the Grotesque." Unpublished doctoral thesis. University of Wollongong, Sydney, Australia. Retrieved from Australasian Digital Thesis Program, http://ro.uow.edu.au/theses/843.

Kleiner, S. (2009). "Thinking with the Mind, Syncing with the Body: Ballet as Symbolic and Non-Symbolic Interaction." *Symbolic Interaction*, 32(3): 236–59.

Kraus, R. (2009). "Straddling the Sacred and Secular: Creating a Spiritual Experience through Belly Dance." *Sociological Spectrum*, 29(5): 598–625. DOI: 10.1080/02732170903051383.

Lilly. (2010). Personal interview: The experience of belly dancing. M. Cowper. Hamilton, New Zealand.

Margaret. (2010). Personal interview: The experience of belly dancing. M. Cowper. Auckland, New Zealand.

Maslow, A. (1968). *Toward a Psychology of Being.* Princeton, NJ: Van Nostrand.

_____. (1970). *Religions, Values, and Peak Experiences.* New York: Viking.

Michelle. (2010). Personal interview: The experience of belly dancing. M. Cowper. Christchurch, New Zealand.

Mulvey, L. (1975). "Visual Pleasure and Narrative Cinema." *Screen*, 16(3), 6–18.

Privette, G., K. Hwang, and C. Bundrick. (1997). "Cross-Cultural Measurement of Experience: Taiwanese and Americans' Peak Performance, Peak Experience, Misery, Failure, Sport, and Average Events." *Perceptual and Motor Skills*, 84(3): 1459–1482. DOI: 10.2466/pms.1997.84.3c.1459.

Ruby. (2010). Personal interview: The experience of belly dancing. M. Cowper. Hamilton, New Zealand.

Sarah. (2010). Personal interview: The experience of belly dancing. M. Cowper. Hamilton, New Zealand.

Sellers-Young, B. (1992). "Raks Sharki: Transculturation of a Folk Form." *Journal of Popular Culture, 26(2)*, 141–152.

Local Performance/ Global Connection

American Tribal Style and Its Imagined Community

TERESA CUTLER-BROYLES

"If one is performing ATS® (or ITS) at all there is always an inherent message of community togetherness and mutual support."—Samantha Riggs, professional dancer

The above statement in various permutations is a commonly held sentiment—tenet, in fact—of dancers in the American Tribal Style® (ATS®[1]) dance community. What makes this singularly intriguing is that this ATS community is a relatively new phenomenon. The dance form gelled in the mid–1980s when San Francisco dancer Carolena Nericcio incorporated elements of costumes, jewelry, music, dance styles, and performance venues from various influences into FatChanceBelly dance, a studio and group specializing in what she called American Tribal Style,[2] and the ATS community spread from its origins in the U.S. to an uncounted number of physical locations throughout the world. While local, national, and international Tribal dance festivals draw hundreds of dancers every year and are venues for many community members to finally meet others they've only previously known through virtual relationships—email, Facebook, YouTube, or by viewing each other's instructional DVDs—the majority of ATS dancers will never meet. They are connected to each other and the community only through their own performance and viewing of the dance, and the knowledge of each other's existence. These elements—participation via performance or the viewing of such, and knowledge of each other—are the core of the ATS dance community, which is understood by each member to be a real entity, spread over a borderless area, undefined and unbounded. And despite this not-uncommon isolation of dancers from each other, ATS dancers often feel firmly a part of the community as a whole, maintaining a sense of belonging that expresses itself through the dance. Along with this comes an oft-stated declaration of an across-the-board experience of equality among the members.

As a long-time though admittedly intermittent dancer, I set out to investigate this phenomenon and what social mechanisms are at work to create the ATS community, to make it cohesive, and to keep it a viable living entity, one that its members know exists despite it having no borders, no constitution, no criteria for membership other than the dance, in fact no elements of what might be considered essential to a traditional understanding of community. I was curious as well about whether the ATS community is truly un-stratified, and whether this sense of equality is actual or axiomatic, practiced or simply professed. As with all investigations of this sort, my conclusions are based strictly on available material; and are not intended to include other forms of community.

So what exactly is it that connects a dancer in Bellingham, Washington, to a dancer she has never met in Manhattan, and them both to another in Austin, Texas or Berlin, Germany? And how can they possibly feel connected, in the sense expressed by Riggs in the opening quote, to dancers in Australia, Ukraine, France, the UK, South Africa, and the many other countries where the ATS community is large and growing larger?[3] Why does this bond exist? How is it possible to call so many people from such culturally, ethnically, socially, and culturally disparate contexts a community at all? How does such a community form? How does it function? What sustains it? And what, in the words of Albuquerque ATS performer Alisa Tan, creates the potential for connection with other dancers — even those halfway around the world?

To answer these questions it is important to look at the construction of the concepts of "community" and "membership" as they relate to the 21st century. What does membership in any community look like in a globalized world, and how is it different today than it might have been before technological innovations such as the internet and YouTube? In order to look at these concepts, I will utilize the theories of Benedict Anderson and Arjun Appadurai as lenses through which to investigate the concept of community and explore how imagination has become a force in maintaining a community in a technologically connected globe.

In his book *Imagined Communities: Reflections on the Origin and Spread of Nationalism,* Benedict Anderson explores the concept of the nation. Anderson sees "nation" as a category of belonging, "*an imagined* political *community—and imagined as both inherently limited* and sovereign" (2006, 6) (emphasis mine). An imagined community in Anderson's usage here means simply "imagined because the members ... will never know most of their fellow-members ... yet in the minds of each lives the image of their communion" (6). In this sense, then, "imagined" is not *imaginary*; nations do indeed exist and Anderson does not dispute that fact. He merely locates their existence in the minds of their members as well as in geographic locations and cartographic representations, and posits that this mental construct of community, far more than geography or maps, is what holds a people together. So while physical nations are bounded by geographical elements, Anderson explores the notion that they constantly and invariably exceed their physical boundaries through their members' travel, migration, military deployment, and even retirement. Regardless of physical location, these members' identity does not shift.

How are these dispersed communities held together? Anderson suggests that a strong force in the binding of nations and their diasporic communities is the ability of people to envision themselves as members of their community. This entails, crucially, a common language and a means of disseminating ideas about identity and belonging to the wider community not connected physically. He speaks of the medium of print, and coins the term *print-capitalism* as the mechanism through which imagined communities enact their existence and enable members to belong.[4] Indeed, in the 18th and 19th centuries, and through most of the 20th, actual print could be said to have fulfilled this role. However, late in the 20th and increasingly more so in the 21st century, the internet and its various outlets such as MySpace, Facebook and especially YouTube have become the mechanism, allowing — perhaps inevitably — communities and even nations to expand exponentially and become virtually borderless, with members scattered throughout the world. Importantly, these members continue to consider themselves unquestionably part of the same nation/community, despite physical distance and lack of physical connection.

One example is the Palestinian people, considered state-less by much of the international community, nevertheless they have a sense of cohesiveness; they identify themselves as Palestinian, part of a real community, bound together by shared history and by their connection to a real piece of land with (arguably tenuous and disputed, but real) borders. They are dispersed throughout the world; the quintessential imagined community made up of members who do not know each other, yet in whose minds exists a strong image or belief in their connection (communion) with others. This community is held together by both media in the form of books, newspapers, and magazines in print or online, and by imagination.

Community through media and imagination is the concept explored by Arjun Appadurai in his book *Modernity at Large: Cultural Dimensions of Globalization* (1996). He focuses specifically on media and migration as forces at work in the production of what he envisions as a stateless future, in which belonging will depend in large part on imagination and on the media. In his discussion of imagination and its importance in holding together communities of various kinds, Appadurai tells us that the world is "...a complex transnational construction of imaginary landscapes," (5) and that "the imagination is now central to all forms of agency, is itself a social fact, and is the key component of the new global order" (31). Without imagination, community as we know it would cease to exist in a world in which relationships of all kinds exist in virtual space and people are spread throughout the globe. Mediated space is the only space in which community can survive, in Appadurai's view, as people become ever less connected to actual geography.

In this context we can ask, what about the ATS community? Can it be compared to either Anderson's idea of nation, or connected in ways similar to Appadurai's mediated, imagined world? Where "nations" are finite and bounded the ATS community is neither—and Anderson suggests it needn't be. Just as readers of newspapers in decades past imagined each other performing the same, ritualized perusing of the daily news, an essential aspect of belonging by participating in the consumption of print-capital, ATS dancers from thousands of actual, physical locations feel themselves to be participating and belonging through a similar "steady, anonymous, simultaneous activity" (Anderson 2006, 26), that of dance. It is truly, then, an imagined community in an Andersonian sense, made up of members whose connection to the community itself and to each other is created not by physical borders and geographic contours, but by imagination—and a common language: the dance and its accoutrements.

As with spoken language, the language of ATS has building blocks that are combined in various ways to create meaning. Where spoken—or written—language has letters, words, sentences, paragraphs, and poetry learned from other speakers of the language, ATS has specific movements of body parts such as hands, arms, shoulders, torso, legs, feet that are learned from a trained ATS instructor via observation and repetition. Again similarly to spoken or written language, as a new dancer becomes fluent in the language her[5] ability to communicate through movements becomes fluid and the steps become second nature, allowing her to "talk" with other ATS dancers from any country. So it is the steps, sets of steps, and body movements that make up the ATS dance, coupled with a distinctive style of costume and jewelry, a distinct type of music, and often the venue at which the dance performance occurs, that are the shared language each community member knows, and while many of the moves and steps are similar to Egyptian or Cabaret style belly dance, and certainly any belly dancer will learn the ATS language more quickly than a novice, ATS is quite different in its end-goal.

For the goal of ATS is communication with other dancers/speakers of the language.

Unlike traditional[6] belly dance, ATS dancers typically do not dance solo; ATS is performed in groups with the dancers in synch or moving in oppositional-but-complementary directions. What looks seamless in performance is in fact un-choreographed. Each dancer watches the lead, determined by position in the group in relation to the direction the dancers are facing — and therefore the lead often changes in the same performance — and reads the cues she gives. These cues are invisible to outsiders who cannot speak this language, sent via specific movements of head, arm, torso, or particular calls, and they communicate the next steps or groups of movements within each conversation/performance. Variations in the cues, and in the specifics of the steps that follow, do exist from dancer to dancer or troupe to troupe; these variations are similar to colloquialisms and accents within a spoken language and can be comprehended by other speakers of the language. Therefore, as they dance with each other or simply watch a performance, each dancer is either speaking or reading the language of ATS and feels connected to those who are present, as well as those who exist in the larger community of ATS dancers, the majority of whom are *not* present and a high percentage of whom they will never meet.

Some additional elements are just as important in communicating and claiming membership in the community. Costumes consist of full, colorful, often layered skirts, a wide tasseled belt with various charms, mirrors, beads, and heavy embroidery, a crop top called a choli, and a turban made of brightly colored veils. Makeup is often highly stylized and includes accents in the form of typically black beauty marks and stylized groupings, often around the eyes.[7] The jewelry is heavy and ornate, often authentically antique from countries such as Afghanistan, Pakistan or others, and frequently includes wrist cuffs — bracelets that enclose the wrist and are typically more than three inches wide. Colorful pieces of glass or stone adorn both clothing and jewelry. The wearing of this style of clothing and these types of jewelry is recognized as Tribal of some sort by all Tribal dancers of any flavor, and as such communicates membership even when the dancer is in street clothes and not performing.[8]

Together, these elements create community through a shared language that is in large part kinesthetic, of the body far more than the brain. Taisa Gontar, an ATS dancer in the Ukraine,[9] tells us that this connection to community "is created by all the points that Dance goes through: Dance itself, movements that [are] familiar to everybody, the costume styling preferred by everybody, by internet communication, by the common love to Dance, and ATS and common Tribal Spirit."

The founder of American Tribal Style belly dance Carolena Nericcio performs with a sword, a traditional prop of this style of belly dance (courtesy Carolena Nericcio).

Inasmuch as the understanding of the many elements of the ATS language, and the connection that stems directly from this understanding, are the essence of the community, it would seem that as a means of communicating identity and belonging, and as an avenue through which to participate in the larger community, the language of this particular dance functions in strikingly similar ways to Anderson's printed word. As such, it could be called *dance-capitalism*.[10]

As the glue that holds the community together, dance-capital — much as print-capital — must have a mechanism for dissemination. Whereas in the 18th century onward, print "provided the technical means for 're-presenting' the kind of imagined community that is the nation," (Anderson 2006, 25) and was in fact what held nations together, in the 21st century, this glue is modern technology. In a globalized world, as Appadurai tells us, "media ... offer new resources and new disciplines for the construction of imagined selves and imagined worlds" (1996, 3). Appadurai tells us that mediascapes — the "the distribution of the electronic capabilities to produce and disseminate information ... and the images of the world created by this media" (35) — offer a series of elements that allow us to create scripts, or metaphors, and help us "constitute narratives of the Other and proto-narratives of possible lives" (36) for ourselves. This is something Tan alludes to when she tells us that after watching ATS dancers on YouTube, the point is to "bring the information to a group of real dancers to try it ourselves." And Gontar says "I really feel connected to the whole community. It is like being a part of a really huge family. And connected to those persons that I got luck to meet on my Tribal way. We keep in touch through internet [sic]."

In other words, the internet has become a globalizing force. Through observing other dancers and incorporating their interpretation of the ATS language into their own dance, community members embody this intersection between "us" and 'them," merging the two and creating out of the mix a unified Us, a global community without geography.

The creation of ATS itself is emblematic of this process. ATS emerged as a synergistic melding of a number of dance moves, philosophies, and styles, combined by professional dancer Carolena Nericcio into a new form in the late 1980s. Nericcio's principal influences were San Francisco dancers Jamila Salimpour and Masha Archer, who drew from a hodgepodge of countries and styles from around the world to create and grow the original Tribal Style. Their adaptations and expansions adopted dance styles, costumes, jewelry and music from a variety of sources ranging from North Africa to Europe and Turkey, from legendary roving bands of gypsies, and from sources both ancient and modern. Performance styles were drawn from the circus where Salimpour began her career as an acrobat, as well as incorporating a freedom from the stage that became a signature part of ATS's appeal. When Nericcio formed her FatChanceBelly dance troupe in 1987, American Tribal Style as such coalesced.[11]

The availability of choices that included such a culturally broad, and indeed historically deep, wealth of sources is itself a product of the process of globalization which was, by the 1970s, becoming a global fact.[12] In combining these various and hitherto unrelated elements, both Salimpour and Archer excelled in what globalization scholars call "hybridization"—"the mixing of different cultural forms and styles facilitated by global and economic and cultural exchanges" (Steger 2003, 5). Through this process of hybridization, both

Salimpour and Archer tacitly admitted, accepted, and used to advantage the impossibility of staying true to any "pure" sense of a dance which, already by the turn of the 20th century, had been dispersed, transformed, and adapted from murky, almost mythological origins in a fantastical Middle East.[13] The result was, and continues to be, what Archer, in reference to costuming, called "acquisitive eclecticism ... a very strong Byzantine tribal look, which was completely invented" (Archer 1995).

This eclectic mix is not only an illustrative example of how the process of globalization can result in something new, vibrant, and positive with its own trajectory into the future, it also has the potential to exemplify an answer to a question that globalization scholars are often at odds about: whether the process of globalization is ultimately equalizing, or whether it widens the divides between peoples. And as ATS is a dance form that itself possesses and embodies a number of the processes of globalization, this question of equality is an important one.[14]

The statement "the best evidence available shows ... the current wave of globalization, which started around 1980, has actually *promoted economic equality and reduced poverty*" (Dollar & Kraay in Wade 2004, 1) is encouraging; when it is juxtaposed against the following, it becomes less so: "Globalization has dramatically *increased inequality between and within nations*" (Mazur in Wade 2004, 1) (emphasis mine). Each of these statements, while speaking most directly to economic factors, participates in on-going debates about the effects of all aspects of globalization — political, social, educational, cultural, and more. As the "compression of the world and the intensification of consciousness of the world as a whole" (Mittelman, in Steger 10) continues, these debates become ever-more heated, with scholars and analysts on both sides contributing ever-more-impassioned points of view. In large part, on which side of this debate one comes down depends on how globalization is perceived. While it is far more nuanced than I present here, essentially three possibilities exist: Globalization is either a top-down process, in which Western and/or privileged — i.e., rich — nations impose their values[15] on Others; a mitigated top-down process in which these same privileged nations export their values to Others who then adapt and modify them, refining them to fit into their own extant value system; or a bottom-up phenomenon in which "in situ everyday activities" that are both informed by and "formative of globalities and, through their interoperation, the global" (Flusty, 2004, 7) is at work; or some combination thereof.[16]

Regardless of which lens one uses, the question of equality arises, and as both a product and an embodiment of the process of globalization, ATS as a point of intersection is a unique lens through which to ask — and perhaps answer — this question. In interview after interview, and on every ATS website

I researched,[17] the dancers express not only a belief in equality, but an experience that seems to suggest that the questions that keep globalization scholars up at night are irrelevant. Equality within this community is understood as foundational and goes without saying, and the underlying belief appears to be that ATS is a forum that not only attracts and enacts, but also projects a non-competitive, non-judgmental inclusiveness that fosters communication and belonging. A random sampling of statements from ATS websites follows:

"ATS celebrates the female form in all its beautiful shapes and sizes, promotes positive self image, and creates community among women" (Techniques Studio 2011).

"The studio classes are tailored to provide a warm, loving atmosphere where women can feel included and safe. Classes are also filled with like-minded women who come to share a great sense of camaraderie" (Devyani Dance Company 2011).

"Some groups might have more experience and natural advantages than others but I don't think that makes them better than other groups. Maybe better / more exciting to watch, but a rag tag group of women having fun with each other is just as valuable" (Tan 2011).

"In fact sisterhood is one of the main features of tribal belly dance" (Tribal-belly dance, http://www.tribal-belly dance.be/, accessed November, 2011).

"Anyone can do it... this is basically a modern folk dance. It is for the folk. All folk" (Riggs, 2011).

"It fosters feelings of liberation and unity, of sensuality and power. ...infuses the dancers with a feeling of power and elegance, the belly dance moves celebrate the artistic sensuality of women, and the tribal nature of ATS belly dance encourages a sense of community" (BTribal 2011).

Though sometimes not credited, these and other writers are almost always dancers themselves and are, for the most part, careful to stay away from language that might hint at judgment of each other as professional dancers, of ATS's origins, of beginning or "baby" dancers, of women who those outside the community might consider too old for belly dance, or of women with body types American society often does not consider attractive. Michelle Morrison, owner and principal dancer at Farfesha World Dance Studio in Albuquerque, New Mexico,[18] says, "I think the ATS community started out being even more 'alternative' as far as society is concerned. It was also very tolerant of things like different body types, piercings, and tattoos, and so attracted a large group that might not otherwise have felt comfortable or welcome in ... 'Cabaret' style belly dance" (Morrison 2011).

In other words, the marginal has become the norm in the ATS community, and whether stated explicitly or merely understood as the underlying foundation that goes unsaid, equality in this liminal community does indeed exist as an experienced phenomenon *between dancers*. There is one important exception, however, in the realm of Tribal Style dance teachers: FatChance-Belly dance, effectively Carolena Nericcio, offers certification for those who wish to learn to teach American Tribal Style. The earning of this certificate is a matter of pride and is something those who have it use as a statement of both dedication and commitment to the form. Dancers who do not have this certification, yet who truly consider themselves part of the community, make a point to note that they are not FatChance certified. This is seen as a sign of respect within the community, not — as far as I could tell — as an admission of any lack. Additionally, dancers who have taken the original ATS form and expanded it, appear always to credit FatChance and ATS as their starting point. Nericcio has recently acknowledged others' changes and interpretations of ATS as a natural growth of the dance while continuing to be grateful to other dancers and teachers as they acknowledge her position as creator. While a certain hierarchy appears to exist in terms of the perception that ATS/FatChance, and Nericcio herself is the core, and the offshoots are in fact peripheral, dancers who perform these peripheral styles do not appear to feel — or be regarded as — somehow inauthentic.

As a student I have found this phenomenon of equality in effect in ATS and other Tribal classes in a number of studios. In Albuquerque, the Tribal dance classes I attend are filled with women of many different ethnic and religious backgrounds who range in age from early 20s through mid–60s, with bodies sized 4 through 40 both quite short — me — and tall, and with an occasional male student; our significant relationships cover the gamut from traditional heterosexual marriages to open relationships to same sex partners. The ATS class I took at Manhattan Tribal[19] in New York was filled with a similar demographic. Not once have I heard a dancer at any level make a derogatory remark, either in or outside the classroom or while performing, nor do ATS or other Tribal websites participate in that level of negativity. Each dancer not only feels but truly *is* a member of the wider ATS community, and the conditions of membership are simple: learn the language, and then ... dance. It could be said that the dance itself, the space of performance, becomes a virtual *contact zone*, constantly evolving in a shifting space of no-borders in which ATS "subjects are constituted in and by their relations to each other" (Pratt 1992, 7).[20] Gontar of the Ukraine regularly attends ATS festivals, and her experience epitomizes this. Wherever and with whomever she has danced, she says, "always I had this beautiful experience of dancing with my new ATS colleagues that I have never dance before. And perhaps this may be called one of the moments when you can feel this ATS® connection the most sharp." And Dayl Workman of Sydney, Australia, discusses her passion for tribal belly dance as "extend[ing] to the love of community, bringing people together to move and dance the same 'language'" (http://www.tribal-hub.com/index.html#sydney, accessed March 2012).

As I have begun to learn the language of ATS and am able to communicate — haltingly and generally only as receiver of cues to date — the community has seeped into my awareness and I into it, a result of both dancing and of viewing others' dances. It is very much like possessing knowledge of a secret code; once I knew that the cues existed, and then learned what moves they initiated, I was able to watch with more understanding, a comprehension not just of that dance but of all ATS dancers. And during open dancing sessions that generally follow ATS performances, in which anyone can participate, though I stumble through the steps, miss the cues, and am anything but graceful, I feel just as much a part of the community as I do of other communities based on more traditional foundations such as family or career.[21]

This equality in ATS seems to stem in large part from an almost vehemently non-political stance. When asked whether she thought her dancing was political on any level, Nericcio answered: "Not intentionally. Perhaps in the beginning I thought it was a statement against repression in the Middle East and Africa. But now I understand that one has to have respect for traditional cultures" (Nericcio 2011). Samantha Riggs says, "if anything, I would say it [her dancing] is anti-political. ... I would hope that our dancing shows that anyone can do it and greater understanding of one's fellow humans can be reached by engaging in this activity" (Riggs 2011). And Mimi Fontana says, "I don't give a rat's ass about who likes what and what is or is not correct. I also don't have a problem with gay people, 'freaks,' anti-establishment folks" (Fontana 2011).

Expressed in different ways, each of these statements fairly screams tolerance — if such a thing is not an oxymoron. It is as though by virtue of being part of the community one is de-facto apolitical and is open to new styles and new people, to expressing power and sexuality, and to exploring non-traditional lifestyles of many sorts. As with marginal figures everywhere, their status as such is what defines them, and their marginality is both expressed and experienced as an all-inclusive sense of belonging that lives in the dance and in the bodies of dancers. This sense is then communicated through the media of both imagination and technology to other dancers in other physical locations, creating a community that is experienced by its members as one of equality and ongoing connection.

The community of ATS dancers, then, is maintained by the dance-capital inherent in the language of the dance itself, and is transmitted through forms of media — YouTube, DVDs — to other dancers who both partake of the community and give back to it in the form of yet another dance. In the words of Carolena Nericcio, "The internet has provided such a great resource.... In the beginning of the web, I couldn't imagine how it could benefit a kinetic thing like dance ... it has really proved to be an almost emotional conduit for dancers to connect" (Nericcio 2011). Michelle Morrison agrees, calling YouTube and instructional videos "invaluable resources to discover other people's styles, see how other dancers are interpreting music and presentation of our art" (Morrison 2011). Gontar agrees, saying "I really feel connected to the whole community.... We keep in touch through [the] internet." "Our" art, a shared dance, a shared community.

The internet functions here as an integral component of the ATS community and the dance can be seen as globalization in microcosm. Its very origins were made possible through access to global music, dance forms, clothing, and history. The hybridization process that melded it together continues in the growth of new Tribal styles, each of them a newly hybridized version that through digital media is disseminated to others.

In the end, ATS and the internet have become virtual contact zones in which exists "co-presence, interaction, interlocking understandings and practices" (Pratt 1992, 7). This is perhaps the promise of ATS: as a (imagined) community, it embodies the promise of equality and positive growth touted by proponents of globalization, rarely met and always contested. In a globalized world ever more connected, the spread of both culture and commodity must be incorporated into daily life on all levels. Setting aside the consumer, political, and economic forces to focus instead on the emergence and ever-changing nature of American Tribal Style belly dance, we can see it as a cultural phenomenon within the larger globalization process, and as such it holds a unique place.

As Steger tells us, "Globalization also refers to people becoming increasingly conscious of growing manifestations of social interdependence and the enormous acceleration of social interactions. Their awareness of the receding importance of geographical boundaries and distances fosters a keen sense of becoming part of the global whole" (2003, 12). By virtue of belonging to the ATS community through performing, teaching, attending dance festivals both local and global, and by speaking the language of ATS in venues both actual and virtual, these dancers participate in the larger world that encompasses them all. In a world such as Appadurai envisions, without nations or borders, and instead maintained and mediated by technology and imagination, perhaps American Tribal Style belly dance[22] is both pioneer and — literal — embodiment of the possible.

Perhaps it is time for all of us to dance.

Notes

1. AmericanTribalStyle® and ATS® are registered trademarks, as are FatChanceBellydance®, and FCBD®. Legal information can be found at www.fcbd.com/about/legal.shtml. For ease of reading, the trademark symbol will not be repeated throughout, but should be understood.

2. The ATS form is often confused with what are in fact offshoots of American Tribal Style. Improvisational Tribal Style (ITS), Tribal Fusion, Tribal Style, or even simply Tribal, are terms used that denote variations of ATS and are later developments. Another dance heavily influenced by Tribal is Goth belly dance, or GBD, a style based on "dark aesthetics" that celebrates "...the terrible beauty of the grotesque and tragically mortal" (Siegel, 2005, 166 in Fruhauf, 2009, 119). To confuse things further, all these dances are always in flux, redefining themselves and their offshoots as new dancers incorporate, adapt, and alter the moves, costumes, or group dynamic often considered essential. For more details on the histories of ATS, ITS, Tribal Fusion, Fusion, Tribal and related dance forms, see many sites online by searching for any of the above keywords.

3. Carolena Nericcio lists sister studios in Taiwan, Japan, Russia, Finland, Germany, and Belgium as well, with new studios emerging on a regular basis.

4. As Anderson explains it, the mechanism here is as follows: in order to maximize sales and circulation, publishers began to print various media — especially books and newspapers — in a vernacular language which allowed for speakers of different dialects to read the same publications, and thereby imagine others who both read and understood the same ideas, concepts, and news items. This in turn created a shared understanding of the world, and facilitated common discourse. This experience was enhanced by the reading of, say, the morning paper, at which time a reader could conceive of others doing the same thing at the same time, or in fact see them doing so, and was thereby "continually reassured that the imagined world is visibly rooted in everyday life" (Anderson, 2006, 36).

5. While some men do perform this dance, they are few, and I will limit my pronoun to the female.

6. By "traditional" I mean what predominantly Western audiences think of when they envision "belly dance."

7. Interestingly, tattoos are extremely common in ATS — and in fact all forms of Tribal — dance. This prompted me to ask Nericcio if they conveyed a meaning of some kind, or whether they were an integral part of the dance. Her response was that no, instead "It's just circumstance. I happened to be tattooed and I attracted other tattooed people. My tattoos don't have any connection to the dance" (interview, 2011).

8. For specifics about the music used in the dance, and its typical venues, see www.fcbd.com/about/history_rr.shtml.

9. Her website can be found here: http://taisa-jah-surya.livejournal.com/.

10. I am using this concept with a bit of a twist here. The capitalist motivation that encouraged, in Anderson's view, the printing of books in a common language does not translate directly. In the case of dance-capitalism, I posit that the common language of ATS dance moves and cues is motivated not by potential future economic profits, but by the potential for future connection with other dancers.

11. For more details, see www.fcbd.com/about/history_rr.shtml and other sites.

12. It should not be forgotten that the process of globalization has been a fact for centuries. While the extent and breadth of this process has increased exponentially since the advent of computers and the connectedness of the internet, it should not be assumed that contact zones between cultures have only just recently been productive of new and previously unknown forms of cultural expression.

13. By the mid–20th century in America, danse Orientale/raqs Orientale/belly dance had been through so many permutations it would have been unrecognizable to dancers of

earlier generations who had actually lived and danced in the "exotic" Middle East. Always already a manifestation of Western imagination and fantasy, Middle Eastern belly dance in the Americas originated in large part to satisfy those same American audiences, and the myth of its origin was in large part what both Salimpour and Archer, and then Nericcio, resisted as they created this new dance style.

14. While "equality" in globalization discussions is often used in an economic sense, within measurements of poverty and income inequality, as well as the questions of power and privilege in a social context, this chapter broadens the concept to a cultural one that has far less to do with power, income, or poverty level than with social/cultural questions of hierarchical status within the ATS community.

15. Political, cultural, social, religious, economic, financial, and market values all fall under this.

16. Globalization as an effect/goal of evil oppressive nations is a familiar characterization. Countering that, Appadurai believes that "as rapidly as forces from various metropolises are brought into new societies, they tend to become indigenized in one form or another" (1996, 32), and Steven Flusty tells us that in fact globalization is a bottom-up process, and that "we must imagine a 'nonsovereign' production of the global that is as increasingly immanent in, and emergent through, our day-to-day thoughts and actions as it is in the mass movement of capital, information, and populations.... The formation of the world must be seen as embedded both in space and in the lives of emplaced persons.... The inhabitants of the world [are] globally formative actors" (2004, 7).

17. Admittedly quite a small percentage of the available sites; at last search, there were more than 174,000 hits for a Google search of ATS belly dance.

18. For more information, see www.farfesha.com.

19. Information about classes and the studio can be found here: http://www.mimi fontana.com/

20. This term denotes a "space in which peoples geographically and historically separated come into contact with each other and establish ongoing relationships" (Pratt, 1992, 6) and was coined by Mary Louise Pratt in her scholarship on colonial dynamics. Pratt imbues the term with inherent "radically asymmetrical relations of powers" (7), and while I do not subscribe to a view that insists on seeing ATS in this light, despite some criticism of belly dance as a whole as an appropriated dance form, I do use the term advisedly, to call into question the perceived equality of the ATS community. The performance of each dance is itself, perhaps, a constantly evolving contact zone. While this chapter does not allow for exploration of this potentially productive arena, the ATS-performance-as-contact-zone hypothesis this will be the subject of further study.

21. And as an aside, as a novice dancer I felt much more part of the ATS community than I often have in academia, wherein levels of accomplishment must precede acceptance.

22. This chapter focused exclusively on American Tribal Style; however, it is my belief that offshoots of ATS have this same potential.

Works Cited

Anderson, B. (2003). *Imagined Communities: Reflections on the Origin and Spread of Nationalism*, Revised edn. London and New York: Verso.

Appadurai, A. (1996). *Modernity at Large: Cultural Dimensions of Globalization*. Minneapolis: University of Minnesota Press.

Archer, M. (2011). www.fcbd.com/about/history_rr.shtml, accessed November 2011.

BTribal (2011). http://www.btribalbellydance.com/, accessed December 2011.

Devyani Dance Company (2011). http://www.devyani.net/pages/About-Us.html, accessed November 2011.

Flusty, S. (2004). *De-Coca-Colonization: Making the Globe from the Inside Out*. New York: Routledge.
Fontana, M. (2011). FaceBook Interview.
Fruhauf, T. (2009). "Raqs Gothique: Decolonizing Belly Dance." *The Drama Review* 53, 117–138.
Gontar, Tasia (2012). Email interview, March 16.
Morrison, M. (2011). Facebook interview.
Nericcio, C. (2011). Email interview/correspondence.
Pratt, M.L. (1997). *Imperial Eyes: Travel Writing and Transculturation*, 4th edn. London: Routledge.
Riggs, S. (2011). Facebook interview.
Siegel, C. (2005). *Goth's Dark Empire*. Bloomington: Indiana University Press.
Steger, M.B. (2003). *Globalization: A Very Short Introduction*. Oxford: Oxford University Press.
Tan, A. (2011). Facebook interview.
Techniques Studio. (2011). http://www.techniquesbp.com/, accessed December 2011.
Tribal-bellydance. (2011). http://www.tribal-bellydance.be/, accessed November 2011.
Wade, R.H. (2004). "Is Globalization Reducing Poverty and Inequality?" *World Development* 32, Issue 4: 567–589, available online at the first link at http://www.google.com/search?sourceid=chrome&ie=UTF-8&q=%22Is+globalization+reducing+poverty+and+inequality%3F%22, accessed 2011.

The Use of Nostalgia in Tribal Fusion Dance

CATHERINE MARY SCHEELAR

In a subculture fraught with romanticism of the other, belly dancers of non–Middle Eastern descent are increasingly drawing inspiration from their own cultural climates. Since belly dance or Oriental dance became especially popular in North America during the 1960s and 1970s, there has been a similar increased scholarly output. As belly dancers seek to legitimize their dance form in the greater culture, this academic trend may contribute to the community's search for origins by creating new concerns for authenticity in the wake of accusations of invented tradition (Hobsbawm 1983). While all tradition can be considered as invented in one way or another, the Tribal Fusion genre has evolved as an overtly 21st century form still in the process of defining its own recognizable and reproducible generic boundaries, often by reacting against the constraints of parent belly dance genres.

Within Tribal Fusion there is an aesthetic known by various names such as Tribal Burlesque, Vintage Tribal Fusion, and Vaudevillian Tribal Fusion, and like other forms under the Tribal Style umbrella practitioners are moving even further away from the Middle East for aesthetic inspiration to "the exotic Occident" (Haynes-Clark 2010, 130). This performance genre's structure and aesthetics are strongly coded to recall past times, but the resulting form "does not refer to a lived reality or even a fictive one, but to a set of previously existing and highly identifiable images" (Dika 2003, 13). In not claiming to reference the modern Middle East this style escapes charges of cultural appropriation and inauthenticity by instead highlighting the West's historical fascination with the Orient, which allows Tribal Fusion to stay relevant to the greater Western belly dance culture. There exists a dialogue between concepts of tradition and modernity as the realization of the Americanness of Oriental dance reminds non-eastern belly dancers of fragments of their own cultural histories through generally lower-class American entertainment genres.

Tribal Fusion belly dance is often described as the genre which allows for the most experimentation (Fazio 2005). However, in the global belly dance community predominantly composed of *raqs sharqi* dancers this flexibility renders Tribal Fusion to be categorized as the least genuine form, derided by purists as both derivative and degenerate with little folkloric influence left to be seen. These sentiments are echoed in the following statement by dancer Asharah:

> This is where I get into trouble and make enemies. I think many newer dancers perform under the moniker of "fusion" because they don't want to put in the work to learn traditional belly dance.... I feel like dancers also use "fusion" as an excuse to do whatever they want without any sort of technical, cultural, or historical foundations under the guise of artistic expression [Kurtz 2011, 13].

A number of writers have argued that individual genres are hierarchically ordered and often tied to social hierarchies (Bourdieu 1991, Kuipers 1990, Leitch 1992). In the Oriental dance family, being able to pinpoint exactly when Tribal Styles such as ATS and Tribal Fusion were formed makes the dance forms appear to some as contrived in comparison to the vague, mysterious, ancient, yet therefore more legitimate-seeming *raqs* (al) *sharqi* (translating from Arabic as "dance [of the] east"), commonly referred to as the world's "oldest dance" (Aradoon 1979, Mourat 2000). Jennifer Haynes-Clark has used Bourdieu's concepts of orthodoxy (which encapsulates a society's current accepted norms) and heterodoxy (beliefs which challenge the accepted norms) to highlight how some adherents of the *raqs sharqi* belly dance genre, still the most popular form of the dance, demand respect for the genre as originators due to the forms widely accepted eastern roots (2010, 43). These forms may be viewed as orthodoxy while more recent branches of the Oriental dance family tree more overtly challenge the acceptable boundaries of belly dance, suggesting heterodoxy.

While belly dance has long represented subversive and feminist desires in the West, Haynes-Clark further argues that "the invented tradition of belly dance must be renewed and revised if it is to remain relevant to American women" (Haynes-Clark 2011, 43). She suggests that American belly dancers could dismantle the rampant Orientalism that permeates their dance forms by acknowledging many Oriental dance forms as unique, modern, and American (Haynes-Clark 2011, 125). Marta Savigliano (1995) noted a similar phenomenon when studying the fascination of North Americans with the Latin dance form tango; that dances can only truly be decolonized when practitioners move beyond the search for origins and authenticity and instead enjoy the dance form as an evolving cultural entity rather than an unchanging artifact of an ethnographic present (9). In describing Gothic Belly Dance and also applicable to Tribal Fusion is Tina Fruhauf's (2009) assertion that modern forms are "unburdened of a debt owed to ethnic dance ... [answering] the demand for a mode of expression that addresses the complexity of the postmodern woman's life" (122). While she admits that "more traditional belly dancers reject GBD," the ongoing transformation of belly dance introduces new concepts of authenticity (Fruhauf 2009, 135–136).

"Origins help articulate identities"

While Tribal Fusion began as testing the boundaries of Tribal Style, a form which itself revolted against the dominance of American *raqs sharqi*, Tribal Fusion is itself evolving beyond simple novelty and play, whereas Stephen Nachmanovitch reminds us "definitions slip, slide, perish, decay with imprecision" (Nachmanovitch 2009, 15). The beginnings of Tribal Fusion (hereafter known as TF) can be traced back to Carolena Nericcio's founding of American Tribal Style (ATS) and her FatChanceBellyDance troupe. Her student, Jill Parker, went on to found the Ultra Gypsy dance troupe in 1996 in the San Francisco, California, area which now acts as a center point for Tribal Style belly dancers worldwide who look West for authenticity, inspiration, and acknowledgement (Zuza 2011, 21). Ultra Gypsy was heavily based on American Tribal Style (ATS) as Parker herself was an original member of it. Many credit her as TF's creator while others attribute the beginnings of Tribal Fusion to Bay area dancer Frederique Johnston, who in the late 1990s began experimenting with the ATS repertoire to then underground electronica music (Zay 2011, 25). At this time inspirational deviation from the ever shifting imaginative geography of the Middle East was still considered taboo. Even within the once avant-garde ATS genre, music from or echoing North Africa and Central Asia (romantically described as the Silk Road Route) remains the norm. While various forms of Silk Road and Arabic music are used in TF, electronica music is the most favored, varying from world fusion to dark industrial. Dance scholar Julia R. Zay suggests that a true change in a dance form doesn't occur without a change in music as the introduction of new music allows for new rhythms and accents "causing some movements to become more prominent and others to fade into the background" (Zay 2011, 25). Contrasting with the hyper femininity of many styles of belly dance which exhibit light, graceful movements, here emphasis is placed on the exaggerated contrast between quick upper body and torso isolations known as locks and serpentine arm and torso movements.

In 2001 Johnston's troupe *Romani* performed at the first Tribal Fest, the largest festival of Tribal/Alternative belly dance in the world, where other troupes were influenced by their idiosyncratic stylization. While various names for the new style floated around such as Electronica Orientale and Urban Tribal Style, it wasn't until around 2003 that the term Tribal Fusion became common, which nods to its ancestors in American Tribal Style while acknowledging innovation. Professional Tribal Fusion dancers do not simply describe their dance as Tribal Fusion but rather are apt to describe their dance style as a fusion of Oriental and non–Oriental dances such as North Indian Kathak, tango, flamenco, jazz, hip-hop, modern dance, and pop and locking (from the funk and breakdance dance street styles of 1960s and 1970s California). Known for infusing the style with intense muscular isolations cultivated through yoga training, Rachel Brice has been credited as the first Tribal Style soloist, spreading the style in major international Bellydance Superstars performance tours from 2003 to 2004. Along with combining movements from various forms of ethnic and popular dance, dancer Jasmine June notes that: "new sounds appeal to the eclecticism of fusion in the dance, and this new combination is both American and global, allowing it to be adopted in a similar spirit of rebellion that spurred Tribal Belly dancing as a movement in the first place" (June & MacKoy 2011).

Professional TF belly dancers have been inspired by and regularly collaborate with experimental American electronica artists such as Beats Antique and Pentaphobe who pepper their dubstep, breakbeat, and DnB (Drum and Bass) music with Arabic and Indian rhythms. And while Balkan music has long been used by belly dancers when performing Roma or "gypsy" dances, in TF performances it blends with glitchy electronica, the contrast making elements of both modernity and nostalgia all the more dramatic. In the last few years elements of the American Jazz Age have popped up; Brice recently performed a sinuous Jazz Age solo at 2011's Tribal Fest, which also saw dancers performing the Charleston to ragtime piano pieces and a few numbers of what has recently been dubbed Flapper Fusion; dancers performing to vintage jazz music while wearing flapper costumes. While this habit may be unexpected to audience members accustomed to *raqs sharqi* or folkloric dress, 1920s Western fashion was heavily influenced by Oriental motifs as evidenced in the popular headdresses, loose flowing tunics and trousers, Egyptian-inspired patterns, and copious use of silks, beading and fringe. These signifiers of a Western past easily resonate with modern TF dancers and may also serve to inspire dancers to learn more about American dance history:

> Obviously, Tribal Fusion is not a traditional Middle Eastern Belly dance form; yet performing to Jazz music is attractive to Tribal Fusion dancers because it comes from the same country as Tribal Fusion itself— America. For some dancers, it can be easier to relate to music from one's own culture than it is to music from halfway

Bedecked in beads, flowers and lace, Saskia Aarts and Laura West of Luna Dance Fusion publicize an event (courtesy Daryl Croft).

around the world.... Performing to Jazz allows a Tribal Fusion dancer to embrace the fashion traditions of her own culture [June & MacKoy 2011].

(Dis)orienting Oriental Dance: The Vaudevillian Aesthetic

Far from being rife with concerns over cultural accuracy and impeccable representation of foreign cultures, Tribal Fusion dancers increasingly reference overtly European and American aesthetics. The most striking difference between *raqs sharqi* and Tribal Fusion is the latter's much darker aesthetic, a look based on Tribal Style but which often draws heavily on gothic, vintage, or vaudevillian inspirations. Very few dancers of the Tribal Style(s) engage in the common Western belly dance practice of adopting an Arabic persona often evidenced by an exotic stage name, and while *raqs sharqi* dancers often foster a hyper feminine look with long hair and tanned skin, Tribal dancers usually style their hair up in elaborate head-dresses (inspired by Art Nouveau artist Alfons Mucha and the Art Deco Flapper style) and cultivate a paler aesthetic reminiscent of the Expressionist film era, often punctuated with tattoos and facial piercings.

As dance scholar Tina Fruhauf notes, "Tribal dancers are not generally accepted in the traditional American performance venue for belly dance, the Arabic-style restaurant or nightclub" (Fruhauf 2009, 133). As little stereotypically Arabic influence remains, professional TF dancers have had to seek out new performance venues that more closely resonate with their aesthetic, such as electronica dance parties (commonly called raves) and nightclubs, countercultural festivals such as Burning Man, opening for rock bands, or performing with traveling road shows, allowing belly dancers opportunities to collaborate and perform on the same stage with other circus performers. Tribal Fusion aesthetics often draw attention to the sensual, sexual, and working class history of Oriental dance as it evolved in early American circus, burlesque, and vaudeville theatre, acting as a signifier for female empowerment by subverting both patriarchy and mainstream feminism through playing with acceptable boundaries of public female behavior (Haynes-Clark 2011, 118). Most contemporary Oriental dancers distance themselves from these origins in aspiring to have belly dance recognized by outsiders as either a classical, codified art form and/or an authentic cultural artifact. At the same time, "the celebration of burlesque within the Tribal Fusion movement is contained within historical signifiers, perhaps in an effort to distinguish this erotic form of belly dance from other modern erotic dances" (Haynes-Clark 2010, 67). This phenomenon echoes a larger trend amongst Tribal Fusion dancers of incorporating aesthetics historically associated with 20th century Western Orientalism, such as the Vamp, the Salomé dancer, and the 1893 World Fair's Little Egypt character. Haynes-Clark suggests that "the modern Middle East has become too 'real' for it to be confused with the exotic Orient of the Western imagination. The interest in vaudeville and burlesque evoke a time in American history when the Orientalist fantasy seemed less cluttered" (2010, 67).

Vaudevillian Tribal Fusion (VTF) costuming and performance styles index the familiar-yet-unfamiliar Victorian (1837 to 1901), Edwardian (1901 to 1910), and the Roaring Twenties or American Jazz Age (1920s), all eras wherein Orientalist imagery was in vogue throughout the domains of art, dance, film, consumer advertising, home décor, and fashion (Adams et al. 2011, Studlar 1997). While this range admittedly covers a broad range of potential histories, they are similar in that the use of aesthetics from these time periods indexes an obviously Western pastness. Much of the popular entertainment of these eras such as silent films and music hall performances both suggested and reinforced the popular view of an expansive, mythical Orient as a liminal space of leisure, luxury, and sensuality. Most interestingly, VTF belly dancers exploit the imagery of European colonialist art and the costuming of early Salomés (which inhabited high culture spaces such as the ballet and opera) and lower-class sideshow cooch dancers alike. With little concern for historical accuracy, a play of references occurs when dancers combine feathers, flowers, lace, pearls, ruffles, brass buttons, stockings, pinstripes, vintage leather boots, bloomers, flapper dresses, art nouveau and art deco clothing, parasols, and burlesque fans. Dancers will often perform to vintage or simulated vintage music and design artificially aged, faded, and damaged sepia poster advertisements, photographs, and videos to circulate within a dance subculture rife with "the desire for desire in which objects are the means of generation and not the ends" (Stewart 1991, 74).

Much like earlier American burlesque and vaudeville performers, VTF dancers also freely combine gendered symbols such as top hats and bustles. Sociologist Paul Connerton (1989) describes the 19th century Victorian clothing these dancers covet as highly gendered: women wore clothing suggesting frivolity and childishness (such as light colors/pastels, ribbons, lace, and bows), which inhibited movement (such as corsets, bustles, and petticoats) rendering the wearer inactive and submissive; these clothes served as both decodable messages and to mold ideal female behavior (33). However, in keeping with American belly dance's histories of alternative feminism (Haynes-Clark 2011), modern belly dancers subvert the messages that these ultra-feminine clothes signify by using them as props in their public performance of female sensuality and freedom. Dancers can create a mysterious aura by disrupting time, allowing them access to bodily knowledge of different realities; the aesthetics of Victoriana can be felt through wearing lace, bustles, and corsets, without the historically apropos level of oppression of women. And in referencing forms of Western pastness rather than attempting to adhere to impossible representations of foreign culture, new understandings of cultural authenticity are possible, as explained by British performer and instructor Rebecca Priest, "We have Steampunk style which, with our background in the Victorian era, is performed with authenticity and quite quirky costuming. Given that the UK is the birthplace of [the] gothic subculture, we have a real affinity with the darker side of dance" (Gativa 2011, 31).

In her study of turn of the century Britain and commodified authenticity, Elizabeth Outka describes

> the late nineteenth century fascination with new ways to construct illusions, and with the corresponding possibilities for reinventing the self. Over the course of the next century, dramatic changes in advertising, marketing, and shopping would encourage consumers not simply to live a life but to select among lifestyles; not to stay within the given circumstances and time of their birth but to live in multiple pasts; not to remain fixed in one identity but to perform within many [Outka 2009, 3].

Similarly, repurposed and recycled materials, movements, and music combine in novel ways to highlight the American cultural value of the never-ending ability to be remade; a form of authenticity defined by innovation (Outka 2009, 10). Outka's term originary authentic is fitting here as Tribal Fusion's avant-garde multitextual aesthetic and movement vocabulary allows dancers access to a form of authenticity while also acknowledging the potentiality for change. Combining various indexes of the past, while seeming paradoxical, allows a modern Tribal dancer to embody certain values in their performance. Instead of having to choose between values associated with the past (such as authenticity, purity and tradition) and the present (such as modernity, accessibility, and continual self-fashioning), they can unite all of these desires and values into one ever-evolving identity through access to previously elite goods such as textiles, jewelry, and cosmetics. The modern dancer can access both the lower and upper classes, both the gypsy and the jewels, or "the distilled essences of other classes" (Outka 2009, 15). While in more traditional-looking belly dance forms dancers play at being gypsies, village dancers, or peasants, in VTF dancers reference historically lower class American forms of public (and often nomadic) performance such as burlesque, vaudeville, and the circus sideshow.

Many dancers know that they are not accurately representing anyone else's culture or even their own historically accurate cultural history, but rather are continually creating something in the here and now through referencing a multitude of forms and combining them in (sometimes) novel ways. The resulting aesthetic is not representational of any actual single past reality but is instead a simulacra, "a copy of copies whose original has been lost" (Dika 2003, 3). The historically signifying aesthetics are so obviously juxtaposed that they could not possibly adhere to *raqs sharqi* notions of authenticity which can occur when "the American imagination demands the real thing and, to attain it, must fabricate the absolute fake" (Eco 1986, 7–8).

As the greater American belly dance culture generally did away with the magical performances that evoked overtly Orientalist depictions of sultan's harems, the *raqs sharqi* genre strove to engage in simulation of a real thing, that is, the culture of the (usually Egyptian) Other. Conversely VTF performers often index phenomena once understood as reality and now realized as real fantasy. Through weaving together various histories of Western Orientalism depicted in transnational media such as Hollywood cinema and antique French postcards, VTF performances bring to light Western dancer's own cultural histories rather than imagined realities of foreign dancers.

While widely considered the lowest genre in the hierarchy of belly dance genres, these Tribal Fusion dancers engage in what can be considered a lower class habit of mixing elements that the high class (*raqs sharqi* dancers) would consider un-mixable. However, these polluting actions can also be seen as even higher class behavior, as by playfully mixing these elements the VTF dancers suggest that they are outside of such class distinctions or frameworks and so have the freedom to mix as they please. In not claiming to represent any one time or place (other than the ever changing present) dancers weave temporal fragments together, temporarily satisfying desires for an appealing aura of tradition while participating in a cutting edge and novel production of cultural phenomena. And to be able to sustain all of these contradictory impulses which flow between authenticity and artifice, performers must on some level acknowledge that all of these embodiments are constructions; these transgressive performances suggest that class position itself is a constructed and unstable performance (Outka 2009, 16–17).

Pastiche of the Past Performed: Introducing Graceful Mistakes

Not only is there a growing trend in TF towards VTF costuming and musical accompaniment, but also indexed are past performance genres integral to the early history of American belly dance. As one informant explained, this theatrical trend is not so much new or cutting edge but rather a return to the roots of belly dance in the West. In a sense the dance comes full circle in referencing the public performers of yesteryear who were not only dancers (artists) but dancer-actor-acrobats (entertainers) who played out stories to their audiences. Individual VTF belly dance performances often exhibit narrative structure complete with campy characters, and it is also becoming more common for whole belly dance theatre shows to evolve (from a night of separate dance performances in secession one after the other) into musical-narrative theatre (with a single cohesive storyline). With more dance troupes labeling themselves as belly dance theatre, the spaces in between the actual dancing grow to highlight the vague boundary between dancing and acting in American belly dance history.

Anthropology of performance scholar Richard Schechner suggests that theatre often acts as a model of and reflection on taboo subjects within a culture such as violence or sexuality (2003, 243). Theatre is also useful in commenting on social hierarchy. While the historically Western "belly dancing body can be read as a subversive body" (Keft-Kennedy 2005, 295), in the larger Oriental dance culture unabashedly and unapologetically mixing styles and confusing origins is largely discouraged, at best written off as fantasy and at worst openly criticized. Likewise, the use of various past narrative elements which historically included Oriental dance such as vaudeville, burlesque, and ballet bring to light the adaptive and escapist history of belly dance.

The emergence and growing popularity of VTF performance can be partially attributed to two West Coast phenomena: Frédérique (The Lady Fred)'s Silent Sirens Theatre and The Indigo's Le Serpent Rouge production. In these and similar pieces, performers use recognizable schematic elements to communicate their concept to the audience such as antique and Art Deco costumes and ample use of props and musical gags. Body language and facial expressions also signal pastness as exaggerated pantomime acting was the style of early 20th century popular performance both in popular theatre and silent films. Dancers will often sport campy, exaggerated expressions and movements and parody serious belly dance performances by pretending to be drunk, tired, to fall or trip, or to not be able to execute the movements properly. When an audience member first encounters such a performance, they may not realize that the dancer's foibles are intentional. To pull this parody off effectively then, a dancer must have excellent control in order to layer and contrast her skill with comedy to ensure that the audience is able to differentiate between sloppy technique and taboo acts as a way of making fun of the established hierarchy and boundaries of belly dance genres.

Anthropologist Gregory Bateson (1972) suggests that the extent to which the artist does not have to consciously control their movements suggests a mastery of the art through repetitive practice or habit formation (120). The movements have been practiced so much that they become second-nature and

Dancer and Silent Sirens Theatre creator Frédérique (The Lady Fred) (courtesy Kristine Adams).

so the artist can then layer on top of them. Therefore by pretending to dance horribly or comically VTF dancers are actually highlighting just the opposite: how well they have mastered the art of belly dance. While many in the audience may view these performances as simple entertainment, this type of VTF performance is most often performed in venues where many of the audience members are likely to be other dancers who are familiar with the degree of difficulty of mastery of movements as well as the various genres of Oriental dance and its degrees of concern over purity.

Performance scholar Annemarie Matzke (2005) states that "to articulate or embody doubt in performance is a mode of creating a sense of trust and evoking authenticity." VTF dancers will often display the preparation and process of theatre by performing warm-ups on stage or intentional mistakes such as pretending to forget choreographies, as well as engage in interventions such as motioning to the audience, highlighting what anthropology of performance scholar Richard Bauman (1986) considers the gap between the narrated event (the script of the dance) and the storytelling event (the dance itself). These gaps allow dancers to slip in and out of their performance frames and in doing so illuminate to the audience the constructed nature of the performance. These transgressive acts highlight the story of the performances construction alongside the aesthetic that the performance would more ordinarily communicate. Through paradoxical juxtaposition of indexed pastness and overtly modern elements, VTF dancers highlight that they are not accurately recreating past or Eastern forms. Much like the theoretical perspective of reflexivity and self-critical awareness in ethnography wherein the researcher describes a study's limits, problems, and failures, the practice of questioning the material lends the author/performer credibility in contexts where it is acknowledged that truth is impossible to define or represent (Franko 1993, 135). The very existence of these performances calls into question the authenticity of Oriental dances, which claim historical or cultural accuracy, by instead highlighting the fact that performers create culture in the present.

A discussion of frames may be helpful in further understanding just how VTF dancers challenge rules, orthodoxy and tradition in the Oriental dance subculture through play and thus create a cultural form wholly their own (Nachmanovitch 2009, 11). Sociologist Erving Goffman (1974) understood frames as basic cognitive structures which guide the perception and representation of reality; by defining a situation it is rendered meaningful to the viewer or participant (10). These frames are not consciously manufactured but rather unconsciously emerge in interaction, and this unconscious selection of a frame structures the viewer's perception of occurrences. While it is continually subject to reassessment and renegotiation, successful frame alignment between the audience and the performer occurs when the audience's expectations about what is appropriate and expected from the performance overlap with what the performer delivers, producing resonance (Snow et al. 1986, 464). When proposed frames do not resonate with the understandings and values of conventional frames the frame transformation process occurs, wherein in order to secure participants and support, new values, meanings and understandings are required (Snow et al. 1986, 473, Goffman 1974, 43–44). For example, the frame of cultural artifact did not resonate with audience members when watching early Tribal Style dancers and so a new (or old, depending on who you ask, as these trends are cyclical) belly dance frame emerged, that of play and fantasy. VTF's habit of engaging the audience through the play frame rather than the cultural artifact frame serves to de-essentialize modern belly dance from the long assertion that the dance needs to have an overtly Eastern influence.

The Emergence of Genres

Rather than being concerned with cultural accuracy towards temporally or spatially distant cultures and their dances, VTF dancers call attention to

Western belly dance's tendency towards fantasy entertainment much like the early burlesque and vaudeville performers who embraced turn of the century Salomania. Through mixing these elements in their performance the dancer/entertainer inadvertently communicates to the audience that the subject of discourse in VTF performance is not only the story that is being told by the dancers, but also reflects upon the entire structure of Oriental dance through highlighting the way a single performance is linked to other performances in the Oriental dance family.

While audience members will not mistake a dancer performing to electronica music while dressed in costuming referencing Oscar Wilde's pearled Salomé for an authentic reproduction of the original 1896 play, audience members may recognize historical elements of American Orientalism and find delight in the temporal paradox and lack of seriousness. They may then perceive *raqs sharqi* performances to follow with a similar critical awareness, noting similarities and differences between the performed genres as displayed through costuming; for example, both performances may reference Las Vegas showgirls through different ways, one through the use of the Wings of Isis prop and the other through large ostrich feather fans, also commonly used in burlesque theatre. In the most extreme sense VTF performances are meta-dances: belly dance performances about belly dancing, as they bring up the question: "What is belly dance? Culture or fantasy, or both?"

This balancing of innovation and tradition is similar to the concept of play, which gives both structure and allows for improvisation, as playing without any sort of structure or "rules" is often meaningless. However, in terms of the emergence of genres we are no longer strictly playing when we deliberately seek a specific end result, as it has become a form to be reproduced as well (Nachmanovitch 2009, 18). After the initial joy of breaking boundaries play now becomes increasingly balanced with defining and refining as the forms become codified and transmittable, adhering to a number of formal constraints for ease of mobility. In American belly dance a style becomes its own genre when an ideal form is sought after and when increasing numbers of practitioners can tell you what it should not be, as the very act of mentioning the following habits means that they are very common:

> Tribal Fusion as a term should not be used in lieu of proper labeling or as an excuse for laziness. Tribal Fusion is a specific style of dance with certain characteristics, and we mustn't forget that it is in its essence still belly dance. Tribal Fusion is not another term for popping and locking, nor is it a justification for dancing to non–Middle Eastern music or not learning more traditional Middle Eastern dance styles. It is also not a catch-all term for a dancer to use to label herself because she isn't sure what else to call her dance [Keyes 2011, 42].

By juxtaposing flapper-inspired costuming with Balkan-infused electronica music, other dancers will know that the VTF performance they are watching is not authentic in the sense that they are genuinely representing another time and place. However, at the same time the performance is authentically modern and American in that it is itself its own cultural form which speaks to the history of the transnational belly dance community and its evolution through various forms of popular media, as well as the contemporary belly dance community's present concerns for authenticity in post-modernity. Tribal Fusion and the Vaudevillian aesthetic have become their own truths and their own forms with both general structures to be replicated and individual overlying textures to be idiosyncratically adjusted, all the while indexing various temporal threads of Western belly dance phenomena.

All American belly dance forms discussed in this study (*raqs sharqi*, ATS/ITS, Tribal Fusion, and Vaudevillian Tribal Fusion) heavily reference both Eastern and Western cultural contexts and histories, and all costuming has the ability to objectify a dense and enduring network of past and present relationships and histories. In his work *Art and Agency*, anthropologist Alfred Gell (1998) discusses how the artist (intentionally or unintentionally) always uses his previous works to inspire his later works (237). These earlier versions, even if considered complete and ideal by the artist, always act as a preparatory sketch for further works. Similarly, this occurs in any form of art or communication. In terms of Western belly dance, in looking back at the Little Egypt dancer, she appears as a fixed character in belly dance history along with Salome and the flapper. Upon closer inspection it becomes apparent that all personas and performances are both (unintentional) preparations for future works, and retrospective to previous works. In hindsight and at the macro-level, we may erase the gradation between ideal types; the more micro-level and detail oriented the researcher becomes, the more they see the processual rather than fixed nature of any history.

For example, while Little Egypt may have seemed to be an ideal type after arising at the 1893 World's Fair, threads of its persona can be seen in the Salomania of ten years later, which then influenced the Oriental Hollywood Vamp and Arabian Nights films of the 1920s, which influenced both Eastern and Western Cabaret music halls, all of which funneled into the greater 20th century transnational belly dance culture. Similarly, while *Raqs Sharqi*/Orientale/Cabaret, Tribal Style, Tribal Fusion, and all genres, subgenres and styles in between may seem as fixed, they rather all exist on a non-linear gradient. And as new research on belly dance comes to light previous accepted histories are subject to revision; while the past leads into the present, so do present actions loop back into and alter our constructed pasts.

Conclusion

While nostalgia has been academically referred to as "an individual's longing for the past, a yearning for yesterday, or a fondness for possessions and activities associated with days of yore" (Holbrook 1993, 245; Davis 1979, Stern 1992), nostalgia is also understood as a reaction to the present. In his sociological study of nostalgia entitled "Yearning for Yesterday," sociologist Fred Davis (1979) suggests that nostalgia can be used as an attempt to manufacture authenticity and tradition as well as contributing toward identity preservation (86–88). Tribal Fusion allows for ample aesthetic exploration and has incorporated movements and elements from a variety of non–Oriental dance and performance styles, such as hip-hop and West African dance. However, in repeatedly referencing the ur-moment or *chronotrope* in time (1880–1920) when belly dance first coalesced as an escapist art form that allowed for the liminality of identity of American women, current belly dancers are able to glean interesting insights into the overall structure of American belly dance; philosopher Alfred Whitehead suggests that "*how* an actual entity (an experience or event) *becomes* constitutes *what* the actual entity is.... It's 'being' is constituted by its 'becoming'" (1979).

As Tribal Fusion dance has evolved since its beginnings in the early 2000s, increasing numbers of TF dancers have put in the time and dedication to become masters of this art. While adherents of other belly dance genres may prefer their versions of belly dance, they may at the same time recognize the grace and skill necessary to properly execute the Tribal Fusion movement vocabulary. Through evoking a cluster of historical Orientalism, the VTF aesthetic allows TF to remain relevant to the Oriental family tree, interacting in a meaningful discursive space with other belly dance genres. In referencing the beginnings of Oriental dance in the West, dancers can reveal and acknowledge a certainty of belly dance; that it is a transnational intercultural creation not wholly Eastern or Western, as well as a fluid and dynamic form of escapist entertainment that ever-shifts according to the tastes of the dancers and the audience.

Works Cited

Adams, K.H., M.L. Keene, and J.C. Koella. (2012). *Seeing the American Woman, 1880–1920: The Social Impact of the Visual Media Explosion.* Jefferson, NC: McFarland.

Aradoon, Z. (1979). *The Oldest Dance: Origins and Philosophy of Dance Orientale (Belly Dancing).* Stanford: CA: Dream Place Publications.

Bateson, G. (1972). "Style, Grace, and Information in Primitive Art." *Steps to an Ecology of Mind: Collected Essays in Anthropology, Psychiatry, Evolution, and Epistemology.* San Francisco: Jason Aronson.

Bauman, R. (1986). *Story, Performance, and Event: Contextual Studies of Oral Narrative.* Cambridge: Cambridge University Press.
Bellydance Superstars. (2011). *About Us: A History of the BDSS.* http://www.bellydancesuperstars.com/content/about.html.
Bourdieu, P. (1991). *Language and Symbolic Power.* Cambridge, MA: Harvard University Press.
Brice, R. (2012). Personal communication, January 25.
Burning Man. (2011). *Burning Man: Welcome Home.* http://www.burningman.com/.
Connerton, P. (1989). *How Societies Remember.* UK: Cambridge University Press.
Davis, F. (1979). *Yearning for Yesterday: A Sociology of Nostalgia.* New York: Free Press.
Dika, V. (2003). *Recycled Culture in Contemporary Art and Film: The Uses of Nostalgia.* Cambridge: Cambridge University Press.
Fazio, G. (2005). "Tribal Power: Bellydance Superstar Rachel Brice." *The Japan Times,* August 3, 2005. http://search.japantimes.co.jp/member/member.html?ft20050803a1.htm.
Franko, M. (1993). *Dance as Text: Ideologies of the Baroque Body.* Australia: Press Syndicate of the University of Cambridge.
Fruhauf, T. (2009). "Raqs Gothique: Decolonizing Belly Dance." *TDR: The Drama Review* 53:3 (T203): 117–138.
Gativa, N. (2011). "Dancers of the Foggy Albion: Tribal & Fusion in the UK." *Fuse: A Tribal and Tribal Fusion Belly Dance Magazine* (Fall): 31–32.
Gell, A. (1980). *Art and Agency: An Anthropological Theory.* Oxford: Clarendon Press.
Goffman, E. (1974). *Frame Analysis: An Essay on the Organization of Experience.* New York: Harper & Row.
Haynes-Clark, J.L. (2010). *American Belly Dance and the Invention of the New Exotic: Orientalism, Feminism, and Popular Culture.* Portland State University, Master's thesis.
Hobsbawm, E. (1983). *The Invention of Tradition.* Cambridge: Cambridge University Press.
Holbrook, M.B. (1993). "Nostalgia and Consumption Preference: Some Emerging Patterns of Consumer Tastes." *Journal of Consumer Research* 20 (2): 245–256.
June, J. (2011). "Not So Steampunk Belly Dance" in Gilded Serpent, posted February 26th, 2011. http://www.gildedserpent.com/cms/2011/02/26/jasmine-june-steampunk-belly-dance/#axzz1ZIH191Rs
_____, and K. MacKoy. (2011). "Belly Dance n' All That Jazz." *Gilded Serpent,* posted June 24, 2011. http://www.gildedserpent.com/cms/2011/ 07/24/jasmine-kim-belly-dance-jazz/#axzz1YnuK7PCQ.
Keft-Kennedy, V. (2005). "'How does she do that?' Belly Dancing and the Horror of a Flexible Woman." *Women's Studies: An Inter-disciplinary Journal* 34: 279–300.
Keyes, A. (2011). "Fusion Confusion: Why Not All Fusion Belly Dance Is Necessarily Tribal." *Fuse: A Tribal and Tribal Fusion Bellydance Magazine,* Winter: 42.
Kuipers, J.C. (1990). *Power in Performance: The Creation of Textual Authority in Weyewa Ritual Speech.* Philadelphia: University of Pennsylvania Press.
Kurtz, K. (2011). "Getting to the Heart of the Fusion Controversy: Four Dancers Weigh in on Fusion in Belly Dance." *Fuse: A Tribal and Tribal Fusion Belly Dance Magazine,* Spring: 12–13.
Leitch, V.B. (1992). "(De)Coding (Generic) Discourse." *Genre* 24 (1): 83–98.
Matzke, A. (2005). *Testen, Spielen, Tricksen, Scheitern: Formen szenischer Selbstdarstellung im zeitgenössischen Theater.* Hildesheim: Olms.
Mourat, E. (2000). "Dance of Ancient Egypt." *The Belly Dance Book: Rediscovering the Oldest Dance.* Ed. Tazz Richard. 42–51. Concord, CA: Backbeat Press.
Nachmanovitch, S. (2009). "This Is Play." *New Literary History,* 40, 1 (Winter): 1–24. Baltimore: John Hopkins University Press.

Outka, E. (2009). *Consuming Traditions: Modernity, Modernism, and the Commodified Authentic*. New York: Oxford University Press.

Saskia Aarts. (2011). Personal communication, November 12.

Savigliano, M. (1995). *Tango and the Political Economy of Passion*. Boulder, CO: Westview Press.

Schechner, R. (2003). *Performance Theory*. USA: Taylor & Francis.

Snow, D.A., E.B. Rochford, S.K. Worden, and R.D. Benford. (1986). "Frame Alignment Processes, Micromobilization and Movement Participation." *American Sociological Review* 51: 464–81.

Stern, B. (1992). "Historical and Personal Nostalgia in Advertising Text: The Fin de Siècle Effect." *Journal of Advertising* 21 (4): 11–22.

Stewart, S. (1991). "Notes on Distressed Genres." *Crimes of Writing: Problems in the Containment of Representation*. New York: Oxford University Press.

Studlar, G. (1997). "Out-Salomeing Salomé: Dance, the New Woman, and Fan Magazine Orientalism." *Visions of the East: Orientalism in Film*. Eds. Matthew Bernstein and Gaylyn Studlar. Toronto: Rutgers University Press.

Whitehead, A.L. *Process and Reality*. London: Free Press, 1979.

Zay, J.R. (2011). *The Balla Guerra Manual I: Combat Dance*. Virginia Beach: RDI Publications.

Zerubavel, E. (2003). *Time Maps: Collective Memory and the Social Shape of the Past*. Chicago: University of Chicago Press.

Zuza, Ms. (2011). "Tribal Fusion's Best Kept Secret." *Fuse: A Tribal and Tribal Fusion Belly Dance Magazine* (Winter): 20–26.

"I mean, what is a Pakeha New Zealander's national dance? We don't have one"
Belly Dance and Transculturation in New Zealand

Brigid Kelly

Throughout the 20th century, as Western fascination with "Eastern exoticism" and desire for an explicitly feminine means of self-expression crystallized "the [Oriental] dancing body became an object of alterity" through which Western women aimed to articulate essential selves (Dox 1997, 151). In the early 21st century, the belly dancer still signifies alterity, but as the dance form has spread around the world, it has become a site for more complex articulations of self. When New Zealand "Oceanic belly dance" troupe Kiwi Iwi fuse Middle Eastern, North American, Latin, Maori and Rarotongan dance movements to interpret a contemporary Maori haka, for instance, they present a fluid, multicultural vision of New Zealand as participant in global culture, while ultimately asserting their commitment to a Pacific identity. Belly dancers who operate within the traditional conventions of the dance, too, may negotiate both performance of cultural alterity and an expression of a locally-situated self.

Most popular and scholarly literature on belly dancing examines only Middle Eastern and North American contexts (for example, Cooper 2004, Dox 2006, Rasmussen 2005, Sellers-Young 1992, 2005, Shay and Sellers-Young 2003). Attention to the development of belly dance in New Zealand, a former British colony in the South Pacific with a population mostly of British and European descent, may lay ground for looking at belly dance as a contemporary transcultural and globalized activity, rather than perpetuating generalizations about "Western" (i.e., North American) versus "Middle Eastern" belly dance.

An analysis of belly dance today must engage with both identity politics and the notion of globalization. I approach both globalization and identity via a hybridity model and draw on Marwan Kraidy's (2005) critical transculturalism, which views all cultures as inherently hybrid or mixed, but also recognizes the effects of power inequity. It aims to understand hybridity at a social level and allows a focus on links between institutions, texts and experiences, while keeping the idea of hybridity as a unifying element; it stresses the role of exchanges between participating entities and takes into account broader societal contexts. Most crucially, it focuses on "complex processes at play" to move beyond "bipolar models" of global/local, power/resistance, imperialism/hybridity (Kraidy 2005, 13).

I use the term "globalized belly dance" to describe belly dance primarily as it has developed outside its indigenous — that is, Middle Eastern or North African — cultures, finding this model preferable to calling such belly dance practice "Western." Belly dance outside the Middle East and North Africa is now practiced in countries not generally thought of as part of the West, such as Japan, China, Korea, Russia and South America. This approach also interrogates the concept of Western homogeneity. To do so is important because positioning all "Western" nations and peoples as part of a single-minded colonizing force ignores significant social and historical (not to mention linguistic) differences between individual "Western" cultures, as well as social differences that exist within those cultures. Globalized belly dance implies a transcultural exchange that may flow in multiple directions. It acknowledges the ongoing, active participation of Middle Eastern and North African people as influential teachers, event sponsors, musicians and performers, rather than restricting their involvement to "inspiration," and also allows us to view non-indigenous belly dancers as creative, not merely imitators or appropriators. It recognizes that belly dance, wherever it is done, is never untouched by what is going on outside the dancing body and beyond the performance space; it is always culturally hybrid, reflecting the idiosyncratic geographic and historical location in which participants and audiences exist.

As any student of belly dance seeking classes in a foreign country knows, belly dance has a culture of its own. Rather than being a Western reinterpretation of Middle Eastern and North African dances, as Barbara Sellers-Young (1992) and Julie Fisher (2003) suggest, belly dance is best considered as the expression of a synthetic culture which centers on the act of belly dancing. Unlike indigenous belly dance, it is institutionalized — centered on structured classes and formal performances — and culturally marked; it takes place in countries where belly dancing is not a culturally normative activity (although it can travel to them, as the development of belly dance festivals for tourist students in Egypt and Turkey attest). Belly dance practice structures the performance and professionalism more than spontaneous, improvised "lighthearted play" (Adra 2005, 41), and codifies movements and dance styles. It also requires the circulation of commodities and wider transcultural networking.

Belly dance as a practice/performance package is decentered, its people, technologies, capital, images and ideas caught up in "global cultural flows" which engage in "continually fluid and uncertain interplay" (Appadurai 1999, 229). The way it operates as a kind of portable package of "myths, semiotic codes, discourses and ... transformative practices" with which people may engage locally to produce their own distinct "meaningful experiences" has features of George Ritzer's "McDonalization" model (Kellner 2003, 38–39). In *Media Spectacle* Kellner (2003, 39) suggests that while the global fast-food franchise McDonald's does signify a "mode of homogenisation, massification and standardisation," it may nonetheless be experienced in different ways due to participants' diverse genders, ethnicities, class and geographic locations. Although identified as originating in the United States, participants from different cultural environments have adapted it to suit their socio-historical contexts and personal identity. When participants in belly dance culture incorporate belly dance movements into their wider movement repertoire, such as when they dance socially, they blur boundaries between performance and individual self-expression, "exotic Other" and "personal identity."

Belly Dance — A New Zealand Thing?

This essay derives from a master's thesis completed in 2008 that considered the directions belly dance had developed in New Zealand. The dancers who participated in that study — who are here identified with initials, not their real ones — frequently identified their dance as hybrid (or "fusion"), and related this to the multiple ways they self-identified as New Zealanders. Extending the idea of hybridity onto identity acknowledges the complex, multiple ways identity is constructed; a "Kiwi" identity[1] might occupy "the contaminated and connective tissue" between the multiple social, cultural and historical elements that structure New Zealand society (Bhabha 1996, 54). A New Zealand belly dancer's identity thus "contaminates," or affects, and "is contaminated" or affected by her engagement with belly dance culture. Several participants identified "the belly dancer" as one of multiple personae with which they identified and on which they could draw; the belly dancer was figured as a performed identity, but one that subsequently became part of a more complex and confident "self."

Belly Dance and Transculturation in New Zealand (Kelly) 141

Kiwi Iwi members Maarie Hutana (rear) and Samadhi Stuart (front) perform with tailed poi. Poi, which is traditionally used by Maori for games, martial training and to provide rhythm in performance, was chosen as a suitably localized prop (photograph by Jason Atkinson).

Belly dance appears to have reached New Zealand in the mid–1970s; resources were few and while there were some Middle Eastern teachers of the dance in its earliest years, North American belly dancers were among the strongest influences (Kelly 2008, 57). New Zealand has a tiny Middle Eastern population; fewer than 1 percent claim Middle Eastern ancestry,[2] and the country has never had a large Arabic restaurant or nightclub scene. Thus, most participants in this study had noticeable difficulty articulating ways in which belly dancing fitted into New Zealand culture when asked directly and viewed it as completely outside or largely alien to New Zealand culture. Conversely, the few Maori or Pasifika (Pacific Islander) interviewees saw (or sought) parallels between Polynesian and Middle Eastern cultural values, particularly surrounding family, hospitality and physical modesty. "The difference is we do kapa haka[3] and they do belly dance," (PX 2007). PX said that for Maori women, "exposing your belly's huge, especially after having children," and felt this was the chief reason for less Maori and Pasifika involvement in belly dance classes. But SB, who is Pakeha,[4] believed Maori women were less likely to participate because they could find satisfying cultural activities, including participation in performance groups, through their marae or extended family, whereas non–Maori could not. "Pakeha women are saying, what makes me a New Zealander?" she observed. "What is culture? If culture is the language you speak, the clothes you wear, the activities you do, the songs you sing, the food you eat, the dances you dance — what makes a New Zealander from that aspect? I think we're worried about that. We can't just bowl off to a marae[5] and say 'can I join your kapa haka group?' ... They don't need or want Pakeha involved in those things" (SB 2007).

Many participants agreed that non–Maori/Pasifika New Zealanders lacked a dance culture of their own, and acknowledged this was a driving force behind their interest in belly dance. These participants had a deep personal investment in belly dancing as a method of self-expression and pleasurable display that they believed was not available within wider New Zealand culture. They were, however, ambivalent about representation when they performed it in public. Some solved this by paying careful attention to the responsibilities attached to "presenting someone else's culture" (QZ 2007) and/or "promoting understanding and tolerance of different cultures" (TC 2007). Several participants spoke of their experiences of belly dancing at multicultural events, articulating the ways this role could be both pleasurable, because of positive responses from Middle Eastern audience members, and anxiety-provoking, for fear of being found insufficiently authentic.

An alternative approach was re-identifying their dance as "fusion," a discursive strategy within globalized belly dance that allows dancers to explore hybridity openly. The term fusion generally refers either to a deliberate mix of belly dancing and another dance style, or using belly dance moves to unconventional, usually Western, music. (WF 2007) felt that the category of "fusion" provided a "wide open arena" in belly dance wherein dancers could explore new ideas without being labeled or judged. For her, fusion belly dance occupies the same position as early modern dance, with its orientalist themes, did a century ago; Meyda Yegenoglu (1998) might observe that the latent Orientalism infusing both these dance forms creates the fertile ground of fusion as a creative category. But participants in this study seemed comfortable also using the term simply to acknowledge that their belly dance was not "authentic" Middle Eastern belly dance, even if it looked traditional. The idea of fusion could be used to locate their belly dance, as when dancers defined their dance as "Dunedin fusion" or "Northland style." The focus group members spoke of fusing belly dance with "Western" dance when they went out socially, observing that "Western" social dance "lacked that sexy sensuousness" they enjoyed in Middle Eastern dance and "looked pretty bad" in comparison (EB 2008). They also noted, though, that music videos from the United States had injected new "sexy" styles into New Zealand social dancing.

Their use of "Western dance" in this context was interesting because the term is more often applied to formal or theatrical dance forms. It was also striking that they appeared to default automatically to the notion of "Western" (rather than "Kiwi" or "New Zealand") versus "Eastern," to describe informal local dancing, suggesting that they, too, did not think of New Zealand as having its own dance. However, their observations that dancing had changed with the addition of music video-inspired movements, and that they were considered good dancers because they could add belly dance movements to their social repertoire, indicated some dancing that, being neither of these things, might be deemed local — such as the "Kiwi handbag dance" one participant and I both identified jokingly to students when teaching a sideways step and touch of the un-weighted foot. A binary definition may also have helped the focus group participants distinguish between belly dancing, which they liked, and other dancing that focused the movement on the torso, which they liked less.

Despite some resentment towards "political correctness," most participants indicated a desire to continue learning and engaging with "others" whose culture contained elements they found attractive, in order not to offend or unthinkingly appropriate. This cautiousness may reflect both socio-political developments towards biculturalism in New Zealand since the 1970s and the growing visibility of migrants from countries where belly dance is an indigenous practice. But some also felt that the dance had "changed with the tides and the location," as (DM 2007) put it, and so did not need to be bound to a material, "authentic" Middle East. The United States origins of many influential teachers, troupes and learning materials reinforces many participants' fundamental recognition of belly dance's hybridity, but also links the dance to some degree to a culturally dominant United States — which can be appropriated and even resisted by using its own tools.

Colonizers Colonized

The focus group dancers demonstrated consciousness of New Zealand's participation, as part of "the West," in a wider global community, but also identified a simultaneous sense of being colonized by the West via American music videos. Some dancers identified colonization within belly dance as well. CW (2007) said she thought American Tribal Style (ATS) belly dance was like "what Americans like to do to things like cheese ... pasteurised and homogenised" with "everything Arabic taken out of it." Others thought changes in belly dance reflected wider developments in a world where cultures and boundaries are increasingly less easy to define. NW, observing that she no longer felt "like a New Zealander doing a Middle Eastern dance so much anymore" but "part of the whole lack of matrix" (2007), indicated that she saw herself as participating in a globalized, decentralized activity.

It appeared that while many dancers felt they should be sensitive to Middle Eastern culture, tribal belly dance, being Western or American, could be appropriated and reworked less problematically. The impulse towards homogeneity and standardization that some thinkers detect in globalization not only creates parallel desire for what is different and local, but, as Kellner (2003, 39) argues of McDonald's,[6] can also provide new methods of articulating a local identity. Within belly dance, differentiation tends to center on places of origin — Egyptian, Turkish — or style — tribal, oriental — rather than articulating a sense of one's own place. CW's criticism that ATS reformulates belly dance into "a network marketing approach," however, also reflects Kellner's (2003, 40) observation that McDonald's both transmits forms of U.S.-centric cultural imperialism and circulates novel and alternative forms that generate cultural hybridity in non–Western cultures. Belly dance provides its digestible experience of cultural otherness to Western and other dancers outside indigenous belly dance cultures, whose tastes, preferences and uses of belly dance will also reflect the culture they live in.

The "carefully constructed hybrid" package of tribal belly dance, readily accessible via websites, DVDs and certification programs, perhaps bypasses ideas of appropriation in participants' minds to some extent because it is always already an acknowledged fusion, and has become a consumer product to boot (Sellers-Young 2005, 291). The Christchurch-based tribal fusion troupe Kiwi Iwi — their name itself a localized reworking of "American Tribal" (American = Kiwi, Tribe = iwi) — was created to explore tribal-style belly dance in a way that would both be "more of our place," and an "up your nose"[7] to the idea of doing something American.

Kiwi Iwi: A New Tribe

Kiwi Iwi was founded in 2002 or 2003, at a time when tribal had just begun to grip the imaginations of New Zealand dancers. Troupe founder CC found ATS exciting and new but felt that viewing the dance through "the cultural eyes" of a New Zealander required "another cultural shift" to restore "a missing factor" (ibid.). Other early members recall disliking "what seemed ... starting out to be an enormous number of rules" in ATS.[8] CC (2008) was particularly uncomfortable with the "mashing" of costume pieces from different cultures, the ATS system of naming moves — "things called the Basic Egyptian, when I felt in my study of Middle Eastern dance that the movement was actually much more Turkish ... it was like calling something the Irish" —

Jane Provan and Samadhi Stuart wear the original Kiwi Iwi costume. Kiwi Iwi's early costume choices imposed upon classic American Tribal Style costuming a troupe-constructed "Kiwi" identity: this incorporated loose hair and feathers, at a time when turbans were de rigueur, paua (abalone) shell jewelry and decorations, a fantasy Maori-inspired chin "tattoo," and hand-felted woolen belts. Colors were drawn from the natural environment and the paua shell (photograph by Jason Atkinson).

and "the highly repetitive nature and ... physical one-sidedness" of some of the movements. She decided to remove some elements and replace them with "our own stuff"—in particular, the Maori performance art kapa haka.

While the troupe has become more overtly "tribal" in its presentation since CC's departure, and has extended its focus to "Oceania," thus creating scope for a wider movement vocabulary, it retains the elements members initially defined as "Kiwi," which relate to music, costuming, props and movement vocabulary. Poi[9] was introduced alongside sword and finger cymbals, along with movements either directly borrowed from kapa haka (such as wiri, a quivering of the hands also found in some North African and Gulf dances) or inspired by them. The latter include a modified tribal movement (pivot-bump): the vertical hip lift is replaced with a horizontal slide, recalling the side-to-side stepping used in kapa haka to make female performers' piupiu, or flax skirts, swing. One early kapa haka-inspired combination featured the leader counting to four in Maori, which reflects how songs are often introduced in kapa haka performance. Contemporary Maori music is used along with more traditional tribal and alternative pieces; the troupe's dance to the Hinewehi Mohi song "Kotahitanga" includes a choreographed haka.

Costuming initially retained an ATS base, with dancers in choli tops, full pantaloons and tasseled hip belts, but in colors they associated with New Zealand, purples, blues and greens, rather than the typical reds and blacks of ATS. Hand-felted wool was chosen for the belts because of the fabric's ubiquity and familiarity in New Zealand. Other modifications included the adoption of paua-shell jewelry in place of imported Afghani pieces[10] and loose hair instead of turbans. FP (2007) observed that Kiwi Iwi would have eschewed shoes even if it were conventional for tribal dancers to wear them, because bare feet were "just so New Zealand as well." The troupe also adopted a fantasy version of the traditional Maori women's chin tattoo, the kowhai moko, in place of the Berber tattoos that ATS dancers conventionally apply to their faces.

The members interviewed expressed some ambivalence about using Maori cultural elements, although two members both said they felt "strong" when wearing their "moko," and when performing the troupe's haka. Conscious they risked being seen as culturally appropriative, they were nonetheless confident about their research, which included liaison with local Maori groups. They agreed that involvement in Kiwi Iwi had encouraged members with little prior understanding of Maori culture to study it further. The sole member with Maori ancestry said she felt personally "strengthened" by the use of kapa haka movements and music with Maori lyrics, and loved "having to" listen to contemporary Maori music to find suitable pieces for new Kiwi Iwi dances. However, she was conscious that her own iwi was comfortable with women performing haka or taiaha (spear), but that if she were living in another iwi's region it might not be acceptable for her to do so.

CC admitted having qualms about mixing Maori cultural elements with tribal belly dance but felt confident she could do so with the same integrity she tried to apply to oriental dance. She observed that it was harder to produce a quality oriental dance show than a Kiwi Iwi one because of the comparative lack of, for instance, people who could help with deeper interpretations of

Arabic songs. It was much easier to get translations of lyrics if a song was sung in Maori. "I could get two or three and compare them, for example, and come up with appropriate gestures to those words. And then the [Arabic] gestures are quite different" (2008).

The Kiwi Iwi participants' references to landscape — one modeled her belt after a favorite childhood haunt — loose hair, barefootedness and natural resources like shells and sheep indicate that their constructions of "Kiwiness" were perhaps no less located in a mythic or idealized past than the Silk Road fantasy of classic ATS. However, their development of new costuming, drawing simultaneously on contemporary international tribal trends (long fringed overskirts, which also evoke the piupiu or flax overskirt, cowrie shells), and retro Kiwiana (shell-encrusted bras, red, black and white kowhaiwhai-patterned ¹¹ribbon), and dances reflecting their other interests and musical tastes, such as a Latin dance, suggests the construction via pastiche of a more globalized and fluid Kiwi identity. While the Kiwi Iwi model presents an idealized reinterpretation of a liberal, happy, homogenous New Zealand where Maori, Pakeha and new migrants are one people, it does so by acknowledging difference and creating a space wherein cultures flow together without fully merging.

Authentically Impure

The achievement of culturally "authentic" performance is highly prized by some in the international belly dance community. Meyda Yegenoglu (1998, 121) asserts that authenticity is a product of Orientalist hegemony, since it centers on constructing difference between the native and the Westerner. Aiming for authenticity, then, still caters to a desire for the "true and authentic" native voice, which for Yegenoglu "is the very gesture by which the sovereign Western subject constructs himself/herself as considerate and benevolent" (ibid.). However, producing such representations is in truth a hybrid sort of work, though not as obviously hybrid as the deliberate fusions practiced by groups like Kiwi Iwi. These dances cannot be "pure" or "authentic" representations of indigenous dance because they are being performed outside their place (and sometimes time) of origin, by culturally-other dancers. Indeed, they more accurately represent an intersection between indigenous belly dance and the accepted standards of globalized belly dance. Like deliberate fusion, such work also requires conscious engagement across cultural conventions.

American Tribal was initially positioned as a feminist or resistant alternative to oriental belly dance due to its less revealing costuming, "earthiness" and, in ATS, emphasis on the projection of unified feminine strength rather than an audience-directed performance of heteronormative femininity (Zussman 1995). As ATS has become mainstream the term "tribal" has retained implications of resistance; new "fusion" offshoots of tribal resist both "traditional" belly dance and ATS, but intersect with them. For Osweiler (2005), "traditional Middle Eastern dance" (by which she means American belly dance emulating indigenous styles) seeks to retain its difference and uniqueness by constructing a binary between itself and "experimental" belly dance, whereas the experimental variants disrupt this binary by constructing lines back into traditional forms. However, as the category "tribal" splinters against the increasing "sedimentation" of ATS into a strictly codified style that also works to maintain a unique and separate identity by adopting tropes of authenticity and purity,[12] it is clear that tribal dancers, too, may create binaries that "hide and at times deny" a mixture of influences.

But it is not only in resistant variants of belly dance that this binary process is deliberately disrupted. As numerous dancers involved in this study explained, their recognition that they were not "authentic" gave them a sense of agency over the conventions of the dance. By dubbing even dances with a traditional look "fusion," they circumvented issues of appropriation and reclaimed the sense of creative self-expression that some felt had been lost in the face of growing political correctness. The participants who mentioned incorporating belly dance into social dancing indicated that long-term practice gave them a sense of entitlement to belly dance movements, which was also informed by their participation in globalized belly dance culture, where such dancing was "normal" behavior. Use of belly dance movements in this way was therefore not constructed as representing the exotic, but as natural for them and personally authentic. Dancers who embraced fusion nonetheless seemed to consider belly dance kinesthetically (or culturally) distinct from other dances, exhibiting concerns at times that the dance could hybridize to a point where it ceased to be belly dance.

Going Forward

The blurring of lines between self/Other, us/them, East/West can occur without neglecting difference and inequality in globalized belly dance's synthetic culture. The globalized belly dance model allows for more nuanced critical exploration that does not reduce belly dancing to a simple Western-versus-Eastern binary. While I have distinguished between dancing that takes places in contexts where it is culturally normative and belly dancing in other contexts, the indigenous and globalized categories are permeable and do intersect and interact with each other.

The responses of the New Zealand dancers in this research showed ways in which involvement with belly dancing has become more complicated than exploring ideas about the self/Other through the enactment of orientalist fantasies. These dancers seldom indicated being consciously invested in fantasies about exotic Middle Eastern Others. They did not seem to think of belly dance as a historical artifact rescued, (re)circulated or even created, as Fisher (2003) argues, by North Americans. Indeed, some participants saw themselves as resisting cultural colonization by the United States through their involvement in globalized belly dancing, fusing belly dance movements into their social dancing rather than copying American mainstream music videos (even though the movements might well look the same) and, in the case of Kiwi Iwi, actively reworking ATS to resist it and conjure a Pacific identity.

Belly dancers who reject "the liberal desire" for authenticity, which Yegenoglu notes remains "the very product of Orientalist hegemony" (1998, 121), in favor of fusion might seem better able to circumvent the problems of Orientalism. The dancers of Kiwi Iwi enjoy freedom to break "rules" about representation and authenticity and about how tribal should be done, and adopt a responsibility not to misrepresent or exploit the less powerful cultures on whose performing arts they draw. But they acknowledge that they risk accusations of appropriation too, particularly given that only one member is Maori. The distinctiveness of the troupe's work hinges on presenting facets of the sometimes troubling Other that is always already present in New Zealand; the one that was there first. The Middle East seems only lightly touched on in a fusion of Maori and Pasifika elements with tribal, possibly because tribal is acknowledged as a reworking of Middle Eastern belly dance, containing it but not really representing it. But because they are still belly dancers, all performers of fusion continue to be seen as representative of Middle Eastern Others; moreover, Others of every kind remain merely "source(s) of inspiration" (Shay and Sellers-Young 2003, 31). Thus, they remain trapped in and complicit with orientalist discourse; they conjure Orientalist fantasies (whether they mean to or not) and any attention to being "morally correct" and "getting it right" involves them in a "colonial gesture" (Yegenoglu 1998, 120).

For Yegenoglu (ibid., 71–72) contradictions in orientalist discourse do not challenge Orientalism's hegemony, merely rearticulate it in different ways. But, to turn her assertion on its head, as much as "each intersection, each disruption, each displacement" fixes Orientalism in place as a unified discourse, it also multiplies and complicates it. It is in this multiplicity and complexity that we can find the potential to think about belly dance's slippery hybridity, and consider ways that belly dancers may engage with multiple ideas of self and other without losing sight of the dance as representative of both a fantasized Orient and a material Middle East.

Notes

1. "Kiwi'— technically a flightless bird found only in New Zealand — is used informally for "New Zealander," and also to describe things and activities seen as particularly typical of New Zealand.
2. The 2006 New Zealand census reported a total of 17, 514 people who claimed Middle Eastern ethnic identity. They constituted the largest sub-group of the MELAA (Middle Eastern, Latin American and African) identity group, which together totaled 0.9 percent of residents.
3. Traditional Maori performance art. Kapa means row and haka is a traditional war dance and chant. Kapa haka, which is practiced by both sexes, usually features singing and the display of prowess with poi — weighted flax balls used to teach club skills — and sometimes taiaha, or spear.
4. Pakeha is one commonly-used Maori word for non–Maori and is used to denote New Zealanders of European origin. It is a contentious term — some white New Zealanders insist on "New Zealand European" or "Kiwi"— and is often used by white New Zealanders who strongly identify with a bicultural or multicultural national model.
5. Traditional Maori tribal meeting place.
6. Kellner is here critiquing George Ritzer's dystopian presentation of McDonaldization as ultimately another version of Weber's "iron cage" of rationalization.
7. FP (2007). Group interview, December 21, Christchurch, New Zealand.
8. FP (2007). Group interview, December 21, Christchurch, New Zealand.
9. In interviews I learned that several Kiwi Iwi members, like me, had been surprised and a little disappointed to discover that some tribal performers in Australia and North America were also using poi, as we were unaware that poi was not solely Maori but used in other parts of the Pacific. However, the Kiwi Iwi members interviewed said that their usage of wrap poi — wrapping the pin around the body to change its direction — with belly dance was, as far as they knew, unique to them. They were also interested in developing further use of short poi, which have a shorter string and are often used either singly or in pairs to add percussive sounds.
10. Dunedin's The Lost Tribe, who are more traditionally ATS in their presentation, have also adopted paua, and have incorporated old New Zealand coins, such as "thrupenny bits," in their costuming.
11. Kowhaiwhai are decorative painted scrolling designs.
12. ATS is an acknowledged "modern style of dance" which differentiates itself from "classical styles ... [or] a traditional version." Creator Carolena Nericcio's reported insistence that "ATS" is used only to refer to her style and that her certified teachers must not teach other belly dance styles, along with her adoption of the term "Tribal: Pura" to describe "an absolute style" based on classical art and scientific guidelines, help keep ATS separate from subsequent developments. See: www.fcbd.com.

Works Cited

Adra, N. (2005). "Belly dance: An Urban Folk Genre." *Belly Dance: Orientalism, Transnationalism and Harem Fantasy.* Eds. A Shay and B. Sellers-Young. Costa Mesa: Mazda Publishers, 28–50.
Appadurai, A. (1999). "Disjuncture and Difference in the Global Cultural Economy." *The Cultural Studies Reader*, 2nd ed. Ed. S. During. London and New York: Routledge.
Bhaba, H.K. (1994). *The Location of Culture.* London and New York: Routledge.
CC. (21 January 2008). Interview (Kiwi Iwi). January 21, Christchurch, New Zealand.
Cooper, L.A. (2004). *Belly Dancing Basics.* New York: Sterling Publishing.

CW. (2007). Interview (Kiwi Iwi). January 21, Christchurch, New Zealand.
DM. (2007). Telephone interview (belly dance). November 21, Christchurch, New Zealand.
Dox, D. (1997). "Thinking through Veils: Questions of Culture, Criticism and the Body." *Theatre and Interculturalism* 22 (2): 150–60.
_____. (2006). "Dancing around Orientalism." *TDR: The Drama Review* 50 (4): 52–71.
EB. (1 June 2008). Focus group (belly dance embodiment). June 1, Christchurch, New Zealand.
Fisher, J.M. (2003). *Orientalism, Representations and Created Fantasies: The Transformation of the Traditional Middle Eastern Dances to Belly Dance* (thesis). Florida Atlantic University.
FP. (2007). Group interview (Kiwi Iwi). December 21, Christchurch, New Zealand.
Karayanni, S.S. (2004). *Dancing Fear and Desire: Race, Sexuality and Imperial Politics in Middle Eastern Dance*. Ontario: Wilfrid Laurier University Press.
Kellner, D. (2003). *Media Spectacle*. London and New York: Routledge.
Kelly, B.M. (2008). *Belly Dancing in New Zealand: Identity, Hybridity, Transculture* (thesis). Christchurch: University of Canterbury.
Kraidy, M.M. (2005). *Hybridity: Or the Age of Globalisation*. Philadelphia: Temple University Press.
NW. (2007). Interview (belly dance). November 9, Tongariro, New Zealand.
Osweiler, L. (2005). "A Theoretical Introduction to Dancing on the Fringe: Connections Forming an Evening of Experimental Middle Eastern Dance." Dance Under Construction, UC Graduate Cultural Dance Studies Conference, UCLA.
PX. (2007). Interview (belly dance). December 19, Christchurch, New Zealand.
QZ. (2007). Personal Interview (belly dance). September 28, Christchurch, New Zealand.
Rasmussen, A. (2005). "An Evening in the Orient: The Middle Eastern Nightclub in America." *Belly Dance: Orientalism, Transnationalism and Harem Fantasy*. Eds. A Shay and B. Sellers-Young. Costa Mesa: Mazda Publishers, 172–206.
Ritzer, G. (1993). *The McDonaldization of Society: An Investigation into the Changing Character of Contemporary Social Life*. Thousand Oaks: Pine Forge Press.
SB. (2008). Interview (belly dance). September 21, Christchurch, New Zealand.
Sellers-Young, B. (1992). "Raks el Sharki: Transculturation of a Folk Form." *Journal of Popular Culture* 26 (2): 141–151.
_____. (2005). "Body, Image, Identity: American Tribal Belly Dance." *Belly Dance: Orientalism, Transnationalism and Harem Fantasy*. Eds. A. Shay and B. Sellers-Young. Costa Mesa: Mazda Publishers, 277–303.
Shay, A., and B. Sellers-Young. (2003). "Belly Dance: Orientalism — Exoticism — Self-Exoticism." *Dance Research Journal* 35 (1): 13–37.
TC. (2007). Telephone interview (belly dance). October 30, Christchurch, New Zealand.
WF. (2007). Telephone interview (belly dance). December 14, Christchurch, New Zealand.
Yegenoglu, M. (1998). *Colonial Fantasies: Towards a Feminist Reading of Orientalism*. Cambridge: Cambridge University Press.
Zussman, M. (1995). "Far from the Pink Chiffon: Reshaping Erotic Belly Dance (Interview with Carolena Nericcio)." *Whole Earth Review*, 34–39.

Quintessentially English Belly Dance
In Search of an English Tradition

Siouxsie Cooper

There are different versions of Belly Dance[1] "history,"[2] most of which describe narratives of the development and impact of it in America (Sellers-Young 2005, Shay and Woods 1976, Carlton 1994, Monty 1986, and Dox 2006). Efforts abound to describe the genesis and relationship of Belly Dance to ancient and modern Egypt (Helland 2001, Buonaventura 1989), presenting selective, anecdotal and anachronistic versions of a Belly Dance past. These narratives describe performance and styles as different cultural embodiments and codifications of their own histories, economic value and socio-politics. It is important to point out that as much as different performance and styles may be seen as complementary and sharing something essential, they are also in constant economic and cultural competition with each other. Therefore, each style of Belly Dance claims authority and authenticity of some sort, and implicitly asserts a different version of history, rejecting and reacting against the claims of other styles: consequently they are not just pieces of the same jigsaw puzzle. For example, Dox's (2006) well-known article *Dancing around Orientalism* offers a narrative of in American popular culture as a complex interweaving of commercial, artistic, contextual readings and narratives of the dance within a relatively short time frame:

> Belly Dancing's history and popularity in the United States can be traced to the late 19th century. For the 1893 Chicago World's Fair Midway Plaisance, Sol Bloom promoted versions of Egyptian, Persian, Moroccan and Tunisian dances, which gave rise to the then-scandalous *danse de ventre* performed in vaudeville houses, burlesque shows, and on film. By the 1920s, variations of Middle Eastern social and folk dances, with the addition of veils, had entered the private sphere of West-

ern salons as a form of exotic artistry and self-expression, a vision reinforced by stage performers such as Ruth St Denis and Maud Allen [2006, 53].

The above is a global picture but one that is also played out in a location like England. There is no single narrative published that recounts the development of "English" Belly Dance, yet there has been an identifiable community of practice in England since the late 1970s, which by definition has required (and created) its own claims to authenticity, ownership, form and tradition: in short, its own narrative(s). Indeed, there are key publications and bodies of work that have been influential and defining in England from the 1980s until the present. They are Suraya Hilal's school of *Raqs Sharqi* (established around 1985 and as of 2001 the Hilal Dance is international trademarked with a training program) and Wendy Buonaventura's internationally popular text *The Serpent of the Nile* (1989, reprinted 2011, translated into 21 languages). Both Hilal and Buonaventura assert their own versions of Belly Dance history, and implicitly the authenticity and value of their own work. They creatively select, reject and react against other narratives of Belly Dance history. They compete against each other in an almost binary fashion, but essentially Hilal and Buonaventura established the English Belly Dance tradition. Our question, however, is how to go about describing that tradition and understanding how it defines current English Belly Dance, including its relationship to "global" forms.

Belly Dance in England is a community that shares an international practice which helps form a specific or local identity-in-practice (Holland et al., 2001). To begin to understand that identity and its tradition, as per Appadurai's (1996) "ethnoscapes" concept, it would be useful to consider the community's identity and tradition in terms of the "changing social [and economic], territorial and cultural reproduction of group identity" (48). Also, Wenger's (1991 & 1996) community of practice model offers key developmental and heuristic processes detailing a community member's transition from peripheral (Lave & Wenger 1998) to core membership, building a sense of self-in-practice and self in relation to a community of shared practice. Thus, by considering the social and cultural milieu of the 1980s against which Hilal and Buonaventura reacted but from which they emerged, their narratives of authenticity, their personal heuristic processes, the creative tension of their perhaps necessary and binary opposition, and considering how they sustained an impact for over twenty years, we will be able to identify the key characteristics that constitute a continuing English Belly Dance identity locally and on a global stage.

Hilal and Buonaventura emerged as leading artists in England when cultural diversity policies and multi-cultural issues dominated the political and arts landscape of Thatcher's Britain. During this Thatcher era of a changing cultural landscape, Hilal and Buonaventura's prominence in the English Belly Dance community signaled a formalization and codification of teaching and performance practices, which in turn trained a new generation of performers, artists and instructors. I argue that Hilal and Buonaventura's ambition to present the "art" in Belly Dance while also resisting the "exotic" associations of the dance genre produced a new paradigm operating in the community which still persists. Both practitioners are more often than not in competition with each other, and their activities and profiles raise questions about the role of individual ideological, political and economic proclivities during the emergent years of Belly Dance in England. Each dancer also has expressed a different politics of representation through her understanding of the form, offering competing opinions on Orientalism, nationalism, class, and gender identity. How Hilal and Buonaventura portray their choices discursively has held as much significance to this inquiry as the choreographic decisions themselves. As such, their public representation of such points and how they had approached them in a teaching context factored into the investigation more than how individual dancers thought about them privately.

The Social and Cultural Context for the Emergence of Hilal and Buonaventura

Early publications of dance biographies, historiographies published on the internet, trade magazines and interviews I have conducted in the field reveal the presence of a vibrant Belly Dance culture in London during the 1970s. The majority of activity reported London as the central location of Belly Dance activities in England (although there were notable regional exceptions). The reason for this was twofold: the relocation of Arab nightclubs to London during the Lebanese civil war; and the arrival of American Cabaret dancers in search of new teaching and performance opportunities (Waldie 2006).

Clearly, there was a Belly Dance "scene" in London pre–Hilal and Buonaventura. It was not specifically a coalesced (English) community of practice, but, as I will describe, it was a background that inevitably informed the early work of Hilal and Buonaventura, partially excluded them and was the catalyst for their creative response and reaction. Another significant catalyst for Hilal specifically was the previous Labor government's experiment that instituted a Cultural Diversity arts policy (before the Thatcher government of 1979) which lasted until 1997. I would argue the Cultural Diversity policy stimulated interest in world dance and other forms of culturally diverse art (Jordan 2000), supporting dance showcases, artists and groups not previously funded. Its impact on the community saw substantial core funds awarded to Suraya Hilal in the late 1980s, in total £80,000 over five years; which was a significant period for her dance experimentation and development. In effect the wave of world dance interest sweeping England, the core funding opportunities in the arts, and the rising presence of women in public life endorsed the ambitions of female-led Belly Dance enterprises: Hilal and Buonaventura were able to reposition their dancing ambitions away from male-owned and male-prescribed clubs and onto stages for a wider and increasingly interested dance audience.

The exclusive Arab nightclubs of the 1970s catered to the international Arab elite, offering a new cultural environment while still simulating the nightclubs found in Lebanon, Cairo and other Middle Eastern countries. The clubs were sites for eating, smoking and socializing, with a designated space for live entertainment. The prime focus of the entertainment was live Middle Eastern music, and then a Belly Dancer would be presented as a secondary focus close to the end of the night.

According to English Belly Dancer Sarah Ward,[3] belly dancing also appeared in a rising number of Greek nightclubs and tavernas, for example the Rendevous in Bayswater and Cleopatra's, in north London Turkish restaurants and dives like Gallipoli, and in the well-known Iranian restaurant Pars Persian in Earls Court (June 2011). In each dancing context the dancer was an accompaniment to food. Her dancing was not the primary focal point, arguably, except for those interested in learning the dance.

As a direct result of the dance's secondary position within the nightclub environment, Hilal and Buonaventura sought alternative performance contexts that would prioritize the dance over the music and "socializing" activity. Their other aim was to raise the status of the female dancer from "late-night, adults-only" entertainment to artist, for both personal and ideological reasons. In a recent interview I conducted, Buonaventura presents her choices:

> I think it [belly dancing] is presented in lots of different places which I wouldn't, personally, be interested in performing in, because you are then compromised. I mean, there is a whole cabaret, restaurant and nightclub scene, which I am sure is very compromising for dancers, but then again you have a choice whether or not to work in these contexts [2009].

Hilal states, in an interview for a channel Four *Rear View* documentary highlighting her recent *raqs sharqi The Beloved* (1991) debut at the Sadler's Wells: "I was shocked [...] It was not the same dance I learnt as a young girl in Egypt. There's too much about the 'erotic' and not enough on the 'art' in the dance. I want people to see the beauty in the dancing, not the sexiness" (1991).

In a filmed interview for Gilded Serpent[4] Charlotte Desorgher (2011) describes a burgeoning London community in the 1980s, with students — like herself— encountering for the first time Arabs (chiefly Syrian and Lebanese) dancing to live music. She contrasts this new experience with her own initial attempts to train in Belly Dance by using a handful of Arabic music audiotapes and one VHS tape of a belly dancer. These new nightclubs provided a new method of training and an expanded musical and movement repertoire sought by Desorgher and her contemporaries. When asked about training with the Arab belly dancers, Desorgher describes a difficult situation in which dancers did not know how to teach it or didn't want to teach (2011). By contrast, Anne White[5] remembers: "I learnt to dance from the [male] musicians; they helped me with the songs, taught me the words and the moves to go with them, telling me what to do with the audience and what this or that meant" (2008). The secondary status given to Belly Dance in the Arab nightclub culture and the reluctance to pursue teaching and instructional work by dancers outside nightclub hours produced a "gap" in the market. As a result, the burgeoning non–Arab English Belly Dance student population had to seek tuition elsewhere. In an interview Desorgher describes the arrival and storm surrounding Hilal's classes and performances ending her description by summarizing Hilal's impact as the first real attempt to professionalize Belly Dance training (2011).

Buonaventura's first Belly Dance teacher was the American Gail Smedley, who within a year returned to America. When Smedley left, she gave an astonished Buonaventura her class, stating: "You've got the gift for it" (2009), in so doing installing Buonaventura as a teacher. In effect, the limited contact for dance tuition from the Arab night club dancers allowed outside dancers, in this case American Cabaret style dancers, to initiate teaching within a relatively short time period from starting to learn themselves. Many teachers were learning on the job. Hilal and Buonaventura's swift rise to teacher status indicates the relatively early stages of the development of the community. At the same time, this afforded Hilal and Buonaventura freedom and room for experimentation and invention. The English Belly Dance community, with more active and visionary community members, now had the potential to "coalesce" (Wenger 1996). Hilal's natal links to Egypt and vision for the dance ensured an unquestioned leadership role. At the same time, the relatively small population of teachers and the expanding opportunities to present the "art" in the dances of the Middle East meant that the implied need for Buonaventura then to identify her personal relationship to the Middle East could be deferred.

To summarize, the early 1970s Belly Dance community in London formulated a unique Arab-American configuration of a "translocated" (Appadurai 1996) dancing context and dance expertise. For a brief fifteen years the Arab clubs and Eastern Mediterranean restaurants[6] provided performance opportunities and the chance for patrons to encounter the dance and culture of the Middle East. These simulations, however, were invariably context-generative due to the translocated clientele, which in time diminished and moved elsewhere. Nonetheless, this context attracted American Cabaret Style talent who offered dance tuition to subsidize their income. The mix of Anglo-Arab sociocultures and performance contexts, together with an American ideological and aesthetic underpinning, were the backdrop, starting point and creative foil to Hilal and Buonaventura's emergent English style of Belly Dance. They took the hybridized, translocated dance genre and context and reconfigured and re-represented it for English theatre contexts. The coalescing focus of the English Belly Dance community was the acquisition, exploration and sharing of dance skill and knowledge rather than the nexus and socializing activities of the Arab nightclub culture. This in turn led to the foundation of their emerging ideological and aesthetic configuration for the "art" beyond the exotic and erotic in English Belly Dance and its community.

The Authentic Naming of English Belly Dance

The name Belly Dance has a troubled etymological past which has allowed the West[7] to create and pose an Orientalist fantasy, complete with harem imagery and reference, as Belly Dance's "historical" narrative of origin and authenticity. Hilal and Buonaventura of course needed to reclaim and rename the art and narrative of Belly Dance in order to empower themselves and realize the value of their own work.

Hilal's arrival in England saw the earliest use of the Arabic words *El Raqs* and *El Sharqi* to form a replacement for "Belly Dance": *Raqs Sharqi*. Its literal translation is "Dance of the East" or "Orient." Remarkably the Orient is still referenced in this new name. The reference may not be visible or heard by those who do not know Arabic, but essentially Orientalism as a concept (Said 1978) is present even in the Egyptian Arabic word for the dance. The reasons for it were similarly paradoxical: Hilal had to borrow a degree of authenticity from the accepted norm and authority of the dance that came before her, at the same time as reacting against and reforming it. Hilal's use of the Arabic rather than its Anglo-French[8] terminology shifts our focus from an American vaudeville past to that of an Egyptian social dance heritage.

Buonaventura experienced the same paradox in trying to rename the dance. Her first publication was *Belly Dancing: The Serpent and the Sphinx* (1983). Six years later, the text was renamed as *The Serpent of the Nile: Women and Dance in the Arabic World* (1989), and Belly Dance was replaced as a term by "Arabic Dance." However, in expanding the socio-geographical scope of the dance (from "Egyptian" to "North African," "Persian" and "Middle Eastern"), Buonaventura needed to reference a greater amount of Orientalist text and imagery in the revised publication.

Both practitioners ended up destabilizing the dominant narrative that preceded them, in order to assert their own chosen narratives. In doing so, they began to set out their unique visions and personal credentials, signaled their intention with regard to practice and refocused the community on the "art" of the dance genre. By way of example, in being individually synonymous with the narratives and dance styles they were promoting, Hilal could only focus on an "Egyptian" origin and authenticity for the dance, when she was of Yemeni-Egyptian origin, and Buonaventura focused on a "pan–Arabic" origin and authenticity for the dance, when she was of Sicilian-Libyan ancestry.

When it comes to Hilal's narrative for Raqs Sharqi, it is clear from early interviews, written manifestos and television documentaries about her work that Hilal looks backs to a pan–Egyptian *raqs sharqi* dance culture, aligning it with both high (Classical Sharqi) and low (Sha'abi) dance culture rooted in the rhythmic language of Egyptian music and tradition. Specifically, she makes reference to (1) the Golden Era of *Raqs Sharqi* aesthetic and dance praxis from the 1930s and 1940s Egyptian films (which portrayed such Cairo dance stars as Tahia Carioca and Namia Akef); (2) old *baladi* compositions (the Tet and Awadi improvised musical forms of the dance); and (3) the Anglo-Egyptian classical orchestrations composed by Abdel Al Wahab and others as the authentic and original *raqs sharqi*. At the same time, however, the paradox remains, for Hilal still uses modern American dance technique and choreographic practice in her classroom.

For Buonaventura, by contrast, Arabic Dance derived from literary, religious and ancient documents she sourced in both the Middle East and in England. She located sources for Arabic Dance in Orientalist paintings, travel writings, her own travel writing from visits to Egypt, Tunisia and Morocco, images and writing from the Great Exhibitions (Paris, London, Chicago), Hollywood film and modern Arab Dancers found in Cairo and further afield including America. Nonetheless, she acknowledged parallels with pan–Egyptian *raqs sharqi* sources such as the Golden Era dancers (named above) and the social dances of rural and urban Egypt, and even Hilal's incorporation of American modern dance pedagogy to formalize Arabic Dance training. However, Buonaventura rejected attempts to "purify" Arabic Dance by aligning it with only Egyptian theatre and aesthetics. The dance form, she maintains, finds its proponents all around the world and part of its hereditary community is the European theatre tradition adopted by Egyptian entrepreneur Badia Masabni in 1926 (Buonaventura 1989, 149).

In Buonaventura's timeline of Arabic Dance, she traces an unbroken chain from ancient Egypt, through the Awalim culture of the 19th century, to present day dancers found in Cairene nightclubs. For Buonaventura, attempts in the 1980s and 90s to improve or modernize Arab Dance offered new ways to build a reputable profile for a dance form previously confined to restaurants, nightclubs and parochial venues. It also offered permission to expand on Arabic Dance traditions beyond Middle Eastern aesthetics and towards a transnational dance theatre inspired by Arabic Dance but not necessarily contingent upon it. A profound sense of Anglo-Arab hybridity accompanied her version of history, which in turn privileged an Oriental mythos (Dox 2006).

Hilal thus eschewed the Orientalist past that Buonaventura celebrated. Hilal located *raqs sharqi*'s authenticating history not in nightclub enterprises found in downtown Cairo in the late 1920s, but in 19th century court traditions, the educated female Awalim tradition (Van Nieuwkerk 1996), and the social dance traditions of regional Egypt, the values of which she still sees as current. For Hilal, the 1920s dancers of Cairo were subject to a colonial system that restricted and degraded them, a context that compromised the "art" of the dance. She thus maintained that the 20th century later became a time of rejuvenation and a post-colonial re-viewing of the past.

Together, Hilal and Buonaventura displaced the dominant configuration of Belly Dance in England. In effect, by destabilizing the term they also afforded a destabilization of its normative structures in order to pursue their own emergent processes of creation. The initial strategy towards *raqs sharqi* and Arabic Dance would both identify a common aim to prioritize the "art" in the dance while simultaneously allowing for their divergent and emergent practices. The core aesthetic and ideological characteristics of Hilal and Buonaventura's practice describes both the formation of present day English identity but also infers deep rooted opposing values concerning ownership and the creative processes of contemporization, a contemporization that often struggles with an Anglo-Egyptian colonial past.

Teaching the Movement Vocabulary of English Belly Dance

By affiliating their practices with those of the Middle East, both Hilal and Buonaventura were raising questions about their own identity in a culturally diverse and "sensitive"[9] political landscape in England. The nature of the identity and narrative each artist represented was played out in the content of their teaching and their approach to teaching, the movement vocabularies they adopted, and their technical construction of their performances. Having successfully displaced the dominant and preceding configuration of the dance, as individuals these artists could then only define themselves as having valuable difference by reacting against each other's work. Increasingly, they adopted a binary opposition to each other. The binary opposition was one of coexistence, difference and complementarity, rather than a competition of similarity.

Beginning with the content of their teaching, Hilal's pan–*raqs sharqi* dance specifically promoted different Egyptian styles, namely *sha'abi*, *baladi* and Classical *sharqi*. Buonaventura's content, like the research for her book, deliberately looked beyond Egypt. Her pan–Arabic dance specifically promoted Tunisian, Moroccan, Oriental Cabaret, Saaidi, Persian and Moorish styles.

Hilal's limited and geographically specific narrative for the dance meant that the movement vocabulary was similarly limited. She focused her students on learning these movement precisely, inevitably using a by-rote teaching style. By contrast, Buonaventura mixed movements from different styles, lyrically and fluidly combining them into new phrases. Her focus was not on technical precision of movement, but upon experimentation for wider expression. Hilal's content and approach lent itself to classes labeled "beginners," "improvers," and "teacher trainers," a student's "level" decided by technical merit and Hilal's personal assessment. Buonaventura's approach and content, by contrast, lent itself to "open" classes, where students could join at any time, as long as they had

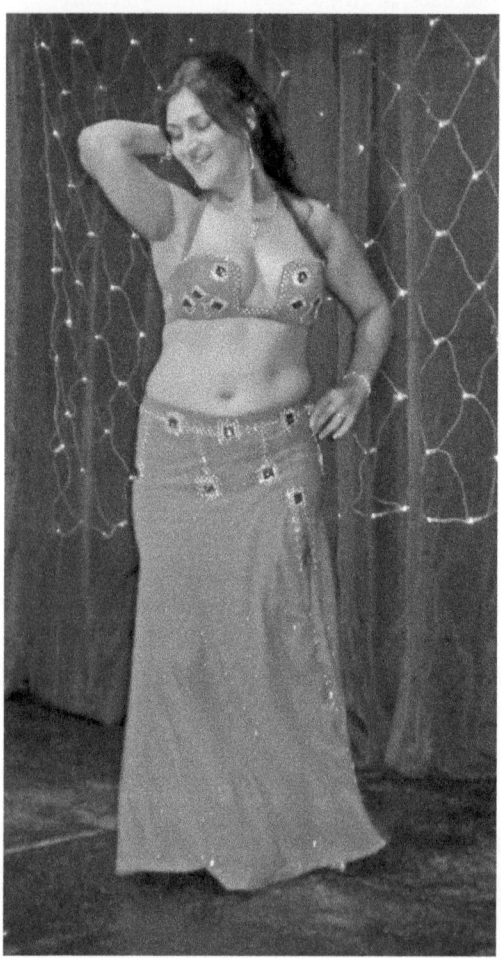

Nafeeseh Rahi-Young at a Hafla, or dance party, in London in which dancers perform for each other (photograph by Caitlin E. McDonald).

dance basics, and there was no required "attainment." In the early '80s, there was a point when both artists were running classes in the same building on the same night — it was made explicit to both sets of students that if they attended one teacher's class, they could not attend the class of the other teacher.[10]

The rigor of Hilal's teaching methods and her tightly choreographed group performances saw detractors label Raqs Sharqi as "Raqs Starchy." On stage, her dancers were dressed uniformly (e.g., the *sha'abi* dancer's costume consisted of a full length circle skirt, tunic covering the midriff, hip belt, bolero jacket and head scarf; the Urban *baladi* dancer wore a galabeya[11] made of assuite[12] material, hip belt and large chiffon head dress; the Classical *sharqi* costume included a full length circle skirt, hip belt and bodice with long chiffon sleeves; there were variations on length, material used and the use of head wear but essentially these costumes — conceived by Hilal's artistic director Jennifer Carmen[13] until 1997 — were largely adhered to), their movements were contained, minimalistic and precise, and their facial expressions had a certain sincerity. It was only when a dancer had reached Hilal's level of dance competence that they might then begin to perform with more improvisation, as indeed Hilal herself did in her solo performances. By contrast, Buonaventura's approach saw her dance-collaborators dressed in a variety of character-specific and themed costumes, their movements were embellished, expansive (highly suited to the theatre stage) and fluidic. Buonaventura asked her collaborators to bring something individualistic and beyond her teaching to the stage, to create a richer whole.

As shown above, each artist configured English Belly Dance based on her own identity, beliefs, constructed narrative and practices. When Hilal started running weekend dance intensives (workshops) in the early '90s, she was the main teacher supported by "Suraya Hilal School of *Raqs Sharqis*" trainees — the dance and the dancers were made in her own image. When Buonaventura set up weekend dance intensives in the mid–'90s, she invited regional dancers to teach and, later, international artists (like Leila Haddad from Tunisia/Paris and Amel Tafsout from Algeria/London) — a democracy of dance based upon her selection.

For all their opposition to each other, Hilal and Buonaventura helped define each other as well as the "art" at the heart of English Belly Dance. Despite their reaction against the dominant American teaching scene that came before them, this American teaching still paradoxically helped to define them. Both artists borrowed from an American dance tradition: Hilal used modern American dance pedagogic practices to develop her movement lexicon and the teaching of it (e.g., Doris Humphrey and Martha Graham); and Buonaventura used American vaudeville "tricks" (e.g., the use of props like sagats,[14] veils and sticks) for her theatre pieces. So, even though English Belly Dance, as developed by Hilal and Buonaventura, looked to the Middle East for its technical dance content and historical narrative, it then framed that content and narrative within a context of Western theatrical codes and conventions.

The Artistic Ambition of English Belly Dance

Both Hilal and Buonaventura's initial ambitions were to reconfigure past Belly Dance practices by moving them towards a more Middle Eastern present. In line with Wenger's model, I argue that each artist constructed her own narrative to authenticate her individual identities as dance artists and her resulting dance practices. Precisely as their individual identities defined the dance and their dance practices, we can understand their artistic ambitions by considering the progression of their *solo* performances over the decades: the solo performances over time can be read as a narrative of their artistic exploration and assertion of their individual dance identities and beliefs.

Buonaventura's solo performances show an artistic preoccupation with the role of the dancing woman in Biblical society, *Revelations* (1991), in British colonial Egyptian society, *Dancing Girls* (1994), in contemporary European society, *Mimi La Sardine* (1999), and global society, *God Created Devil Woman* (2004) and *I Put a Spell on You* (2006). The characters portrayed include Salome, Ishtar Priestess, a North African dancer, Kuchuk Hanem,[15] a restaurant and/or theatre dancer, a self-harming dancer and a mature dancer looking back on her life. The sequence of characters could be read as a female equivalent to Shakespeare's seven stages of a man's life. They could be seen as an individual life story. Indeed, on the front page of the *Revelations* theatre program, there is a *belle epoque* image of a veiled woman surrounded by words illustrating the seven "stages" of a woman's life: virgin, mother, siren, muse, goddess, whore and Amazon.

Given such an arguably personal narrative across these solo performances, it is not surprising that in an interview Buonaventura (2009) considered the dance to be the domain of women, and laments the arrival of the economically astute Egyptian male expert, stating: "There is this very, very female movement, which you cannot reproduce it if you are a man" (2009). The "female," "femininity" and "woman," specifically the dancing woman, are core to Buonaventura's art in English Belly Dance.

Hilal's solo performances are a repeated search and return to some idea of a pure and essential pan–Egyptian dance form: *Return of the Spirit* (1985), *The Nai Taqasim* (1987), *Celebration of the Nile* (1989), *Jewels* (1989), *Divine Rights* (1990), *Colours of Cairo* (1991), *The Beloved* (1991), *Spirit of the Heart* (1997), *Al Janoub* (2002), *Aseel* (2004), *Oscillations* (2008). The titles of the performances talk about a spirit, a soul, a hidden jewel, a center around which all revolves. Different terms and metaphors are used for the same concept, the same journey to discover some lost and sacred art.

Just to give one key example of Hilal's endeavor, I will describe her performance referred to as the *Nai Taqasim* solo[16] (1987). The Nai, an Egyptian flute, is an old reed instrument that produces haunting melodies, is culturally emblematic of the Egyptian musical tradition and is associated with human frailty and mortality. Hilal wears a large gold skirt, a wrap-around halter neck top with exposed midriff and a golden veil. Initially, she holds postures reminiscent of Pharonic Egypt (both godly and of the tomb), complete with a golden veil that alludes to images of the ancient Egyptian Goddess Isis. Then, she shifts her weight from side to side, and lowers her body, while rocking her hips side to side. She pauses, continues and changes direction with various Pharonic poses in slow motion. She turns away from the audience, center stage, and with lowered lighting begins arm undulations precisely and continuously. We witness her skill, musculature and the beauty of her *raqs sharqi*-dancing-self. The *Nai Taqasim*, performed at the Arab Women's Council (at the British Commonwealth Institute, London), cleverly repositions images of fantasy and nostalgia while simultaneously signaling the arrival of Arab women's creative dancing potential. All of Hilal's solo performances are lengthy and characterized by the use of live Egyptian music, and a display of her physical prowess and improvisational ability. She channels the ancestral memory of a golden age of pan–Egyptian dance.

Where Buonaventura has insisted that Arabic Dance can only be embodied by women, Hilal (2008) remarked in a brief interview that the inclusion of men into her classes was a recent change. Market forces in tandem with changing gender definitions and norms have seen an increase in men engaging in the Belly Dance community as dancers, entrepreneurs and volunteers. Hilal now celebrates a new generation of *raqs sharqi* disciples emerging in the West, maintaining that the dance is rightfully the domain of women and men regardless of class. She therefore draws on the tactics of anti-colonial Arab nationalism through the act of "rescuing the dance from extinction" (Heinle 2000)[17] and finding in it the glories of a shared tradition that could unite a diverse global *raqs sharqi* ethnoscape. Hilal Dance incorporates male with female exponents of the contemporary Egyptian dance form.

English Belly Dance and Globalized Belly Dance

As shown, there is a unique and recognizable Belly Dance tradition in England. We can describe it as being recognizably "English" or not. Particular

English Belly Dancers today follow the Hilal tradition, others follow the Buonaventura tradition. There are others still who, even as they are influenced by their predecessors, choose to resist their predecessors, just as their predecessors before them resisted and were influenced by the likes of American modern dance and theatrical tradition. Some borrow from both the Hilal and Buonaventura traditions, and others accept extra influences from outside England (e.g., American Cabaret Style Belly Dance or going to the Middle East to conduct their own research).

There is an identifiable, wide and vibrant English Belly Dance community of practice: where Hilal and Buonaventura represented a tradition based upon a very binary opposition, there are now more shades of grey, more artistic nuances, more complex social and political allegiances, and more pluralities in the opposition. There are still issues that will always survive in English, some issues quintessentially English (e.g., an initial encounter of Arab-American in England, post-colonial relations with Egypt, etc.) and some issues that are global but where England will have its own position and form of dance expression (e.g., religious themes, economic value, race, class, gender and sexual orientation). English Belly Dance takes part in the contemporary negotiation of these global issues, and competes for its own "ethnoscape" of international audiences—just as Hilal Dance, with work like *Aseel* (2004) and *Oscillations* (2008), has now become an international brand and contemporary dance expression; and just as *The Serpent of the Nile* is now reprinted in 21 different languages around the world, thereby gaining Buonaventura an increasing number of international workshop and performance bookings.

Notes

1. I use and capitalize the term Belly Dance throughout the text because it is the most commonly used although problematic idiom applied to this dance genre. It is a term which participants in all global communities of practice and their audience members commonly use even when presented with alternative terms like *raqs sharqi* or Arabic Dance., in effect, is a default setting used by both Western and Eastern dancers to name a specific form of dance that indeed has a troubled Anglo-Egyptian past. This colonial etymological past is a set of competing narratives embodied in the term Belly Dance. Via the capitalization I am drawing the reader's attention to this constantly troubled and embattled term. The capitals "nag" at the reader.

2. I reference Amy Koritz's "Re/Moving Boundaries: From Dance History to Cultural Studies" in *Moving Words, Re-writing Dance*, ed. Gay Morris (London: Routledge, 1996) and a collection of cultural and historical texts concerned with dance found in *Moving History/Dancing Cultures: A Dance History Reader*, ed. Ann Dils and Ann Cooper Albright (Connecticut: Wesleyan University Press, 2001), all of which are dedicated to the "cultural turn" in dance history during the turn of the 21st century and expose previous hierarchical evaluations of the past in favor of a more plural and narrative-driven continuum of both past and present practices.

3. According to English Belly Dancer Sarah Ward (2011), who worked in the London

Arab Clubs in the early to late 1980s, Pars Persian was a particular "hotbed of talent," hosting dance artists like Safa Yusry and musicians like Wadir al Safi. Mona Said, another famous dancer, used to work at Gallipoli, and her presence encouraged more Egyptian dancers to come to London. Previously the majority of dancers were Syrian and Lebanese.

4. http://www.youtube.com/watch?v=ZEPfxYjge50, date accessed October 3, 2011, Charlotte Desorgher (interview June 2011) is an English dancer based in south London who began her career in the early 1980s.

5. Anne White (interview 2010). Anne was originally taught by Suraya Hilal and studied the music and dance under the tutelage of Arab musicians (at her insistence) in the early 1980s. She is a key practitioner based in North London and has developed *Planet Egypt*, a monthly international Belly Dance showcase in London for over eight years.

6. The Turkish, Greek, Levant and Egyptian influences both broadened the cultural experience of the dance and music as well as limiting access to dance instruction. By the time English Sarah Ward worked as a belly dancer at the old Turkish bath house of Gallipoli, around 1988, Mona Said was no longer there. Sarah reports: "Its glory days were long gone. It was still a beautiful place, it reeked of faded grandeur, but it was rarely busy. The owner, Joseph Mourat, used to tell me about the old days and the stars. There were wonderful black and white photos on the wall of the rich and famous that frequented the place in those days" (facebook.com posts June 13, 2011).

7. Names include: Oriental Dance, La Danse du Ventre, Egyptian Dance, Arabic Dance, Hoochie Koochie, Middle Eastern Dance, *baladi* Dance, and *sharqi* Dance, to name but a few.

8. Allegedly originally coined by Sol Bloom, the international impresario importing Moroccan and Middle Eastern dancers for the 1893 Chicago Great Exhibition (see Shay & Woods, *La Danse du Ventre*, 1976, for further reference).

9. I use the word "sensitive" to describe the growing acknowledgement of culturally appropriate practice, including the use of contexts, terminology and supporting ethnic minorities in cultural production during the decade of cultural diversity policy in England and through non-governmental agencies like the Arts Council of England.

10. Again, field notes and interviews are illustrative of the point not evidence for the point.

11. A galabeya is a floor-length tunic or loose dress regularly worn in Egypt as both daily wear and domestic wear. The galabeya is usually tightly fitted around the trunk of the body with slits on either side to allow freer leg movement for the dancer.

12. Assuite is a gauze material covered with silver and nickel metal folded into patterns, creating a woven carpet-like detail and decoration. Motifs of camels, candelabras, people and papyrus were commonly found. The weight of the metal patterns makes the assuite material into a heavy, shimmering, opaque material that catches the light and replicates the fluid action of water. The assuite galabeya is usually two galabeyas, one undergarment galabeya made from cotton with the opaque patterned assuite galabeya on top. Hilal dyed the performer's galabeyas in bright hues: red, pink, blue and purple.

13. Jennifer Carmen (interview 2005) was instrumental in attaining core funding from the Arts Council England for Hilal. Jennifer Carmen also designed the costumes to suit Hilal's athletic "boy-ish" figure, sourcing images and designs found in the Victoria and Albert museum, especially 1920s and 1930s designs which featured long lines, low waistlines, and the use of chiffon and extravagant materials to produce drape effect and flowing movement.

14. Sagats are Egyptian finger cymbals worn by dancers and musicians and used to percussively accompany the music and dance (they are differently tuned and are considered a musical instrument not only a dance accessory).

15. Kuchuk Hanem is a famous figure appearing in Orientalist painting and literature during the late 19th century. She was a well known dancer from Upper Egypt who danced

for Flaubert and other Orientalist travel writers of that period. Her name Kuchuk Hanem is Turkish for "little woman" which was probably a term of endearment used by Westerner travelers. Buonaventura recreates a scene in which an Orientalist text describing an encounter with the notorious Kuchuk Hanem is read while she vibrates her hips continuously to the shimmering sound of the quanoon (a zither-like instrument) in low lighting.

16. In conversation, the *Nai Taqasim* is one of the few early Hilal performances commonly praised for its accomplished composition, presentation of a confident Classical Sharqi style and Hilal's exceptional physical dexterity. The use of the imagery of the ancient goddess Isis, especially in the second part of the *Nai Taqasim*, was an unusual and never repeated motif that Hilal rejected as she pursued a more "contemporary" Egyptian expression in her later performance work.

17. Heinle's (2001) article, found in a Hilal Dance newsletter (no. 3), articulated a brief historical heritage from which the inception and trademarking of Hilal Dance as a contemporary expression of Egyptian dance emerged. In effect, Heinle eulogizes Hilal's efforts to "rescue" a near and far Egyptian dance past.

Works Cited

Adeshead, J., ed. (1988). *Dance Analysis: Theory and Practice*. London: Dance Books.
Appadurai, A. (1996). *Modernity at Large: Cultural Dimensions of Globalisation*. London: University of Minnesota Press.
Aull Davies, C. (2009). *Reflexive Ethnography: A Guide to Researching Selves and Others*, 2nd ed. London: Routledge.
Bacon, J. (2003). *Arabic Dance in an Urban English Landscape*. PhD Thesis, Surrey University.
Bruner, P. (1996). *The Culture of Education*. Massachusetts: Harvard University Press.
Buckland, T.J., ed. (2006). *Dancing from Past to Present: Nation, Culture and Identity*. Wisconsin: University of Wisconsin Press.
Buonaventura, W. (1983). *Belly Dancing: The Serpent and the Sphinx*. London: Virago Press.
_____. (1989, 2011). *The Serpent of the Nile: Women and Dance in the Arab World*. London: Saqi Books.
_____. (1998). *Arabic Dance in Performance*. Bristol: Cinnabar Productions, private VHS collection.
_____. (1999). *Mimi La Sardine*: rehearsal video. Bristol: Cinnabar Productions.
_____. (2003). *I Put a Spell on You*. London: Saqi Books.
_____. (2009). Interview, London.
Carlton, D. (1994). *Looking for Little Egypt*. Bloomington, IN: IDD Books.
Dox, D.L. (2006). "Dancing around Orientalism." *Theatre and Drama Review* Vol. 50, No. 4 (Winter): 52–71.
Hilal, S. (1987). *Nai Taqasim: Arab Women's Council*. London: Suraya Hilal, private VHS collection.
_____. (1991). *Colours of Cairo*. London: Suraya Hilal Raqs Sharqi, private VHS collection.
_____. (1992). *Devine Rites*. London: Suraya Hilal Raqs Sharqi ensemble, private VHS collection.
_____. (1998). *Spirit of the Heart*. London: Hilal Dance, private VHS collection.
_____. (2002). *Al Janoub*. Germany: Hilal Dance, private VHS collection.
Holland, D., D. Skinner, W. Lachicotto, Jr., and C. Cain, eds. (1998, 2001). *Identity and Agency in Cultural Worlds*. Massachusetts: Harvard University Press.

Lorius, C. (1996). "Desire and the Gaze: Spectacular Bodies in Cairene Elite Weddings." *Women's Studies International Forum* Vol. 19, 3: 513–523.
Maira, S. (2008). "Belly Dancing: Arab-Face, Orientalist Feminism and U.S. Empire." *American Quarterly* Vol. 60, No. 2 (June 2008): 317–345.
Monty, P. (1986). *Serena, Ruth St. Denis and the Evolution of Belly Dance in America (1876–1976)*. PhD Thesis, Tisch New York University.
Morris, G., ed. (1996). *Moving Words, Re-writing Dance*. London: Routledge.
O'Shea, J. (2006). "Dancing through History and Ethnography." *Dancing from Past to Present: Nation, Culture and Identity*. Ed. T. J. Buckland. Madison: The University of Wisconsin Press.
Paul, K. (1998). *A Survey Arabic Dance as a Community Dance Practice in London*. Surrey: Surrey University.
Shay, A., and B. Sellers-Young, eds. (2005). *Belly Dance: Oriental, Transnational and Harem Fantasy*. Costa Mesa: Mazda Publishers.
Shay, A., and L. Wood. (1976). "Danse du Ventre: A Fresh Appraisal." *Dance Research Journal* Vol. 8, No.2 (Spring-Summer): 18–30.
South Bank Show *Rear View Window* series (1991). Suraya Hilal and Raqs Sharqi Dance. London: Channel Four Productions.
Waldie, H. (2006). *An American Odyssey: A History of Modern US*. www. eurotib.com/story/2006/10/30/102410/10, accessed June 24, 2008.
Wenger, E (1998). "Communities of Practice: Learning as a Social System." *Systems Thinker*. www.co-i-1.com/coil/knowledge-garden/cop/lss.shtml, accessed December 6, 2011.
_____. (1998). *Communities of Practice, Learning, Meaning and Identity*. Cambridge: Cambridge University Press.
Wenger, E., and J. Lave. (1991). *Situated Learning: Legitimate Peripheral Participation*. Cambridge: Cambridge University Press.
Wenger, E., R. McDermott, and W.M. Snyder. (2002). *A Guide to Managing Knowledge Cultivating Communities of Practice*. Harvard: Harvard Business Press.
White, A. (2008). Interview, London, England.
Van Nieuwkerk, K. (2003). "On Religion, Gender, and Performing: Female Performers and Repentance in Egypt." *Music and Gender: Perspectives from the Mediterranean*. Ed. T. Magrini. Chicago: The University of Chicago Press.
_____. (1996). *A Trade Like Any Other*. Cairo, Egypt: The American University of Cairo Press.

Workshops Attended

Buonaventura, W. (June 1998). *Source of Fire Choreography: A Dance Intensive Week* (Bath: Bath University).
_____. (March 2005). *Choreography Master Class: A One to One Master Class* (Glastonbury, Somerset: Majma Dance Festival).
Hilal, S. (November 2008). *Ashra Baladi: A Two Day Baladi Workshop* (London: Hackney Arts Centre).

Delilah
Dancing the Earth

Barbara Sellers-Young

> *Women have been taught that, for us, the earth is flat, and that if we venture out, we will fall off the edge.* — Andrea Dworkin

Arts activism in support of the environment can be traced to Rachel Carson's *Silent Spring*. Published in 1962, the book documented a world that was increasingly losing the habitats that protected native species — human, plant and animal. This volume made artists and those who support the arts including producers, technical experts, government, and policy makers aware that the environment to which they were emotionally and psychologically attached was in jeopardy. The concern for the changes in the natural environment led many visual and/or performance artists to produce a set of individual and collective art projects focused on the environment. The exhibitions and installations were places where members of a community mixed with each other to consider environmental issues, appreciate different aesthetic dimensions and expressive possibilities.

The goal, as suggested by environmental activist and researcher John Grande, was to create a dialogue "to engage the borderline between art and what is perhaps the most pressing global concern in the new millennium — the quality and sustainability of the environment. These dialogues highlight the political, aesthetic, social, and scientific depths of their thought and work" (Grande 2004, 12). Beth Carruthers has documented many such place specific projects in "Mapping the Terrain of EcoArt Practice and Collaboration" (2006). Performance was incorporated into both site specific and political activities such as those engaged in by Green Peace, but the EcoArt movement of the 1970s and 80s was primarily limited to visual artists. An exception to this is Delilah and her desire to unite dance and an earthly ecology with a woman's body. As such, she contributed to the development of a social movement, often referred to as ecofeminism, in which the conscious awareness of body in relationship to its environment was part of the discourse which challenged systems of oppression including the exploitation of nature and the suppression of women.

Early History

Delilah's initial introduction to belly dance took place while working her way through college in southern California. In 1972, a friend told her about a belly dance class being offered at Grossmont Junior College. The dance's movement style and vocabulary came easy to her and ultimately she was hired by a group of Lebanese musicians based in San Diego to perform with them as entertainment for birthdays and weddings. Her position within the belly dance community continued to evolve as she danced in restaurants throughout southern California, ultimately winning the 1977 Belly Dancer of the Year contest and appearing in the 1979 movie *China Syndrome* with Jane Fonda, Jack Lemon and Michael Douglas. During this period, she also met rock musician Steve Flynn and they jointly decided to move to Seattle.

Like other dancers who started performing in the 1960s and '70s, Delilah learned by doing. Moving with the expressive capabilities of her body, she adapted the movements of other dancers and invented new movements of her own. And, like other women of her generation, she was influenced by the second phase of the women's movement and a desire to create new narratives for women. In her case, she integrated two major influences in her life, dance and nature. As she phrases it, belly dance is "after all, of Earth Mother origins. Anyone who takes issue with this is missing the connection with body: in the dance we are focusing on the use of hips, breasts, belly and arms, all mothering equipment" (1998).

Earth's Ecology, the Body and the Dancer

Gathered in a circle, thirty women define hips and torsos as they move in a counter-clockwise circle as the drum keeps up a steady rhythm. Shaking their shoulders, they gather into the center of the circle and back out again returning once more to the movements of hip and torso. Within the room there is a deep concentration and quiet dignity in the bodies of the dancers as Delilah's movement phrasing for "Birthing and Reclaiming Dance" is repeated again and again. This group of dancers has come to the big island of Hawaii and to the quiet of the 120-acre Kalani retreat to be guided by Delilah in a communion with each other and with nature. The dance retreat is for Delilah a commitment she made in 1992 to bring women to an environment away from the distractions of their daily lives that allows them to investigate their relationship to their personal natures through an environment set in nature; and, ultimately an inner awareness of the ecology of their being. A level of individual awareness in relationship to nature or ecofeminism, which Delilah believes, will challenge the social/cultural binaries associated with self/other, culture/nature, man/woman, humans/animals, and white-/non-white.

Ecology comes from the Greek word "oikos," a reference to the complex relationship between the individuals and the context in which they live which includes the geography, plant, animal and human life of the environment. As Giovanna Di Chiro notes, "Thinking of the body as home/ecology, especially in consideration of those bodies, that have been reviled, neglected and polluted, provides an apt metaphor and material grounding for constructing an embodied ecological politics, that articulates the concepts of diversity, interdependence, social justice and ecological integrity" (2010, 200). Delilah's approach to nature lies within the framework of this branch of eco-activism. In its exploration of women's relationships to nature, Delilah's vision is inspired by a unique combination of the writing of challenger to scientific orthodoxy Rupert Sheldrake and his publications including *The Presence of the Past: Morphic Resonance and the Habits of Nature* (1995), the appreciation of native wisdom as articulated by anthropologist Robert Lawlor's *Voices of the First Day: Awakening in the Aboriginal Dreamtime* (1991) and Dora Kuntz's conception of healing touch *The Spiritual Dimension of Therapeutic Touch* (2004). Delilah has concluded from reading these authors that it is only in integrating a conscious awareness of nature associated with indigenous communities and the spirituality inherent in new somatic therapies such as therapeutic touch can an avenue be found to discover the potential of the self's correspondence with nature; and, therefore a more sustainable life style for the individual and for the planet. For this reason, Delilah organizes opportunities for women from around the world to dance in and with nature in a process that brings the dancer into conscious awareness of her internal kinesthetic aspect of bodily aliveness and its relationship to the world around her. As she phrases it, "The process of dancing in nature is to be in-tune with the natural world around you, to invite nature to inspire your dance. The student learns there is a difference between dancing with nature and dancing in front of nature" (1998).

Delilah integrates her eco-feminist approach with material from a variety of sources including Joseph Campbell's myth structure (1991), Susan Griffin's poetic discourses on women and nature (1978) as well as such exponents of the goddess religions as Jean Shinoda Bolin, *Goddesses in Everywoman: Powerful Archetypes in Women's Lives* (2004) and archeologist Marija Gimbutas, author of *The Goddesses and Gods of Old Europe: Myths and Cult* (1982). Specifically, Gimbutas' research into the myths and related artistry of old Europe has inspired feminists to bring to life in the modern world the narratives from this era of European history. As such, Gimbutas' conceptions of the religions of old Europe was incorporated into the second wave of the feminist thought associated with the Goddess movement in which the Earth or Gaia is considered a complex ecological system in which a change in one aspect of the system influences the total system.

The primary issue for Delilah and others who believe in Gaia consciousness is the manner in which global politics of power have created a lack of respect for the environment and have contributed to the context of global warming. The goal of ecofeminism is to move the global conversation from having power over the earth and its resources to being in harmony with the earth and its resources. In this regard, eco-feminism is closely allied with other areas of the feminist movement in a desire to readjust the global conversation from the cultural hierarchy of the past dominated by men to discursive relationship of equality.

Delilah's project is a similar reclamation in a desire to reconnect the body of the dancer with the primal belief in a relationship between the body as body and body as an "extension of" and an "at oneness with" the earth and its forces. And, belly dance as a means to reveal this connection. In 1997, she wrote:

> Belly dance is older than any culture known today. The steps, the music, the politics it's been subjected to, the language spoken, the religions of its practitioners; none of these have remained the same over the great span of time during which this dance has been practiced. One thing has remained the same, however: the expression, through the dance, of the feminine experience [1997].

This combined belief in the force of the earth and women is central to Delilah's method of teaching belly dance. In Delilah's approach, the power of the earth moves from the feet into the pelvis and from this place of creativity throughout the upper torso, arms and head. She often uses images of water moving through the body of the dancer to connect them to an earth's consciousness and by extension their own creativity. The basic stance to create this movement of awareness comes from acknowledging the center line of the body that penetrates the head, torso and pelvis. She illustrates this central core by using a pole to demonstrate its vertical dimension. The pelvis is engaged around this core through a release of the knees and the movement of the coccyx which allows for what she refers to as slack in the area between the knees and the rib cage. The slack created by this position allows the hips and pelvis to move fluidly in a variety of directions that she suggests emerges from an internal mapping of the individual's creative forces. The movement vocabulary of belly dance — its circles, spirals, twists, lifts, shimmies — are an expression of the complex muscle system that integrates the pelvic floor with the spine and provides the strength for women to hold and give forth life. Delilah guides the students through what she refers to as "mapping the internal realms of the body"; a process that unites the individual consciousness with a kinesthetic experience in an enhancement of a dancer's felt presence.

According to Delilah, these internal dimensions of consciousness are not new conceptions of the female body. Instead, they are expressions of the ontology of the female principle in history as expressed through the body and reminiscent of ancient symbols which archeologist Marija Gimbutas brought to public attention in her books on the goddess cults of Europe. Using examples of symbolic shapes of spirals, triangles, circles, and double spirals borrowed from the illustrations provided by Gimbutas' writing, Delilah helps the dancer to traverse these ancient image pathways within the internal kinesthetic and proprioceptive experiences of her body. The culmination of this deep, internal, kinesthetic awareness of the movement within the pelvis and hips she suggests is a journey through a personal labyrinth.

Although most often associated with the Cretan myth of King Minos and Minotaur, the elaborate design of the labyrinth was symbolically etched on the walls of caves as well as incorporated into the designs of ancient and contemporary pottery. Historically, labyrinths were used to trap malevolent spirits, define a path for a ritual dance or in medieval times symbolize a path to God. The average medieval person could not afford to travel to holy sites and lands, so labyrinths and prayer substituted for such travel. Labyrinths are used by modern mystics to help achieve a contemplative state of transcendence. Walking among the turnings, one loses track of direction of the outside world, and thus increases a contemplative internal focus. This is the state that Delilah, through the labyrinth exploration, guides the dancer. Yet, it is also her goal for the dancer to experience a revelatory awareness of the labyrinth as a representation of the complex interweaving of the moving body, which is a corporeal version of the labyrinth and a metaphor for earth's complexity.

Delilah expands the dancer's internal mapping of consciousness by borrowing from nineteenth century French movement theorist François Delsarte's system. A French musician and teacher, Delsarte evolved a performance style that endeavored to connect the inner emotional experience of the performer with a structured set of gestures. As noted by dance historian Nancy Lee Ruyter (1999), Delsarte's work had an impact on such early modern dancers as Isadora Duncan, Ruth St. Denis and Ted Shawn in connecting the inner emotional experience of the dancer with the various parts of the body. The goal in Delilah's incorporation of Delsarte's approach is "to give voice to the body." Within the Delsarte system, the body is divided into sections. The head is the origins of the intellectual, spiritual and mystical. The torso is the emotive and personal and the legs are the vital relationship to the earth. This tripartite division is further extended as the torso is divided into the intellectual upper torso, emotive middle torso and vital lower torso. These designations are reversed for the legs and feet, as the upper leg is the vital, the calf and knee the emotive and the feet reflecting an intelligent relationship to the earth. The arm is in a similar correspondence as the legs, with the vital connection in the upper arm and its attachment to the torso, the emotive in the forearm and the intelligence represented by the hands and fingers. The head is also divided into three areas with the forehead and the eyes as the place of intelligence, the cheeks as emotive and the chin and neck with its connection to the torso as vital.

Delilah teaches dancers to engage these different areas by guiding them through an ongoing improvisation that begins with the hips and pelvis and moves up and out through the head, arms and hands. As the dancers improvise, she encourages them to explore the various kinesthetic pathways of their body. She reminds them to appreciate the support and balance provided by the legs and how the placement of the feet impacts the alignment of the pelvis, hips and torso. She asks them to explore the possibility that emotions are coming from their central torso, supported by the upper arm and acknowledged by the forearm before the hands add the final communicative touch. She also points to a phrase repeated in many Asian aesthetic forms such as Bharatnatyam and Nihon Buyo "where the eyes go the body follows." She expands on this advice by noting that the direction and gaze of the eyes communicate a relationship between a dancer and their body and the dancer and the audience. As she guides them through a deeper relationship to themselves, she never critiques their personal method of exploration. Delilah's goal for the dancer is to bring them to a conscious realization of a deep kinesthetic consciousness that she believes empowers them and allows them to creatively express their unique individuality in dance and by extension in life.

Empowering Lives

Empowering others is a central theme of Delilah's approach to teaching belly dance. It is an extension of her liberal upbringing in which she was taught to be inquisitive and investigate the possibilities inherent in any idea. For example, she comments, "We read the Bible, but not as absolute truth, but as one way of knowing" (2008). In her frame of reference, there are many ways of experiencing life and her goal is to help those who study with her to discover their personal potential. Initially, she acts as a guide for the dancers in their individual discovery, but she enlarges their experience of empowerment in group explorations that commune with nature and ultimately in celebrations that bring the ethos of her teaching to the community of Seattle and beyond.

The group explorations require that the dancers take responsibility for the bodies of one another. One example is an exploration she refers to as "veil therapy." It is one she discovered while teaching a class for children in which her youngest daughter was participating. Delilah needed to find a way of attending to her daughter without disturbing the flow of the class. Her solution was to have her daughter lie down in the middle of the floor while the other children carefully draped and removed large pieces of light fabric, referred to as veils. When the last veil was removed, her daughter sat up saying she was all better. The kinesthetic awareness the dancer has learned in mapping the internal dimension of the self is shared with the recipient of the veil therapy, as individuals or groups of two or more carefully lift three-foot-long pieces of light fabric and place the fabric across the body of the fellow dancer lying on their back on the floor. They then slowly pull the fabric over the dancer's body. The fabric may cover the entire body or only sections. The different arrangements of the fabric provide a varied kinesthetic experience for the dancer on the floor. The dancers' focus throughout the exercise is one of empathetic intensity as they silently become increasingly aware of their body and their body's response to another. This same focus is brought to other ensemble work in which the dancers are required to stay physically connected to each other while they improvise to music. Dancers learn to extend an internal focus outward from self to other and ultimately to nature.

Within the dance and nature retreats she organizes in Hawaii, Costa Rica, and the Pacific Northwest rainforests, this connection with each other is extended to nature in sunrise rituals as well as dances in the sea, gardens and forests. The dancers are in each instance taking the deep, internal, kinesthetic experience of nature imagery provided in the studio — the hips as earth revolving around the body's sun core or the positioning of the arms as hugging a redwood tree — of the studio to an interaction with nature. Their quest is to allow a personal correspondence between the movements of their body and that of the tides and waves of the ocean or in relationship to the grass, trees, and other plant life. In the process of dancing in nature, they discover, as Delilah phrases it, the "sacred-interconnectedness" between self and the environment. She believes this realization can lead to a transformation of consciousness that empowers the life of the dancer as it increases their appreciation for their place within the earth's scheme. At the same time this expanded sense of self enlarges their sense of empathetic response to the earth and its fragility.

Living in the Seattle Community and Beyond

Seattle's belly dance community incorporates a variety of different approaches to the dances of North Africa and the Middle East. For example, there are groups such as Kamand that presents the music and dance of Iran, the Anadolu Turkish Folk Dancers, St. Demetrios Greek Folk Dancers and Shahrazad Dance Ensemble which perform the folk dances of the region. Within these groups, there is the desire to present the authentic dances of North Africa and the Middle East in stagings that replicate the style of national dance companies from the region. On occasion, they have brought noted choreographers such as L'Emir Hassan Harfouche of Lebanon or Mahmoud Reda of Egypt to create pieces for the ensemble. At the same time, there is also within these companies a crossover into the creative ethos of the belly dance community. Shahrazad Dance Ensemble provides an example in their alter ego company named the Wild Women of Wongo. Inspired by ethnic fusion and alternative music, the ensemble has integrated the dance vocabulary of North Africa and the Middle East with costumes that are works of art for performances at venues as varied as science fiction conventions, Halloween parties, and by special request at an evening billed as oriental dance.

The Shahrazad Dance Ensemble reflects the crossing of cultural boundaries that exists throughout the Seattle belly dance community. Individuals are attracted to the dance form as its lack of consistent vocabulary and improvisational history provides an open space for the imagination. Seattle dancers can embody the dance as representative of women's history, as an expression of nature and therefore the natural, and even combine its vocabulary with other ethnic forms such as Polynesian or borrowings from Bollywood films. There is also its incorporation into the Goth community or as part of the politically satiric performance of neo-burlesque. Seattle's belly dancers have the option to define themselves within a particular style of the form and related community or explore the diversity of styles of expression.

Delilah focus on nature fits comfortably into this belly dance community and as a performer she performs with other Seattle dancers at the Northwest Folk Life Festival; an annual June event which brings ethnic and folk companies from throughout the Pacific Northwest to the Seattle Center's stages. However, Delilah also has an international presence and communicates with the global belly dance community through her website titled *Visionary Dance*

Productions. She created the website and associated Production Company in order to promote the image of her philosophy and her approach to the dance, an image that is resistant to mainstream television. For example, Delilah was able to perform and record "The Dance to the Great Mother," a piece she performed at concerts in the Seattle area in 1985 when she was pregnant with her second child. In conversations, she notes it was not a project that would have been supported by the average production company as it does not reflect the media image of the seductive belly dancer. The video performance does, however, represent Delilah's aesthetic philosophy of the magnificence of the female body and its ability to be creative whether in giving birth or in devising solutions to social problems; besides which, 25 percent of the profits support women's causes through "Birth and Life" women's shelters and the March of Dimes.

Beyond allowing her to promote video/digital projects about which she is passionate, the website also provides opportunities for correspondence between Delilah and the dancers who she meets in person at workshops she is teaching across the globe. In blogs and in a large interactive group of essays referred to as Alexandra's Library, a reference to the famous library of Egypt, there are essays by Delilah and other dancers. They incorporate personal reflections of individual dancers' experiences of dancing in nature, the role of the dance in empowering their lives, references to dancing and pregnancy, dancing and body image, and health in general. The site is also where those interested in being political activists with such events as the Fremont Parade and "Billion Belly March" stay in contact with each other.

The extensive web and production services also include a series of DVDs that offer different levels of instruction and performances by Delilah as well as CDs by musicians based in North Africa and the Middle East (Hakim Yaho) and renditions by American musicians (Sirocco, House of Tarab, Brothers of the Baladi), some which fall into the global beat category such as Necmi Cavli. She also sells belly dance accessories — costumes, veils, etc. Income generated from web sales is a fundamental supplement to the classes and workshops she teaches in Seattle and elsewhere.

Ecology, Dance and the Community

Delilah does not limit her involvement with eco-belly dance to teaching dance; it is the basis of her environmental activism. In 1994, she entered and won the National Public Radio broadcast on the environment. She has also sent letters to the mayor of Seattle or the governor of the state of Washington with suggestions on how to solve the increasing energy crisis. Her approach is not defined by a specific "to do list" often associated with the three Rs of environmental activists — recycle, reuse and reduce. Delilah believes that the earth is a consciousness and the human quest is to understand how individual bodies are related to that consciousness. In an interview, I asked her whether or not she ever did urban style site specific industrial performances; anticipating that someone who organized nature retreats would respond no. She replied, "There is nothing on the planet that is not an extension of Gaia consciousness. This includes contrivances some might consider aberrant; to celebrate earth and the goddess is to celebrate her in all her aspects" (1998).

Her philosophy of the "self in the world" extends to dancers being politically active in the world. In a gathering of dancers in Hawaii, Delilah asked if anyone knew just how many belly dancers there were in the world and speculated on what a political force they could be if they all united in a common cause. What would happen she asked if instead of signing peace and environmental agreements on a piece of paper, governments were required to sign them over the belly of a pregnant woman? She added, "with this process and the symbolism of the belly the consequences to the future generation would not get lost as it sometimes does" (2008).

Delilah's approach to dance as an integral part of nature is in comfortable correspondence with the city of Seattle. Seattle is often associated with two international corporations, Starbucks and Microsoft, but to those who live there it is also known as the Emerald City for the evergreen forests and mountains that surround it, and the harbors and lakes that reside within it. A port city, Seattle is located on the Pacific Ocean with Lake Washington to the east at the mouth of the Duwamish River, which empties into the city's chief harbor, Elliott Bay. The Kitsap Peninsula and Olympic Mountains are to the west of Seattle, and east beyond Lake Washington are Lake Sammamish and the Cascade Range. Despite the wet climate, Seattleites participate in an active outdoor culture of sailing, skiing, bicycling, camping, and hiking in the wilderness areas that are accessible almost year-round.[1]

Historically, Seattle has been focused on the environment, from issues associated with timber and agriculture in the city's early years in the 1800s, to a more recent concern with sustainability. The Office of Sustainability and the Environment works with city agencies, business groups, nonprofits, and others to make Seattle a model of healthy, environmentally sustainable urban living. The city also has neighborhood groups such as the Fremont Art Council that sponsor festivals which celebrate the arts, nature and the urban environment. Thus, there is a community spirit of environmental activism which is an extension of the city's geographic location. This activist stance regarding arts and the environment is a cultural focus in Seattle, but specifically in the Fremont area where Delilah makes her home.

Delilah brings together the belly dance community and Seattle with her involvement in events such as the Fremont Summer Solstice Parade. The Summer Solstice Parade and Pageant is an annual event sponsored and produced by the Fremont Arts Council (FAC), an organization that supports the arts and artists in the Fremont neighborhood where Delilah has her studio. Started in 1989 by Barbara Luecke and Peter Toms, the parade quickly grew to over 80,000 participants. This local event with an international reputation is held the Saturday prior to summer solstice and culminates in the two-day Fremont Fair, a benefit for the Fremont Public Association. The event is distinguished by a sense of freedom in which anything goes, with the exception of no printed words or logos, animals (except guide animals), motorized vehicles, weapons and/or advertisements.

Delilah's contribution has been to participate with other dancers from Seattle and elsewhere in theme based performances that are integrated into the parade. More recently, she has been referring to their performance as the "Billion Belly March" as the number of dancers has increased to over 200-plus participants. Each year is a different theme. In 1999, it was the color blue and within this focus the dancers acknowledged the "Tuareg" of North Africa in deep blue costumes, in 2004 the dancers dressed in red as the symbol of women's power. Delilah's message to the dancers that year was, "We need new energy; we need new ideas and creativity. We need women to be more present. We need the Mother energy. It is time for women to step up and take their turn. It isn't even a choice anymore, it is a responsibility.... Start talking to each other about politics more" (2008).

A symbol of this power was the 2007 project to build a model of an ancient Egyptian temple which could be set up and taken down as the parade moved through the streets of Seattle. Dancers came from a variety of styles within the belly dance community from tribal to ethnic to cabaret. Over 200 dancers from across the United States participated. Some of these dancers received a DVD prior to the event that taught the choreography to be used in the dance. All of the dancers converged in Seattle prior to the Fremont parade to rehearse and to participate in a ten-day combination of workshops and classes. The 2008 event was dedicated to Peace in support of the woman's organization code pink and using the color hot fuchsia pink. The 2009 event used veils and blue costumes with a series of undulations to depict the oceans of the world. In 2010, Delilah formed the Belly Dancers for what has become known as Obama care in support of health care for everyone. As with earlier projects, Delilah's goal is to revise the vision of women as incapable of taking on the issues of the day, and replace it with an image of a woman who like in Delilah's image of her alter-ego, Aphrodite, is pleasant, feminine, and charming, but is also powerful. In her activist stances, she activates the critiques of instrumental rationality, abstract individualism, and the related exploitation of people and places and replaces it with an interactive strategy that moves from individual to collective within a community that increasingly incorporates dancers from throughout the world.

A State of Being: Ecological Thinking

Philosopher Lorraine Code has coined the term ecological thinking for a state of being in which an individual acknowledges the variety modes of engagement "which pervade and reconfigure theory and practice" (2006, 24). Ultimately, ecological thinking that applies to themselves and the context of their lives is the goal of Delilah's teaching. For example, one afternoon as the dancers in the Hawaii workshop were sharing their stories about the significance of dancing with nature in the understanding of their lives, Delilah suggested that a flexible body helps evolve a flexible mind and spirit. A flexible stance is necessary to understanding the complex interrelationship between earth, wind, water, plants, and animals and, therefore, provides an opportunity for individuals to explore the possibilities of the flexible integration of their body, mind and spirit. This ecological thinking is what Delilah brings to her performance as dancer, teacher, artist, and political activist. She has not limited herself to specific stages or venues or styles. Instead, she has performed in restaurants, on stages in choreographed pieces, created movement rituals, and performed in other venues both within the Seattle community and in other locations throughout the world to help women learn to express the joy and power of the female body. In this variety of performance modes, she serves to remind dancers to stay flexible as they are the embodiment of earth's supple consciousness. In doing this she is finding the rhythm of the earth and as she would phrase it "turning my conscious attention toward Her" (1997) and dancing with earth's rhythms instead of dancing at the earth. Her goal for students is that they remain open and conscious and willing to be flexible enough to learn how to dance with the earth's ever changing rhythm.

Notes

1. Culturally, Seattle came of age in 1962 with the Century 21 World Exposition. Located at the foot of Queen Anne Hill, the fair was the brainchild of Al Rochester who had worked in one of the concessions for the Alaska-Yukon-Pacific Exposition held on the University of Washington campus in 1909. Focusing on the theme of modern science, the fair's organizers were able to attract the participation of thirty-five foreign countries. The ten million people who attended the fair traveled on a high speed monorail through the fairgrounds and took a glass-walled elevator to the top of the famous Space Needle. Designated a historic landmark in 1999, the Space Needle at 605 feet high was the tallest building west of

the Mississippi in 1962. It was built to withstand winds of up to 200 mph (320 km/h) and earthquakes up to 9.5 magnitude. Visitors also visited the separate World of Tomorrow at the coliseum and the Worlds of Industry and Art at separate installations throughout the twenty-eight acres of the fair site.

A major remnant of the 1962 exposition is the Seattle Center, which has become the heart of Seattle and the Pacific Northwest's cultural life. The seventy-four acre Center is a visual metaphor for Seattle as it combines open space with fountains and exhibit space and performance spaces. Visitors have the potential to travel quickly to Seattle's downtown area via the monorail or view the panorama of lakes and mountains that surround Seattle from the top of the Space Needle. The Seattle Center's mission statement is "to delight and inspire the human spirit in each person and bring us together as a rich and varied community." The diversity of the Center's offering is apparent in its support of a variety of performing arts groups including the Seattle Opera, Ballet and Repertory Theatre companies. Beyond the performing arts, it is the home of Seattle's men and women's basketball teams (Storms and the Sonics) as well as the ice hockey team the Thunderbirds. Twenty separate ethnic communities hold their annual festival at the center. It also promotes two large cultural festivals — Bumbershoot in September on Labor Day weekend and Northwest Folklife festival held in May during Memorial Day weekend. http://www.expomuseum.com/1962/.

Works Cited

Bolin, J.S. (2004). *Goddesses in Everywoman: Powerful Archetypes in Women's Lives*. New York: William Morrow.
Campbell, J. (1991). *The Power of Myth*. New York: Anchor.
Carruthers, B. (2006). "Mapping the Terrain of Contemporary EcoArt Practice," Canadian Commission for UNESCO.
Carson, R. (1962). *Silent Spring*, New York: Mariner Books, Anniversary Edition (2002).
Code, L. (2006). *Ecological Thinking: The Politics of Epistemic Location*. New York: Oxford University Press.
Delilah. (1997). "Belly Dancing with Nature." http://visionarydance.com/archive/dancingwithnature.html.
_____. (1998). Interviews in Seattle, Washington.
_____. (2008). Hawaii workshop.
_____. (2008). *http://www.visionarydance.com/solsticeParade_04.html*,
Di Chiro, G. (2010). "Polluted Politics? Confronting Toxic Discourse, Sex Panic, and Eco Normativity." *Queer Ecologies: Sex, Nature, Politics, Desire*. Catriona Mortimer-Sandilands and Bruce Erickson. Indiana: Indiana University Press.
Gambutas, M. (1982). *The Goddesses and Gods of Old Europe: Myths and Cult Images*. California: University of California Press.
Grande, J. (2004). *Art Nature Dialogues: Interviews with Environmental Artists*. New York: State University Press of New York.
Griffin, S. (1978). *Women and Nature*. New York: Harper.
Kunz, D.K. (2004). *The Spiritual Dimension of Therapeutic Touch*. Rochester, VT: Bear and Company.
Lawlor, R. (1991). *Voices of the First Day: Awakening in the Aboriginal Dreamtime*. Rochester, VT: Inner Traditions.
Rutyer, N. (1999). *The Cultivation of Body and Mind in Nineteenth-Century American Delsartism*. New York: Praeger.
Sheldrake, R. (1995). *The Presence of the Past: Morphic Resonance and the Habits of Nature*. New York: Park Street Press.

Negotiating Female Sexuality
Bollywood Belly Dance, "Item Girls" and Dance Classes

SMEETA MISHRA

> *It's not just men. Women also give us that gaze. They look at us as if we are doing something wrong. At the dance studio, parents call us and tell us "teach my daughter well." First, I did not get what they actually meant. Later I found out that they were basically worried that we would teach their daughter something socially inappropriate. Some parents even come over and want to be present during class to see what we teach them. Few husbands also come over to see what we are teaching their wives. They sit in the waiting area from where they can see the inside of the studio. After watching a class or two, they are convinced everything is fine.*—Sakshi Malik, Belly dance instructor, Banjara School of Dance, New Delhi.

This chapter interrogates representations of hybrid forms of belly dance in Bollywood cinema and also narrates experiences of belly dance instructors in India. To begin with, it briefly outlines the journey of various forms of belly dance in Bollywood cinema from the late 1950s onward. It then analyzes two highly popular "item songs," which comprised Bollywood belly dance numbers released during the past five years. Moving on, this essay compares the representations of belly dance in Bollywood films with recent claims made by Indian belly dance instructors in the media. It explores how such claims, while seeking to battle stereotypes about the dance form and appeal to Indian middle class aesthetics, end up unintentionally reinforcing Indian patriarchal values and the associated notions of purity, ideal Indian womanhood and morality.

First, it's important to highlight that while definite changes are noticeable in Bollywood cinema in the past decade, song-and-dance sequences remain an important feature of this genre. Fusion is a marked characteristic of such

Bollywood dances as industry choreographers draw from various sources and put them together to create an entertaining number. According to Dhar, "Bollywood dance is a mix of Indian classical, folk and international dance forms. So you have the squats and dips of Bharatnatyam, eye movements of Kathak, the 'Indian lotus' and 'deer' hand mudras [poses] common to most classical styles and Western elements like square jazz and pirouettes" (2011).

Bollywood dances often combine sensual belly dance movements such as hip and breast lifts, thrusts and undulations with other Indian dance movements to portray female sexuality. Such hybrid forms of belly dance are primarily portrayed as a form of entertainment located in bar or nightclub settings (male space), and presented as markedly different from Indian classical dance forms such as Bharatnatyam or Odissi that are considered to have religious significance. For the purposes of this study, belly dance in Bollywood films will be referred to as "Bollywood belly dance" to acknowledge elements of fusion and hybridity. In fact, Bollywood belly dance is becoming popular not just in India but in the West as well. For instance, many belly dance companies in the U.S. now offer "Bollywood Bellydance" apart from traditional belly dance classes.

"Vamp" vs. "Heroine" in Bollywood Cinema

In her book titled *Bombay Cinema* Ranjani Mazumdar (2005) argues that analyzing dance numbers in Bollywood films is very important as they are central to the narrative of almost every film. One must keep in mind that the style and settings in which the female protagonist danced was very different from those used by the "vamp." Rigid binary characterizations of the leading lady and the vamp, who was often portrayed as a nightclub dancer, continued until the 1980s (Mazumdar, 2005). In fact, cabaret numbers by vamps, which emerged in the late 1950s, became standard in many films during the 1960s and 1970s (Mazumdar 2005).

Mazumdar (2005) explains that the vamp "occupied a hypersexualized yet illicit space" and was pitted against the female protagonist on the morality plane (80). The vamp was a symbol of uncontrolled sexuality which was portrayed as something alien to Indian women: "While the heroine was the site of virtue and 'Indianness,' the vamp's body suggested excess, out-of-control desire, and vices induced by 'Western' license" (Mazumdar 2005, 86).

While the settings in which the leading lady or the heroine could break into a song or dance were limited to spaces such as her father's home, her husband's home, in the midst of Mother Nature or in imaginary sequences within the film (Pinto 2006), the sexual aggressiveness of the vamp was often brought out in nightclub settings. Mazumdar (2005) elaborates:

> The night club is one of Bombay cinema's fascinating creations — an illicit landscape of gambling, gangsters, and smugglers, on the one hand, and the excessive and dangerous display of female sexuality on the other. The representation of the purity/spirituality of the nation was negotiated through the image of the heroine, and the woman's body became the site of conflicting value systems. Images of the chaste woman and the nightclub vamp continued to inform Indian cinema right up to the early 1980s [Mazumdar 2005, 86].

To further understand the development of the vamp as a character type in Bollywood cinema, it is important to understand the position of women in the Indian nationalist project. Partha Chatterjee (1989) explains that Indian nationalism's answer to the British colonialist project involved demarcation of Indian culture into material and the spiritual realms. While the material sphere would aspire for industrial and technological modernization like the West, the spiritual would be protected from all change. This material-spiritual distinction was based on the division of the inner and outer spheres — the home and the outside world — with Indian women being the custodians of the inner spiritual world. They were given the responsibility of guarding timeless Indian traditions that make the home/inner world sacrosanct. Thus, the ideal Indian woman would remain selflessly devoted to meeting the needs of her husband and children and harbor no desires of her own. Even as the ideal Indian women became the symbol of sexual purity, female sexual agency had to be transferred to another character type — the vamp. Thus, Datta (2000) argues that the "nationalist project constitutes the female body as a privileged signifier and various struggles are waged over the meaning and ownership of that body" (73).

Gokulsing and Dissanayake (2004) explain how Bollywood does an effective job of portraying this ideal Indian woman/vamp dichotomy constituted by the Indian nationalist discourse:

> This ideal wife must be sexually pure and the epitome of sexual fidelity.... The opposite of the wife is the vamp, normally a decadent modern woman, generally with a name like Rosie or Mary.... She drinks, smokes, visits night clubs and is quick to fall in and out of love. She is portrayed as a morally degraded person and had come to be associated with everything that is unwholesome about the west. And she is almost always punished for her unacceptable behavior [79].

The first such vamp in Bollywood cinema was played by an Anglo-Indian actor, Cuckoo Moray, during the 1940s and 1950s. The dance moves of vamps in Bollywood films were hybrid in nature, combining steps from many sources such as the Indian dance form of kathak (which was popular in Mughal courts), belly dancing and tribal dances (Pinto 2006). After Cuckoo came the queen of all vamps, Helen J. Richardson, a young woman of Franco-Burmese-British-Spanish origin (Pinto 2006). Many of the popular vamp numbers in the 1960s, 70s and early 80s were played by her: "An instant crowd puller, a Helen sequence in a movie guaranteed full house — a phenomenon unseen for any vamp preceding or succeeding her" (200). Helen mastered many core belly dance moves and combined them with other dance forms to create an erotic display of a woman's sexual assertiveness. One of Helen's most popular performances is a gypsy-style belly dance number titled "Mehbooba Mehbooba" from the film *Sholay*, which was released in 1975 and became one of the biggest hits in Bollywood history. In this film, Helen played the role of a gypsy dancer who performs for a dreaded dacoit or bandit, Gabbar Singh. Dressed in a green sequined costume, she enthralls the dacoit with her seductive moves even as the two male protagonists use the time to plant bombs and blow up the place. As her performance ends, an explosion fills the screen and nothing more is said in the film about Helen and her troupe. An interesting contrast between the characters of the vamp and the heroine is brought out in this film. When the bandit captures one of the male protagonists in the film and his lady, he commands that she dance in front of him or he will kill her man. The hero tells her not to dance for them. Of course, she dances to save his life even as they throw glasses on the floor to make her feet bleed.

Thus, female sexual agency was primarily located on the body of the vamp/cabaret dancer in Bollywood cinema until the 1980s. In contrast to the vamp, female protagonists had to be "presumptive virgins" (Pinto 2006, 26). While the vamp could make sensuous movements in provocative clothes, the heroines were depicted as asexual beings that were draped from head to toe (Pinto 2006). Meanwhile, vamps were dressed in revealing outfits. They rarely ever wore saris, which is often presented as the Indian national dress for women. Saris were reserved for the heroine. Female actors who played the virtuous heroine did not play the role of vamps and vice-versa (Mazumdar 2005, Pinto 2006). The women were labeled both in reel and real life and there was little border crossing between the two.

Pinto points out that the actress playing the vamp was rarely a Hindu until the late 1960s. Within the film too, they were portrayed as outsiders, as Christians or of Arabian descent:

> Thus, if you wanted a vamp, it would be best to draw her from that "degenerate" community and to also portray her unequivocally as belonging to that community. It would then be natural for her to sing and dance for men, to be part of a gang, to wave a gun, to show a bit of body, to coquette and pirouette without in any way endangering the patriarchal notions of virginity as an attribute of the Indian woman [2006, 54].

Commenting on how Helen was always portrayed as an "outsider" (tribal, Christian, Anglo-Indian, foreigner, etc.) in Bollywood, Pinto argues that such othering and eroticization represents a mirror image of Orientalism (68). He points out that Bollywood cinema could "take an alien who looked Western and whose name fortuitously rang with resonances of destructive femininity (she even acted as Helen of Troy in Pradeep Nayyar's 1965 film of the same name) and make of her the woman our mothers warned us about" (68).

This is one example of the multiplicity within Orientalism. Shay and Sellers-Young (2003) emphasize that images of the Orient can be distorted in a multiplicity of ways by a variety of sources. For example, they point out that while a lot of critical attention has been paid to the West's Orientalist preoccupations, few have focused on the ways in which Russian artists, both tsarist and communist, misrepresent their own colonized Muslim populations (20). Similarly, India's orientalist representations of its own religious minorities and marginally placed populations cannot be ignored. Bollywood cinema often served as the site for stereotypical portrayal of minorities, especially minority women.

Introducing the "Item Girl" and the "Item Number"

In the 1980s and 90s, a new trend emerged in Bollywood cinema when female leads or heroines started appearing in sexualized dance numbers. The dancers of this era included: Zeenat Aman (*Qurbani* in 1980, *Shalimar* in 1978), Praveen Babi (*Shaan* in 1980, Namak Halal in 1982) and Rekha (*Jaanbaaz* in 1986) was taken forward by Madhuri Dixit (*Khalnayak* in 1993, *Shailaab* in 1990), Urmila Matondkar (*China Gate* in 1998, *Lajja* in 2001), Raveena Tandon (*Rakshak* in 1996, *Ghaath* in 2000) and Sonali Bendre (*Bombay*, 1995) in the next generation (Mohanty 2011).

However, in several ways, a heroine performing a sexually provocative number was different from what Bollywood now refers to as an "item number." While the heroine is central to the film, the item number usually shows a dancer performing for a mostly-male audience. Her character has little to do with the plot of the film. The woman performing the "item number" is referred as the "item girl" in Bollywood vocabulary. Although the heroine may decide to do an item number for a film, Bollywood today boasts of "item number" specialists such as Malika Arora Khan (Helen is her step-mother-in-law), Mallika Sherawat, Rakhi Sawant and Yana Gupta, among others (Mohanty 2011).

Important differences can also be identified between a sexually suggestive dance by a heroine and by an item girl. When the heroine dances provocatively, she is often depicted as someone who is herself unaware of her sexualized body and displays child-like behavior (Govindan & Dutta 2008). Secondly, the male protagonist engages with the heroine when she does an item number. On the other hand, if the item number is performed by the item girl, the hero is usually a mere spectator. Even if he does a few dance steps with the item girl, the latter never manages to win the hero in the film. Thirdly, when the heroine performs an item number in a bar or nightclub, she is usually rescued by the hero. She is not depicted as someone who is naturally comfortable in a bar or nightclub, unlike the item girl. The following case study offers an example of how the hero attempts to rescue the heroine while she is doing an item number showcasing Bollywood belly dance.

"Rescuing" the Female Lead from Belly Dance and "Rape with the Eyes"

"Sheila ki Jawani" or "Sheila's youth/oomph" is a song from the film *Tees Maar Khan*, which is a remake of Vittorio De Sica's 1966 film *Caccia Alla Volpe* or *After the Fox*. The Hindi action comedy was directed by Farah Khan and released in 2010. The male lead in the film, Akhsay Kumar, plays the role of a master conman who involves an entire village in the robbery of precious antiques from a moving train while making the gullible villagers believe it is part of a film shoot. Kumar's girlfriend, played by Katrina Kaif, enacts the role of a dumb girl and wannabe actor.

"Sheila ki Jawani" shows Katrina Kaif/Sheila shooting an "item number" for a film within the film. The dance combines many core belly dance moves with Bollywood style dancing. The first scene shows her wrapped in a white satin sheet that she loosely holds on her chest with her left hand. She is on a pink rotating bed surrounded by men in black. The song opens with a tease that no matter how much men want her, they will never get her. The next scene shows her in a new outfit. (It is typical of Bollywood heroines to change their outfits several times during a song-and-dance sequence.) She now wears a belly dance costume, a tight-fitted golden blouse and harem pants. Most of the belly dance moves she performs focus on her bosoms and hips, with little artistic movements of the hands. The song is fast-paced and she continues to gyrate to the beats. The men form a chorus behind her. The camera focuses on her torso, hips and navel even as she thrusts and shimmies. After some fast-paced belly dance moves, she changes into a white satin shirt, a black hat and tie. The male protagonist, Kumar, makes an entry into the film set at this moment. He utters some profanities at the director and objects to their watching the dance and covers the eyes of people who are looking at Sheila dancing. Fighting the film staff, he joins Sheila on stage with the aim of getting her off it. They are shown dancing together in Bollywood style.

However, soon Kumar is dragged off the set and Sheila resumes her belly dance with another change in outfit. Kumar re-enters the set and tries to again rescue her from the stage even as she sings that she needs a man who can give her a good life. Kumar responds with a promise that he will provide her with everything she needs but first she must leave the stage and accompany him out of the place. At this point, Kumar is again dragged out by bouncers. Sheila changes into a red outfit and resumes her belly dancing even as men surrounding her throw water on her. Bollywood films have often used drenched women to depict female sexuality, especially by showing them singing and dancing in the rain. In this number, even as a drenched Sheila continues dancing, Kumar beats up the director and finally manages to rescue her by carrying her on his shoulder out of the set. The song ends with a repeat of the male and female chorus. The next scene shows Sheila and Kumar home with Kumar explaining to her that she should not engage in such acts as it would have landed her in the hotel room of the director.

While the film got bad reviews from several quarters, the dance received rave reviews. The film's song stayed on top of charts for months. Farah Khan, who choreographed "Sheila ki Jawani" won the Zee Cine Award for Best Choreography in 2011 (Bollywood Hungama News Network 2011). In fact, Sheila's dance sequence became more popular than the movie, which after a spectacular run the first week did not do well in the box office. Well-known critic Rajeev Masand criticized the movie for its insensitivity and low-brow humor. However, he was all praise for the film's choreography: "The Sheila ki Jawani number is one of the film's early highlights—a sight to behold not only for the dance movements but for the complete staging of the production—the music, the costumes, the lighting, and the editing" (Masand 2011). *The Times of India* awarded the number "the hottest item song of the year" title based on a readers' poll comprising 343,000 votes ("Hottest item," 2011). The report remarked that "songs don't just need lyrics to create a stir; the latka-jhatkas [lifts and drops] and the bump-n-grinds have become intrinsic to success on the charts" (ibid. 2011). The dance sequence bears testimony to the way belly dance is often perceived in Indian society. When the good Indian woman represented by the female lead in the film belly dances, she has to be rescued by the hero.

Mayya Mayya: A Belly Dance Performance in an Istanbul Bar

"Mayya Mayya" is a belly dance number from the film *Guru*, a Hindi film inspired by the story of one of the largest business houses in India. The film was directed by Mani Ratnman and the music was composed by A.R. Rahman, and released in India in 2007. Well-known Bollywood couple Aishwarya Rai and Abhishek Bachhan played the female and male leads respectively. The belly dance number titled "Mayya Mayya," or "Water, Water" in Arabic, shows a professional dancer performing in a Turkish bar. The role is played by Mallika Sherawat, who is not a professional belly dancer in real life. She is a Bollywood star, more known as an "item girl" in Bollywood parlance. In fact, an article titled "Mallika, the Richest Item Girl" in *The Times of India* stated: "Mallika Sherawat may be settled in Los Angeles, but Bollywood actually sees her as nothing more than an item girl" (Ganguly 2011).

The eponymous hero of the film, Abhishek Bachhan, nicknamed Guru, works in Istanbul before he decides to stop working for a white man and returns to India to start his own business venture. It is in Istanbul that he visits a bar where Mallika Sherawat is performing a belly dance number. As Abhishek enters the bar, Mallika is shown lying on the glass floor. She is wearing a belly dance costume and she unveils her face in the first scene of the dance. The camera focuses on her bosoms and hips as she lies on the floor performing a few serpentine movements with her arms and singing. She compares her lover to the blue ocean and herself to the shore. She urges him to take her in his arms as she has been thirsty for a long time. For a while, she is joined on a stage by a chorus of dancers. She then goes to the tables of the men in the bar, rolling on the tabletops and making eye contact with the guests. She is shown dancing and teasing people in the bar. The lyrics of the song refer to the physical intimacy shared between her and her lover. She urges him to go slow through the night. The song often refers to the moon and the moonlight to set the romantic mood for the night the two will spend together.

It is at this point in the song that the entire cast appears along with visuals of the male protagonist. The visuals show the male protagonist doing well at work and celebrating with his friends, including the belly dancer, as the "Mayya Mayya" number continues in the background. The belly dancer is never shown in the film again and the lead does not even say goodbye to her before leaving Turkey for India to start a new venture. The male protagonist does not engage with Mallika's character nor is the dance relevant to the plot of the film in any way.

The film received good reviews. A review published in *The New York*

Times stated: "You might think it would be difficult to fashion an entertaining account of the life of a polyester manufacturer, even a fictitious one. But the Tamil director Mani Ratnam, known for intelligent political dramas, has done so with 'Guru,' an epic paean to can-do spirit and Mumbai capitalism" (Webster 2007). The film won several awards including one for best music by A.R. Rahman. *Guru* grossed over 800 million Rupees (18 million USD) and made over $2.1 million from America, which is considerably higher than what typical commercial hits and super hits of Bollywood make ("BO Report," 2008).

Comparing the Two Numbers: Restricted Notions of Female Sexuality

A comparison of the above two belly dance numbers highlights the restricted notions of female sexuality in Bollywood cinema. While the female protagonist, Sheila, has to be rescued from her own sexual assertiveness, sexual invitations by Mallika, the item girl, are considered acceptable. Thus, roles performed by female actors continue to be either pure (asexual) or dirty (sexually assertive). There are very few films that make complex subject positions available for female actors. Govindan and Dutta (2008) argue that the representations of female sexuality in Bollywood cinema are "governed by a paradox: actresses are expected to represent globalized images of a liberated female sexuality, but are still circumscribed by shifting yet narrow definitions of 'Indian femininity'" (180–181).

When a female actor who usually plays the role of the heroine happens to play the character of a sexually assertive female, she makes it a point to use various media outlets to distance her reel personality from her "real" one (Govindan and Dutta 2008). To highlight their point, Govindan & Dutta (2008) offer the example of Bollywood actor Priyanka Chopra and her character in the film, *Aitraaz*, which is loosely based on the Hollywood film *Disclosure*. Chopra performs the character of the sexually aggressive and manipulative Demi Moore. When Chopra received an award for "Best Performance in a Villainous Role," for *Aitraaz*, she emphasized in her acceptance speech that her real personality was very different from the sexually aggressive character she played in the film. She added that she was worried she would be perceived as a cheap woman because of her role and promised never to play the role of a sexually aggressive woman again (Govindan & Dutta 2008). Here, Chopra constructs the image of a "virtuous" Indian woman so that she could continue to bag the role of the heroine instead of being relegated to a secondary character or an "item girl" (Govindan and Dutta 2008).

Similar statements were made by Katrina Kaif, the female actor who belly danced to the tune of "Sheila ki Jawani." After doing a kissing scene in a 2009 film *New York*, Katrina, who is one of the top female actors in Bollywood today, said she was not comfortable doing it and would never do a kissing scene in the future (Rao 2010). She added she would never wear a bikini either, further reinforcing the separation between the sexualized "item girl" and "virtuous" heroine. Analysis of such representations of female sexuality in Bollywood cinema shows that while female actors are expected to appear sexually attractive and erotic to ensure that the film sells, they must simultaneously display a rejection of sexual agency in keeping with the constructed image of the "virtuous" Indian woman, especially if they want to make it to the top of A-list actors in Bollywood (Govindan and Dutta 2008). These female actors cannot ignore the expectations of Indian society in their reel life. The following section demonstrates the contradictory pulls and pressures faced by Indian women, specifically belly dance instructors.

Belly Dancers and Belly Dance Classes in India Today: "Preparing the womb for birth"

Most big cities in India, especially Delhi, Mumbai and Kolkota, have belly dance schools where young Indian women can take classes. Demand for these classes is driven by the phenomenal success of the Bollywood number "Sheila ki Jawani," and by dance shows and competitions on several television channels which bring belly dance into the living rooms of Indian families. Although gypsies in Western India have always incorporated belly dance vocabulary in their folk dance forms and academic literature on belly dance also mention Western India as one of the places of its origin and practice (Shay and Sellers-Young 2003, 14), Middle Eastern belly dance as an independent dance form is viewed as a contemporary, global dance style in India today. Newspaper features refer to belly dance along with hip hop, lyrical jazz, b-boying as one among the "many new forms of dance" coming to India (Mishra 2012).

The news media also frequently publish feature stories on how such contemporary dance forms such as belly dance are a great way to keep fit or mend a broken heart (Patel 2011, Rege, 2011). A newspaper report titled "Hips Don't Lie" promoted a belly dance workshop in the following words: "If you could never summon the courage to burn the dance floor because you simply don't know how, check out Fayruz Nur, a two-day workshop on Egyptian Oriental Dance that begins this afternoon.... And you can even breathe a sigh of relief if you're not size zero. The original belly dancers flaunt a luscious shape while moving seductively to a mix of Turkish and Egyptian beats" (Majumdar,

2008). However, such belly dance classes are more popular in north India today than in the south where classical dance forms such as Bharatnatyam maintain their stronghold.

The Banjara School of Dance run by Meher Malik is a popular belly dance studio in New Delhi with several branches in various parts of the city. The word banjara refers to gypsies, especially gypsies in Western India. The school advertises "Egyptian Oriental Dance" as its forte and claims to have more than 300 students. During the period of this study, Meher was a contestant on an extremely popular dance competition titled *Just Dance* on national television hosted by Bollywood star and dancer Hrithik Roshan. Prior to this, Meher was also a contestant on another show— Season 2 of *India's Got Talent* in 2010. Here is an excerpt of her Q&A session with the judges of *India's Got Talent* immediately after one of her performances on the show:

FEMALE JUDGE: Are you Indian?

MEHER: I was born in Delhi but we lived in the Middle East for 17 years. We came back to Delhi in 2006.

FEMALE JUDGE: Did your parents not object to it [belly dancing]?

MEHER: Not at all. That's the best part.

FEMALE JUDGE: Belly dance is not considered a traditional art form in India. People view it as a form of cabaret. That's why I asked you this question.

MALE JUDGE: Do you face prejudice?

MEHER: A lot. The thing is that it is looked at as just an entertainment for men. That's not true. Belly dance is an art that a mother passes on to her daughter to prepare her womb to give birth.

Meher Malik of the Banjara School of Dance in New Dehli (courtesy Meher Malik).

MALE JUDGE: I agree. It's an art. It's a dance form. And, such prejudices must be removed from India (Malik 2012b).

Meher's responses show how a belly dancer has to continually provide justifications to an Indian audience. Her comments may be understood in the context of what Shay and Sellers-Young (2003) point out: "The choreographer often expresses a deeply felt wish to prove to those unbelievers in the various Middle Eastern communities that oriental dance truly constitutes an art form and not merely lightweight, low-class entertainment" (26). They explain that "claims of ancient roots, dances of fertility, and ritual dances for ancient deities lend dignity to a dance genre with obvious erotic and sexual content" (Shay and Sellers-Young 2003, 32). The fact that belly dance is not viewed as a traditional art form in India but as mere entertainment for men in bars is highlighted in the home page of Meher's studio website. The home page states: "Belly dancing is pursued as a dance form across the world except India. Banjara [her dance school] intends to change that by promoting it as a professional dance form" (Malik 2012a). In an interview with the author, Meher Malik lamented that Bollywood focuses on only one variety of belly dance — cabaret.

Meher returned to India from Egypt in 2006 and started offering belly dance classes in New Delhi. She pointed out that at that time parents would not want their offspring to learn belly dance. "It's less difficult now. It's less difficult also because I have made a name for myself. They see that we are doing good work. But we have to keep providing justifications," she added (2012b). Sakshi Malik, another belly dance instructor at Meher's studio, gave further details:

> People think belly dance is a slutty form of dance. It's cabaret. Even Kathak went through a mujrah phase (a sensual dance performed by a courtesan for a male audience) before it began to be accepted as a classical dance form. May be, belly dance is going through that phase now. It's already a classical dance form in the Middle East. It's called *raqs sharqi*. It's only Americans who gave it this term belly dance and the reputation it has today [2012].

While Sakshi claims that *raqs sharqi* is treated as a respectable dance form in the Middle East, lived reality suggests otherwise. Karin van Nieuwkerk's (1995) book titled *A Trade Like Any Other: Female Singers and Dancers in Egypt* highlights how approval or disapproval of performers was often determined by their gender, time and place of the performance and the nature of the audience. Female performers in nightclubs and other all-male audience venues were not considered respectable. Like in the case of India, Nieuwkerk's extensive field work in Egypt showed that while Egyptians love singing and dancing, "professional performers are regarded with ambivalence" (2). Another instructor at the Banjara School of Dance, Akanksha, said that it was not just difficult for the students. Even instructors had to struggle to win approval of their families. "It was difficult to convince my parents," she said. "They did not want me to become a professional belly dancer. Even now, whenever my mother feels I am in a good mood, she tries to convince me out of it. People must understand that sensuousness is not the only thing about belly dance. These are exercises that mothers passed on to their daughters to prepare the womb for birth" (2012). When this researcher asked the instructors why they felt it was wrong to associate belly dance with sexual agency, Akanksha replied: "This is a society where you are expected to be a virgin until marriage although reality is something else. It's a society of hypocrites. Whatever it is, any dance form which is associated with sensuousness will not be socially approved" (2012).

These responses show how belly dance instructors in their attempt to battle stereotypes about the dance form end up reinforcing Indian patriarchal values and notions of purity, ideal womanhood and morality. To escape the label of a sensuous dance, such belly dancers sanitize belly dance and deprive it of all sexual content—letting the state and other custodians of patriarchy take back the assertion of female sexual agency from the individual dancer. However, a few belly dance students are using novel ways to make belly dance more socially acceptable in India. For instance, Nitisha Nanda, an Odissi dancer who recently started learning belly dance at Meher's studio, performed a short, unusual dance number at the *Just Dance* show mentioned earlier. She presented a piece that combined the classical Indian dance form of Odissi with belly dance. Her performance was well-received. Nitisha, 20, explained her decision to the author:

> I have never seen classical Indian dance forms combined with anything. I did not know how people will react. Usually, classical dance teachers are very orthodox but my teacher was supportive. It was a risky step. But I did not wear provocative clothes. I wanted to remove the whole feel that belly dance is sexy. I knew I was combining a classical Egyptian dance form with a classical Indian dance form. I wore classical Odissi jewelry. Only my top was part of a belly dancing costume. I wore a salwar [loose pants] along with it [2012].

Nitisha survived the first round of the dance show but did not make it any further. She was auditioning for another television show at the time of this interview.

While some play down the sexual nature of the dance, others find the same characteristic empowering. Meher said, "I get students who have just broken up with their boyfriends and they want to learn belly dance. They want to feel free about their bodies. My work is about opening of minds. It is a byproduct of my work here. In 20 years, belly dance will go pro here"

(2012). Nigar (name changed upon request), a 29-year-old hijabi Muslim female who completed beginner's belly dance classes, echoes Meher's views. She said: "I was brought up as an asexual creature at home. In the belly dance class, I felt aware sexually. It was liberating for me" (2012). At such a juncture, it's too early to comment whether belly dance is already creating a new framework for the conception of the feminine in certain segments of Indian society. However, one can say with some certainty that belly dance classes, as Öykü Potuoğlu-Cook (2006) points out in the case of Turkey, are offering a kind of "cultural and economic proximity to cosmopolitan culture" to elite students and practitioners although the same privilege may not extend to professional belly dancers or instructors (644).

Thus, belly dance in India seems to be traversing a contradictory and complex terrain — one where instructors and students play down its sensual nature while simultaneously claiming that it can empower a woman sexually. The contradiction seems to be caused by addressing multiple audiences. While the custodians of patriarchal values need to be assured belly dance lessons will not lead their daughters and sisters astray, those who actually enroll for belly dance lessons also need to feel empowered. After all, they also have access to a multiplicity of images of belly dance made available by the media. As Arjun Appadurai (1996) said, "Lives today are as much acts of projection and imagination as they are enactments of known scripts or predictable outcomes" (61). It in this context that the complex and contested image of belly dance in India needs to be located.

Works Cited

Akanksha. (2012). Interview, New Delhi, September.
Appadurai, A. (1996). *Modernity at Large: Cultural Dimensions of Globalization.* Minneapolis: University of Minnesota Press.
BO Report. (2008, January 7). *Box Office: The 2007 Box Office Report and Classifications.* Retrieved July 11, 2011. http://www.ibosnetwork.com/newsmanager/templates/template1.aspx?articleid=21086&zoneid=4.
Bollywood Hungama News Network. (2011, January 14). *Winners of Zee Cine Awards 2011.* Retrieved August 5, 2011. http://www.bollywoodhungama.com/features/2011/01/14/7016/index.html).
Chatterjee, P. (1989). "Colonialism, Nationalism, and Colonized Women: The Contest in India." *American Ethnologist* 16(4): 622–633.
Datta, S. (2000). "Globalisation and Representations of Women in Indian Cinema." *Social Scientist* 28, 3/4 (April): 71–82.
Dhar, S., and B. Dubey. (2011, February 19). "Desi Thumka, Global Thunder." *The Times of India.* Retrieved June 12, 2011. http://www.timescrest.com/culture/desi-thumka-global-thunder-4802).
Ganguly, P. (2011, February 19). "Mallika, the Richest Item Girl." *The Times of India.* Retrieved August 10, 2011. http://articles.timesofindia.indiatimes.com/2011-02-19/news-interviews/28614638_1_mallika-sherawat-bin-bulaye-baarati-numbers.

Gokulsing, K.M., and W. Dissanayake. (2004). *Indian Popular Cinema: A Narrative of Cultural Change*. Staffordshire: Trentham Books.
Govindan, P.P., and B. Dutta. (2008). "'From Villain to Traditional Housewife!' The Politics of Globalization and Women's Sexuality in the 'New' Indian Media." *Global Bollywood*. Eds. Anandam P. Kavoori and Aswin Punathambekar. New York: New York University Press.
"Hottest item numbers of Bollywood." (2011, July 9). *The Times of India*. Retrieved August 11, 2011. http://articles.timesofindia.indiatimes.com/2011-07-09/news-interviews/29751513_1_numbers-sameera-reddy-saif.
Majumdar, A. (2008, November 8). "Hips Don't Lie." *Indian Express*. Retrieved February 10, 2012. http://www.indianexpress.com/news/hips-dont-lie/382908/.
Malik, M. (2012). Banjara School of Dance. Retrieved February 5, 2012. http://www.banjaradance.com/banjara.php
_____. (2012b). Interview, New Delhi, September.
Malik, S. (2012). Interview, New Delhi, September.
Masand, R. (2011, January 1). *Masand: "Tees Maar Khan" Has Puerile Humour*. Retrieved July 5, 2011. http://ibnlive.in.com/news/masand-tees-maar-khan-has-puerile-humour/138540-47-84.html.
Mazumdar, R. (2005). *Bombay Cinema: An Archive of the City*. Minneapolis: University of Minnesota Press.
Mishra, A. (2012, January 16). "Many New Forms of Dance Coming Up in India." *The Times of India*. Retrieved February 10, 2012. http://articles.timesofindia.indiatimes.com/2012-01-16/news-and-interviews/30631544_1_contemporary-dance-latest-trend-new-mantra
Mohanty, P. (n.d). "Bollywood Item Numbers: From Monica to Munni." Retrieved August 11, 2011. http://www.pixelonomics.com/bollywood-item-numbers-monica-to-munni/.
Nanda, N. (2012). Interview, New Delhi, September.
Nigar. (2012). Interview, New Delhi, September.
Parasara, N.J. (2010, December 23). *Tees Maar Khan review*. Retrieved July 12, 2011. http://www.nowrunning.com/movie/7451/bollywood.hindi/tees-maar-khan/2872/review.htm.
Patel, A. (2011, December 23). "Dance Is a Great Way to Stay Fit." *The Times of India*. Retrieved February 9, 2012. http://articles.timesofindia.indiatimes.com/2011-12-23/fitness/30382725_1_belly-dancing-dance-academy-bharatnatyam.
Pinto, J. (2006). *Helen: The Life and Times of an H-bomb*. New Delhi: Penguin.
Potuoğlu-Cook, Ö. (2006). "Beyond the Glitter: Belly Dance and Neoliberal Gentrification in Istanbul." *Cultural Anthropology* 21(4), 633–660.
Rao, A. (2010, March 2). "I don't feel comfortable doing kissing scenes, says Katrina Kaif." Retrieved June 14, 2011. http://www.topnews.in/i-don-t-feel-comfortable-doing-kissing-scenes-says-katrina-kaif-2252848.
Rege, H. (2011, November 8). "Mend Your Broken Heart." *The Times of India*. Retrieved February 9, 2012. http://timesofindia.indiatimes.com/life-style/relationships/man-woman/Mend-your-broken-heart/articleshow/9323936.cms.
Shay, A., and B. Sellers-Young. (2003). "Belly Dance: Orientalism: Exoticism: Self-exoticism." *Dance Research Journal* 35, 1 (Summer): 13–37.
"*Tees Maar Khan* Sets Box Office Ablaze." (2010, December 24). Retrieved July 12, 2011. http://www.boxofficeindia.com/boxnewsdetail.php?page=shownews&articleid=2363&nCat=box_office_news.
"*Tees Maar Khan* Shows Humongous Drop on 8th Day." (2010, December 31). Retrieved July 12, 2011. http://boxofficeindia.com/boxnewsdetail.php?page=shownews&articleid=2393&nCat=box_office_news).

van Nieuwkerk, K. (1995). *A Trade Like Any Other: Female Singers and Dancers in Egypt.* Austin: University of Texas Press.

Webster, A. (2007, January 15). "Polyester and Power at Play for a Mogul and His India." *The New York Times.* Retrieved July 11, 2011. http://movies.nytimes.com/2007/01/15/movies/15guru.html.

Digitizing *Raqs Sharqi*
Belly Dance in Second Life

CAITLIN E. MCDONALD

As we have argued throughout this volume, in an increasingly globalized world it is necessary to study belly dance in the new, transnational contexts in which this cultural practice is now performed. The traditional anthropological conception of cultures as bounded wholes is losing relevance in the face of new technologies that are altering the possibilities of thinking about locality. New conceptions of culture that include innovative liminal spaces must become the anthropological paradigm, without losing sight of the ways in which individuals' relationships with locality and community are still tied to physical geography (Robertson 1995, Appadurai 2001, Lewellen 2002, Robertson 1992 #340, Abu-Lughod 2005, Appadurai, 2005). Perhaps the best summary of this argument in the context of emerging technologies is in Tom Boellstorff's ethnography of the online virtual world Second Life:

> Anthropologists have long berated themselves (and been berated by others) for assuming that cultures are bounded wholes...
> Yet it is also clear that persons around the world understand themselves to belong to cultures that are discrete even if their boundaries are porous [Boellstorff 2008, 241].

Boellstorff's summary of the complex and evolving layers of meaning represented by the word "culture," taking into account both the sublimation and the continuing relevance of physical locality in forming shared understandings in an increasingly globalized and technologically dependent world, is particularly pertinent to this chapter.

In 2009 I became aware of a thriving belly dance community in the online virtual world Second Life. The active belly dance community met at regular intervals in various locations within the world of Second Life during the week to watch each other dance (Poole, 28 January 2009). Compared with my previous fieldwork at physical dance meet-ups in Egypt, the United States and Britain, and even with virtual fieldwork in online social networking sites for dancers to communicate and share video content, this idea of a virtual dancing avatar seemed at first alien.

The most recognizable example of dancers engaging with remote localities through technology is their use of digital media: nearly all my research participants reported watching video clips on YouTube as a way of researching what the rest of the belly dance community around the world is doing. Video clips can be like (un)sourced, extracted sections of text; often they do not bear any referent to their origins. In these instances the dancer is operating on a truly global stage: instead of engaging in a participatory exercise bound to a specific space and time, the audience can be scattered throughout the globe and watch the performer at any time.

But even in online video clips with no references to the time or physical locality of performance, the dancers represented are real. In contrast, in Second Life users can buy or create animations that cause their avatars to belly dance, unlike real life where dancers need to take classes to increase their skill. Animations are computer scripts that cause a dancer's avatar, the digital representation of self within the game, to perform an action. In addition to dancing these animations control all sorts of gestures such as giggling, smoking a cigarette, running the avatar's hand through its hair, and so forth. Background scripts within the game also cause avatar movements to appear naturalistic even when at rest. Instead of standing rigidly stock-still like an inanimate object when not being actively moved about, the avatar will fidget, gently bounce, and move its limbs around in a way that mimics unconscious real life movement. As technology progresses, digital representation of motion is becoming increasingly realistic. Though, as I shall discuss later, there are still shortcomings in the way animations are made that prevent them from being true simulacra of movement.

How Does It Work?

Second Life is not technically a game because it doesn't have a goal, objective, or set of conditions to satisfy in order to "win." There is no one set of activities a player needs to accomplish, but there are many activities in which a player can participate. One of these is dancing. In fact, going to virtual clubs and pubs to dance is one of the most common Second Life activities (Boellstorff 2008, 16, 106).

Like many activities in Second Life, dancing in virtual clubs and pubs — or at belly dance meet-ups — is accomplished through the animations

Zarafa Merryman, Caitlin E. McDonald's avatar, belly dancing in Second Life (photograph by Caitlin E. McDonald).

described above. Because these animations are scripts, they run exactly the same way every time and there is no need to put in effort to increase skill, except by collecting as many animations as possible and varying the order in which the user runs them. Most people are not advanced enough programmers to make their own animations, so nearly all the gestures performed by users are exactly the same because those are the animations that are available. There is an ever-increasing range of animations as new ones are created all the time, but the market for certain kinds of gestures is larger than others. The range of belly dance animations available is particularly slim, meaning that there is a comparatively limited virtual movement vocabulary. Some animations are free, but the majority of them are purchased using Linden Dollars, the currency in Second Life.

While it is free to sign up for Second Life and there are many activities to do there without spending a single Linden Dollar, it does have a cash-based economy. In 2009 *USA Today* reported that online retail sales were on the rise, unlike the retail slump in the real world. While it may seem that this would have little or no effect on real-world economics, Linden Dollars are in fact purchasable for real-world currency. Market research by Inside Network reported approximately $1 billion in sales of virtual goods in 2009, most of which cost less than a dollar in "real" money (O'Donnell 2009). Inside Network's updated projections suggest that the sale of virtual goods in the United

States could reach up to $2.1 billion in 2011 (Smith and Hudson 2011). The exchange rate for Linden Dollars hovers around 250LD to the U.S. dollar. There is a lot of money to be made selling not only physical objects like clothing or houses or pets in Second Life, but also by selling, for example, different hairstyles, avatars that look like sharks, and animations like belly dance movements. One of my research participants had bought, using real money that she changed into the game's currency, dance costumes for her avatar.

After speaking to my initial informant Lyssa Poole (Poole 2009), I learned that there were films of people's avatars performing animations on YouTube (jimmyjetaimel, 9 August 2009; JenanfromCanada, 11 November 2009; slmoviecom, 29 January 2010). These images of virtual belly dancing began to open new questions about the essence of what is dance: here is a "film," actually a program that has been instructed to capture certain aspects of events within another program, of someone "belly dancing." Suddenly, expertise in the field requires a completely different set of skills from those in the real world of belly dancing. Someone who had never once put on a hip scarf in real life could potentially be the Second Life world expert on belly dance, because she or he has the programming skills to create innovative movements, costuming, and accessories, has enough contacts to organize dance events within the online world, and the ability to capture images of the avatar dancing which can then be used for self-promotion.

All of this is so contrary to an experiential, lived engagement with belly dance that categorizing it with the range of knowledge and practices that my other research participants reported was initially a challenge. However, contrary to my speculation above, my research indicates that the vast majority of people who take an interest in belly dancing online are the same as those whom it interests in real life. People who are motivated enough to put together an online community around this subject are guided by the same motivations in their non-digital lives.

My original assumption was that people would only engage in a hobby online if it were an impossibility or an activity in which they did not normally engage in non-virtual life. This assumption that virtual realities are entirely bound by escapism is a common one, refuted by Tom Boellstorff:

> It is true that some persons spend time in virtual worlds to be something different: women becoming men or men becoming women, adults becoming children, disabled persons walking, humans becoming animals, and so on. However, many who participate in virtual worlds do not seek to escape from their actual lives. Such negative views of virtual worlds fail to consider forms of escapism in the actual world, from rituals to amusement parks to daydreaming: the degree to which an activity is "escapist" is independent of whether it is virtual or actual [Boellstorff 2008, 27].

Members of the Second Life belly dance community engage in all the internal group debates about standards of decency, tradition and historical accuracy that my real-life participants theorize in the course of their interaction with the dance community; this is not escapism at all but participating in a normative behavior for the global belly dance community.

I indicated above that a series of relatively few belly dance animations are being run on many people's avatars. Several videos are available on YouTube of dancers using the same sequence of movements, though the shapes of the avatars themselves and the music they use vary.[1] This can make it difficult at first to realize that the movements are in fact the same, but after watching them together, it becomes clear that though being "performed" on avatars' bodies of different shapes, the motions are of the exact same duration and in the exact same sequence. I found turning the sound from the video clips off helps: once the viewer stops looking for the avatars to respond to musical cues the way a live dancer would, the similitude between their routines becomes apparent. These animations are for sale, though there are a few available for free through "newbie" areas in the game. One of the most popular outlets for buying animations in Second Life is a digital animation company called Animazoo.

Animazoo is a motion-capture corporation based in Brighton, United Kingdom, where they take sequences enacted in real life and digitize them to create animations for a variety of platforms, including animated films and animations for sale to individuals in Second Life. Animazoo worked with Brighton-based dancer Galit Mersand in February 2008 to create the basis of their first line of belly dance animations. Paul Collimore, the director of sales at Animazoo, told me that at the time they approached Galit to do some animation work with them, they already had a very successful store based in Second Life selling animations to players of the game (2010). They were selling other types of dance at that juncture, like hip-hop, jazz and waltz. Dance animations are not their only product: they also sell animations that cause the avatar to make a gesture of surprise, walk like a crab, flick cigarette ash, and much more. Paul indicated that they decided to commission Galit after several Second Life users requested belly dance sequences. There was enough market interest to motivate Animazoo to create a whole new range of belly dance animations. These animations are about 30 seconds to 1 minute in length and they tend to run on a loop, or the user can queue up several different clips one after the other to create a longer sequence (Collimore 2010). It is also possible to have a custom animation generated but obviously this is a much more expensive process depending on the needs of the customer. Prices for single belly dance animations are 250–300 Linden dollars, and packages of dances that come in a set run between 2300 and 2500 Linden dollars.

(That is U.S.$1–1.50, or U.S.$9–10.) Custom animations would be priced based on the complexity of the buyer's specifications, but would be exponentially more expensive.

The biggest-selling animations in Animazoo's Second Life retail store are hip-hop and what Paul called "drunk" dancing, which basically makes a player's avatar look like a slightly tipsy person dancing in a club. Apparently when Animazoo first began this project of selling animations and dances for avatars, they initially brought in professional dance artists of various styles like hip-hop, waltz, salsa and so forth to do very high-quality performances upon which to base the animation sequences. However, they received feedback from customers saying that what they really wanted was the kind of amateur dancing you might do at a nightclub. This corroborates Tom Boellstorff's findings that participating in this virtual world is not confined to those who wish to escape from their "real" lives or to perform only activities that they would be unable to in their offline lives. Rather, there is a high degree of overlap between players' offline and online activities. Similarly, the Second Life belly dance community were clamoring for some animations to use at online haflas (belly dance parties), which are structured in a very similar way to their offline counterparts. Like general Second Life users, the subset of Second Life belly dancers was looking for activities similar to those in which they participate in real life. But in contrast to users who are not affiliated with a particular dance style offline, belly dancers were looking for professional-caliber sequences recognizable as belly dance rather than the informal improvisational sequences that appealed to the general Second Life public.

Galit Mersand, the dancer upon whom Animazoo based their animation sequences, spoke to me about her experiences filming the dance sequences. She indicated that it was not a lengthy process, but only took three hours. She dressed in a suit she compared to a diving suit, upon which points had been picked out for the cameras and sensors to track. Galit brought a music CD with her and improvised movement while the camera captured them. Animazoo did several takes because they discovered that at times the points on the suit appeared distorted and weren't processing correctly. They were also only able to use certain types of moves: some movements were too subtle to be captured by the motion capture technology. Any finger movements, anything with the head, and belly undulations were all too delicate to be captured by the suit or the suit did not have capture points in that area. The head and the fingers, for example, were not covered by this particular suit, so neck slides and intricate finger movements were not part of Animazoo's original animations. Thus large hip lifts and drops, bumps, big arm movements and big circles were what worked best with the technology at the time. Galit had never heard of Second Life before getting involved with the project with

Animazoo, and she told me that she hadn't really thought about it again until she heard from a student of hers that her animations were getting very widely used by digital dancers in Second Life.[2] (Mersand 2010a). Galit remains pleased that her own moves are getting used around the world, even though the people using them may not be aware of her involvement with the project. After watching several different avatars do "her" dance, Galit told me that she is excited about the creative ability to enact one's imagination through the extreme costumes and images people have invented for themselves within Second Life. She also said, "I find the idea of secondlife [sic] a bit 'wrong' in the sense that people live their lives in cyber space instead of here and now. BUT I feel that maybe these clips show the nice and creative aspect of secondlife, now all they is need to go attend a belly dance class in real life. :)" (Mersand 2010). (Like many people, Galit made the assumption that a person's online and offline lives have little or no overlap.)

How Doesn't *It Work?*

The motion capture technique used to create dance animations is not without its problems, and cannot produce a perfect facsimile of a real-life dancer. Though successful at capturing large motions, as I mentioned, smaller and more intricate movements couldn't be captured using the technology Animazoo worked with to create the animations based on Galit's involvement in 2008. Once the motion-capture is created, there is limited ability to vary timing to suit the music, and none of engaging with the spontaneity and improvisational quality that is so important in a real-life dance performance.

Perhaps most importantly the methods used to create these animations had no gestural input for facial expression. Conceptually, dance is often reduced to bodily performance. When defining dance, the face or head are rarely mentioned explicitly, and motions of the torso, legs and arms are usually emphasized. For examples of definitions of belly dance performance, I refer to those cited in the introduction to this volume: facial expression is not a component of any. While in many dance styles facial expression is expected to remain neutral or consistent throughout performance, in belly dance facial expression works in concert with movement vocabulary to create a cohesive expression of meaning. For this reason advice is often given to dance students performing to music in foreign languages concerning the importance of obtaining an accurate translation in order to appropriately interpret and express the lyrics (Asra 2011, Shira 2011). Face is as intrinsic to belly dance as are other aspects of movement vocabulary. Without the ability to capture facial expression, the animations created through motion capture are incomplete.

Though avatars in Second Life perform bodily motions that would be recognizable as part of the belly dance movement vocabulary, without corresponding facial expression they appear like automatons, who can perform a sequence of actions accurately but without understanding.

In many ways, this question of successful dance performance by an avatar parallels a concept in computer science known as the Turing Test (Oppy and Dowe, 2011). Alan Turing posited that if a computer and a human are able to perform a test of intelligence with equal success such that an observer is unable to reliably and consistently tell the difference between which is the human respondent and which is the computer, it can then be said that the computer thinks in the way a person does (Turing 1950). From this test could be extrapolated the concept that any task a computer is able to perform indistinguishably from a human raises the question of what is unique about humanity. However, Turing was dubious about the utility of making a computer that can mimic a human physically as well as in terms of thinking capacity: "We should feel there was little point in trying to make a 'thinking machine' more human by dressing it up in ... artificial flesh" (435). A true Turing Test considers only the ability of the computer to mimic human intelligence, not any form of physical similitude.

What Turing did not address, though, is whether a *representation* of a "thinking machine" might successfully mimic a *representation* of a person. A YouTube video of a dancer can be badly pixelated, have delay between sound and picture, stop suddenly, load badly, and in many other ways create disjuncture between the experience of watching a live performance and a recorded one. Yet viewers generally look beyond the quirks of technology to accept the performance within the video as real. If the limitations of avatars that I described above (lack of intricate small motions, lack of pace or timing variation, lack of facial expression) were overcome to the point where an observer couldn't distinguish between the film of an avatar dancing, and the film of a real person dancing, would the avatar then have passed a modified Turing Test? As the technological possibilities of communication become increasingly prevalent, with face-to-face interaction being only one of a growing range of ways to connect with others, this modified Turing Test may take on new significance.

Dance Discourse in a Virtual World

On some levels, the animations created based on motion capture dances like Galit's are successful dance performances. They contain a movement vocabulary that is recognizable to any member of the belly dance community.

In fact, because they are completely automated, there is no possibility for the dancer to err in performing those aspects of the movement vocabulary. However, given the limitations of motion capture technology I discussed above, the belly dance performances on Second Life are in another way unsuccessful: the avatars look like marionettes more than dancers. But the measure of success within the belly dance community in Second Life is not solely, or even mostly, based on successful performances: how could it be, when those performances are unvarying for everyone using the same animations? Rather, there is a significant component of community engagement amongst Second Life belly dancers including the same kinds of discussions and debates that are held in other online forums, in dance classes, and at dance festivals, paralleling the experiences of belly dancers around the world in real life. Arriving at this conclusion led to a true paradox: though initially being an unexpected result, the deeper I delved into this research the clearer it became that the reason behind the discursive parallels between the international belly dance diaspora and those in Second Life was that they were in fact drawing from the same population. I expected Second Life belly dancers to be those who couldn't or wouldn't dance in real life, but, as with other forms of dance and other hobbies or activities in Second Life, it turned out that people mainly replicated their offline leisure activities.

Non–belly dancers within Second Life may try the animations for fun, just as individuals may take dance taster sessions or try a new hobby in real life. However, during my research I did not meet any users who joined belly dancing groups or became involved in arranging events online whose real lives did not also include belly dance. This is primarily based on my findings with the group Enlightened Divinity, which is also a location within Second Life. Enlightened Divinity was founded by a woman whose avatar is called Karen-Michelle Lane. They host belly dance meet-ups in the Enlightened Divinity space weekly. She started Enlightened Divinity after two years in Second Life as a haven for people who are interested in belly dance. In an online interview KarenMichelle told me, "I've always loved ancient history so the [Middle] East holds a strong attraction for me thus my wish to also keep Belly Dancing alive here in SL" (Lane 2009). Clearly, KarenMichelle also has a big interest in the spiritual aspect of belly dance and its connections with the ancient divine. Even in a medium of emerging consumer technology designed to create an artificial CGI world, there remains a fascination with the past, evident through the continued attachment to ancient divinity myths in the belly dance community within Second Life.

I also researched two other Second Life belly dance groups. The first was Serenity Belly Dance, who were very much in keeping with the Enlightened Divinity model focusing on the spiritual and feminine-empowering aspects of the activity. The second, called Belly dancers, was more "professional": they held events that users of Second Life would pay to attend, and it cost money to join the group. Just as in real life, there are a number of different reasons that people get involved with belly dance and people approach it multiple layers of understanding about what dance means. A comparison of the group charters of the three groups mentioned should clarify some of these contrasts.

- **Enlightened Divinity charter:**
  Enlightened Divinity
  The Gods have graced us with the knowledge and power to bring healing and peace to the lands we own. Join us at Enlightened Divinity to experience the joy of true friendship and love.
  Karen Michelle[3]
- **Bellydancers group charter:**
  For those that love the art of Belly dance!
  Belly dancing is an exotic art, erotic, sexual and most beautiful. A way for a woman to speak with her body and nothing else.
  A solo dance performed by a woman and characterized by sinuous hip and abdominal movements.
  The noun belly dance has one meaning:
  Meaning #1: a Middle Eastern dance in which the dancer makes sensuous movements of the hips and abdomen (Belly dancers).
- **Serenity Belly Dance charter:**
  A belly Dance troup [sic] for hire for clubs, parties and shows. We are NOT exotic dancers nor prostitutes so do not ask. We are artists.
  The dance which we [sic] know as "belly dance" has many names. The French named it "dance du ventre," or dance of the stomach, Turkey as rakkase and Egypt as Raks Sharki. (from http://www.bdancer.com/history/)
  Many dancers today do a fusion of many types of dance including some very non tradional [sic] moves.
  The Serenity Belly Dance Troup Welcomes you. Salam [Serenity Belly Dance].

These charters typify similarities between community approaches to understandings of belly dance in real life and those that arise in virtual community interactions. It is possible to see parallels between the commonly differing or even conflicting narratives concerning what belly dance means and what it could and should mean; discussions which take place in Second Life as in real-life classes, at dance events, and through other digital media.

Conclusion

Boellstorff's argument about the relative escapism of a virtual world quoted above (Boellstorff 2008, 27) does not address why participants would want to engage in a physical activity like belly dance in a virtual reality where the measures of success, skill, or reward are so at odds with their non-virtual counterparts. One solution suggested by my research might be that rather than engaging with the physically rewarding aspects of belly dance — exercise, positive body image, and so on — participants in Second Life are looking for the community-building aspects of the hobby, such as those experienced when partaking in global dance community debates. This is a type of engagement with belly dance and with the belly dance community that does not require a physical embodiment to achieve. This is in fact an aspect of "dance" that many dancers engage in online but outside virtual worlds, through message boards, Facebook groups, popular dance websites and so forth. I am not ruling out the possibility that it also appeals on an escapist or "overcoming the impossible in real life" level as well: individuals could also be attracted by actions the embodied avatar can perform that the individual is unable to in real life, such as a particularly complicated backbend. Another prospect is that the ability to customize the physicality of the avatar with relative ease compared to doing so to one's own body in real life — for example, buying virtual costumes for four or five U.S. cents instead of a real one for many hundreds of dollars — appeals to some Second Life dancers. This would parallel the above-cited popularity of online retail among the general public who use Second Life and other virtual worlds (O'Donnell 2009, Smith and Hudson 2011).

This conclusion is bolstered by the commercial popularity of the "drunk" dancing animation sold by Animazoo, requested by users who wanted to appear as they would in real life when dancing in clubs. This is their most popular item, outpacing animations based on motion capture of professional hip-hop, waltz, and jazz dancers (Collimore 2010). This is an example of how people use Second Life to behave similarly to what they might do in real life but with fewer constraints: complete control over personal appearance including physical characteristics, the ability to keep dancing in the virtual nightclub forever without paying real money for drinks. Users of Second Life, including the belly dance subculture, do not appear to be looking for a complete escape from their everyday lives. Rather, it appears that what users want is a version of themselves in which they have the ability to do enhanced versions of what they do offline: to be a slightly upgraded, glamorous version of themselves. This holds true for the belly dance subculture in Second Life as well as other users. They too replicate their real-life behaviors online, but with a focus on the community-building rather than physical rewards of belly dance. Not all dancers will want to connect with the international community in this way, but it is similar to the way that dancers connect with each other in real life and by using other forms of technology. There are still aspects of a real dance performance that cannot be replicated through motion capture, but the ultimate conclusion of my research was that the experience of dancing incorporates more than the bodily enactment alone.

Notes

1. For three examples, see the videos embedded in my article on *Gilded Serpent* (McDonald, 16 February 2010).
2. This happened because the student noticed a series of movements that appeared to resemble a routine she learned in Galit's class. She saw these in videos I referenced in my article for digital belly dance magazine *Gilded Serpent* (McDonald, 16 February 2010).
3. Both Bellydancers and Serenity Belly Dance have charters that are visible on the Second Life Groups website as well as within the game itself. Enlightened Divinity's charter did not, at time of writing, have a listing on the Second Life Groups website. To refer to the group charter directly it is necessary to sign in to the game and search for the group while in the game.

Works Cited

Abu-Lughod, L. (2005). *Dramas of Nationhood: The Politics of Television in Egypt.* Chicago: University of Chicago Press.
Appadurai, A. (2001). "Grassroots Globalization and the Research Imagination." *Globalization.* Durham, NC: Duke University Press.
_____ (2005). *Modernity at Large: Cultural Dimensions of Globalization.* London: University of Minnesota Press.
Asra. (2011). "Song Lyrics." Retrieved December 17, 2011. http://www.asra-bellydance.com/song%20lyrics.html.
Bellydancers. "Bellydancers [group charter]." Retrieved August 5, 2010. http://world.secondlife.com/group/304aabb9-6c59-cdc8-9624-85cc16e2302c.
Boellstorff, T. (2008). *Coming of Age in Second Life: An Anthropologist Explores the Virtually Human.* Princeton: Princeton University Press.
Collimore, P. (2010). Telephone interview (belly dance animations in Second Life; Animazoo animation company's role in creating and marketing). Exeter and Brighton, UK, April 13.
JenanfromCanada. (11 November 2009). "Second Life @ belly dance club." Retrieved December 10, 2011. http://www.youtube.com/watch?gl=GB&v=383yX7IXz6I.
jimmyjetaimel. (9 August 2009). secondlife sheena bellydancing.
Lane, K. (2009). Interview via Second Life Chat (KarenMichelle's experiences with belly dance in Second Life and setting up Enlightened Divinity). April 10.
Lewellen, T.C. (2002). *The Anthropology of Globalization: Cultural Anthropology Enters the 21st Century.* Westport, CT: Greenwood.
McDonald, C. (16 February 2010). "Digital Dancer! Belly Dancing in 'Second Life.'" http://www.gildedserpent.com/cms/2010/02/16/caitlin2ndlife/.
Mersand, G. (2010a). Telephone interview (filming a motion-capture belly dance sequence for Animazoo). Exeter and Brighton, UK, April 13.
_____. (2010b). (Email questions about Second Life belly dance motion capture. April 14.

O'Donnell, J. (2009). "Avatars Are in a Buying Mood, Unlike Reality, Virtual Retail Sales Are Hot." *USA Today* (December 24): 1B.
Oppy, G., and D. Dowe. (2011). "The Turing Test." *Stanford Encyclopedia of Philosophy*. E.N. Zalta. Stanford, CA: Stanford University. http://plato.stanford.edu/entries/turing-test/.
Poole, L. (2009). Interview (reflections on Oriental dance, internet communities). Clearwater, Florida, January 28.
Robertson, R. (1995). "Glocalization: Time — Space and Homogeneity — Heterogeneity." *Global Modernities*. Mike Featherstone, Scott Lash and Roland Robertson. London: Sage.
Serenity Belly Dance. "Serenity Belly Dance [group charter]." Retrieved 5 August 2010. http://world.secondlife.com/group/b8306196-cae3-8fe8-9bc6-b6ac3d71d226.
Shira. (2011). "About Translations." Retrieved 17 December 2011. http://www.shira.net/music/music-articles.htm#Translations.
slmoviecom. (29 January 2010). Egypt — Second Life — SL Belly Dance Movie — Machinima.
Smith, J., and C. Hudson. (2011). "Inside Virtual Goods: The US Virtual Goods Market 2010 — 2011." Retrieved 27 August 2011. http://www.insidevirtualgoods.com/us-virtual-goods/.
Turing, A. (1950). "Computing Machinery and Intelligence." *Mind: A Quarterly Review of Psychology and Philosophy* LIX (236): 27.

About the Contributors

Candace **Bordelon** began studying belly dance after 12 years as a modern dancer. She holds a Ph.D. in dance from Texas Woman's University, with additional coursework in Middle Eastern studies at the University of North Texas. Her dissertation, with fieldwork conducted in Egypt, explores the relationship between Oriental dance, classical Arabic music, and *tarab*, or musical ecstasy. She is interested in exploring how belly dance can be utilized as a form of movement therapy for women who have suffered from eating disorders, cancer, and sexual abuse.

Siouxsie **Cooper** is a professional performance artist and teacher specializing in Middle Eastern, Central Asian and West African dance. She has performed all over the United Kingdom; in London for Planet Egypt, and in Manchester, Liverpool, Birmingham, Nottingham, Somerset, Cornwall and Devon. Her dissertation from the Dartington College of the Arts focused on belly dance in the UK and its relationship to dance found in Egypt between 2000 and 2010.

Marion **Cowper** is the author *of Shining through the Prism of Belly Dance: Voices from Aotearoa New Zealand*, the first in a series on belly dance as a source of inspiration. It sets out a pathway to spiritual awareness and offers insights on healing, addiction, the mystical and the transpersonal. The book is a combination of the author's own voice and the voices of other belly dancers as they speak of inspirational moments they have experienced through belly dance.

Teresa **Cutler-Broyles** has a master's degree in cultural studies and comparative literature and is a Ph.D. candidate in American studies. She has been writing professionally since 1992. Her credits include fiction as well as nonfiction travel essays, book reviews, screenplays, and interviews with various news-makers and shakers. Her latest book is *A Dream That Keeps Returning*, a series of travel essays about Italy. She teaches film classes at the University of New Mexico.

Lynette **Harper** is a dance artist, author, ethnographer, and educator teaching anthropology at Vancouver Island University. Her creative work and scholarship explores cultural geographies in arts, education, and museums, with a particular focus on the Arab diaspora. After three decades of dance studies, teaching, and performance, she continues to encourage dialogue among cultural communities, dancers and non-dancers, Canada and the Middle East.

Virginia **Keft-Kennedy** holds a Ph.D. from the University of Wollongong, and won the prestigious University Medal in 2001. She has published academic and popular works on belly dancing and cultural studies. Her research interests include women's studies, the politics of representation in literature, and cultural studies. The director and principal of Cinnamon Twist Belly Dance, she is working on a book, "Representing the Belly-dancing Body: Feminism, Orientalism, and the Grotesque."

Brigid **Kelly** has been studying belly dance since 1998. She cites as influences and inspirations Tahia Carioca, Suher Zaki, Tito Seif and Randa Kamel, and Dr. Mo Geddawi. She completed a master's degree at the University of Canterbury with a thesis titled "Bellydancing in New Zealand: Hybridity, Identity and Transculture."

Caitlin E. **McDonald** holds a Ph.D. in Arab and Islamic studies from the University of Exeter. Her findings about the international belly dance community have been presented at several international and interdisciplinary conferences. She has published a book titled *Belly Dance and Globalization: Constructing and Reproducing Gender in Egypt and on the Global Stage*. An avid writer of nonfiction and a blogger for U.S.–based *Skirt! Magazine's* website, she lives in London.

Carolyn **Michelle** is the convener of women's and gender studies at the University of Waikato and co-convener of SOCY202 Popular Culture. Her research interests are in the area of gender and new technologies, particularly human assisted reproduction and emerging biogenetic technologies. She has conducted research on documentary representations of domestic violence (with C. Kay Weaver), discursive constructions of "motherhood" and "the family," and television audiences.

Smeeta **Mishra** holds a Ph.D. from University of Texas at Austin and is a visiting faculty member at A.J.K. Mass Communication Research Centre, Jamia Millia Islamia University, New Delhi. She previously taught at Bowling Green State University, Ohio. Her research interests include media coverage of Muslims, Internet studies, and gender. Her work has been published in *Journal of Broadcasting & Electronic Media*; *International Journal of Cultural Studies*; *Journalism Practice*; *Gender, Place and Culture*; and *Journal of Communication Inquiry*.

Noha **Roushdy** has an M.A. in anthropology and a B.A. in Middle East studies from the American University in Cairo. Her master's thesis, "Dancing in the Betwixt and Between: Femininity and Embodiment in Egypt," on the meaning of belly dance in Egyptian culture received the Magda al-Nowaihi Award for best graduate work on gender studies from the American University in Cairo in 2010. She is also involved in research and advocacy with local and international NGOs in Egypt.

Catherine Mary **Scheelar** has a master of arts degree in cultural anthropology from the University of Alberta. She became involved in Middle Eastern dance through Arabic music and studied it through *tabla, sagat,* vocals, and dance with the University of Alberta's Middle Eastern and North African Music Ensemble (MENAME). Her M.A. thesis, "The Use of Nostalgia in Genre Formation in Tribal Fusion Dance," focuses on the Victorian, vintage, and vaudevillian aesthetic in modern Tribal Fusion.

Barbara **Sellers-Young** is dean of the Faculty of Fine Arts and a professor in the Dance Department at York University, Toronto, and a former professor and chair of Theatre and Dance at the University of California, Davis. She has also taught at universities in England, China and Australia. Her publications include *Teaching Personality with Gracefulness, Breathing, Movement, Exploration* and she is co-editor of *Bellydance: Orientalism, Transnationalism and Harem Fantasy*.

Index

Abdou, Fifi 24
Abu-Lughod, L. 32, 48, 67, 197, 208
Adair, Christy 11
aesthetic 3–6, 9–13, 19–22, 27–30, 66, 73, 100, 118, 121, 126–129, 132, 135, 157–159, 168, 173, 176, 181
Afro-Brazilian 59
agency 37, 109, 134–136, 148, 166, 183, 184, 190, 193
Al-baladi 17, 18, 20–31
Al-Farqui, Lois Ibsen 5
Al-gadid 33, 34, 40
Alves-Masters, Judy 11
amateur 4, 21, 22, 89, 202
American Cabaret Style 156, 157, 164
American Tribal Style 106–109, 111–117, 123, 124, 143, 145
Anderson, Benedict 107
Anglo-Arab 157, 159
Anglo-Celtic 84
Anglo-French 157
Anglo-Indian 183, 185
animation 198–207
anthropology 12, 50, 130, 131
Appadurai, Arjun 3, 7, 8, 12, 13, 27, 168, 107–109, 112, 117, 140, 153, 156, 194, 197
Arab-American 70, 156, 164
Arab-Canadian 49, 51, 59
artifice 129
Asia 48, 69, 123, 173
Australasian 69, 93, 95, 101
Australia 9–12, 68, 93, 95, 103, 107, 116
authentic 22, 24, 27, 43, 45, 81, 84, 85, 110, 115, 121–126, 128–134, 142, 143, 147–149, 152, 153, 157–162, 175
avatar 198–207
Awalim 159

Badawia 56
Bakhtin, Mikhail 86, 87
baladi 12, 17, 18–29, 57, 58, 158, 160, 161, 176
ballet 7, 9, 50, 55, 56, 58, 102, 127, 130
Banjara School of Dance 181, 191–193
Bateson, Gregory 130
Bauman, Richard 131
beledi 37, 39
Bernstein, Carol 42
Bhabha, Homi 7, 140
Bharatnatyam 173, 182, 191
Bollywood 49, 175, 181–194
Bordo, Susan 12, 71–74, 76, 87
Bourdieu, Pierre 9, 70, 122
Brice, Rachel 124
Buonaventura, Wendy 152–164
Butler, Judith 79

cabaret style 56, 109, 114, 156
career 34, 52, 53, 112, 116
Carioca, Tahia 12, 18, 33, 158
Carruthers, Beth 168
Carson, Rachel 168
celebration 6, 13, 79, 114, 159, 163, 177
Chatterjee, Partha 28, 183
China 19, 139
choreophobia 5, 19
Christ, Carol 78
Clifford, James 8
community 1, 2, 4–9, 12–14, 23, 37, 40, 48, 49, 54, 58–69, 76, 106–117, 121, 122, 134, 143, 147, 153–159, 164, 168, 174–179, 184, 197–207
Connerton, Paul 128
cosmopolitan 10, 29, 194
creative 9, 12, 43, 44, 49, 50, 56, 64,

213

75, 98, 100, 139, 142, 148, 153, 154, 157, 159, 163, 172, 173, 175, 176, 203

Dahlena 69, 73–75, 80, 83, 85
Dallal, Tamalyn 75, 89
Daly, Mary 78
Danielson, Virginia 41
Danse du ventre 7
Davis, Fred 135
debkeh 35
Deliah 168–179
Delsarte 172, 173
desire 4, 6, 7–9, 11, 19, 25, 49, 74, 75, 88, 122, 127, 129, 138, 143, 144, 147, 149, 168, 169, 171, 175, 182, 183
Diamond, Nicky 77
diaspora 5, 6, 8, 12, 14, 33, 48, 49, 205
Di Chiro, Grovanni 170
digital 117, 176, 198, 200, 201, 203, 206
diversity 49, 54, 66, 82, 153, 154, 170, 175, 180
Dox, Donnalee 9–11, 48, 94, 138, 152, 159
Duncan, Isadora 9, 172

eco-feminism 171
ecstasy 33, 45, 80, 99
Egypt 3, 4, 5, 8, 12, 17–29, 33–43, 49, 50, 52–56, 58, 59, 60, 65, 68, 82, 109, 124, 127, 129, 134, 140, 144, 152, 155–164, 175–178, 190–193, 198, 206
electronica 123, 124, 126, 133, 134
El Safy, Shareen 34, 40, 41
embodiment 9, 71, 89, 98, 113, 117, 129, 152, 179, 207
emotion 9, 33, 34, 35, 36, 40–45, 77, 83, 99, 117, 168, 172, 173
empathy 40
empower 10, 11, 14, 69–71, 73, 74, 80, 82, 88, 97, 126, 157, 173, 174, 176, 193, 194, 205
England 152–164
environment 4, 10, 34, 42, 53, 78, 102, 103, 140, 145, 155, 168–171, 174, 176, 177
ethnicity 23, 24, 35, 42, 48, 50, 55, 56, 58–61, 65, 84, 107, 115, 123, 124, 140, 175, 178, 180
ethnoscape 13, 153, 163, 164
Europe 10, 17, 21, 48, 68, 112, 126, 127, 138, 158, 162, 171, 172
exotic 7, 9, 23, 48, 49, 62, 80, 83, 84, 93, 96, 101, 121, 126, 127, 138, 140, 149, 153, 154, 157, 206

Facebook 13, 206, 108, 165, 207
fantasy 7, 10, 50, 85, 96, 97, 127, 129, 130, 132, 133, 145, 146, 147, 157, 163
FatChance Belly Dance 106, 112, 115, 123
Fazio, Giovanni 122
feminism 5, 49, 62, 68, 69, 70, 71, 73, 77–79, 82, 83, 86–89, 127
festival 3, 12, 13, 21, 48, 59, 106, 115, 116, 124, 126, 140, 175, 177, 180, 205
fetish 69, 76, 84, 96, 98
Finland 11
Fisher, Julie 139, 149
fitness 21, 29, 68, 69, 71–77, 88
flamenco 49, 56, 61, 124
Flaubert, Gustave 3, 4, 166
flow: creative 42, 43, 44, 94, 99, 100–102; cultural 12, 19, 28, 29, 139, 140, 147
folk 13, 39, 40, 49, 55, 57–59, 114, 152, 175, 182, 190
Fouad, Nagwa 12, 34, 38, 44, 46
France 107
Fremont Summer Solstice Parade 176, 178
fusion 8, 13, 48, 49, 52, 56, 64, 103, 121–124, 126–129, 133–135, 140, 142, 144, 147–149, 175, 181, 182, 206

Gaia 78, 171
Galabeya 161
Gamal, Samia 12, 18, 27, 33
Geertz, Clifford 19
gender 4, 5, 23, 24, 28, 30, 37–39, 49, 50, 61, 70, 73, 80, 84, 88, 94, 102, 127, 140, 154, 163, 164, 192
gentrification 10, 14
Germany 64, 107
Gimbutas, Marija 171, 172
globalization 3, 12, 20, 112, 113, 114, 117, 139, 144
goddess feminism 71, 77, 78, 79
Goffman, Erving 132
Gothic Belly Dance 13, 123
Graham, Martha 161
Greece 60, 82
Greer, Germaine 8
Grosz, Elizabeth 11, 79
grotesque 86–88
gypsy 123, 124, 128, 184

Index

haka 138, 141, 142, 145, 146
Hamed, Nora 39
Hamera, Judith 3, 6
Hanem, Kutchuk 3, 162
Hawaii 8, 170, 174, 177, 179
haya 18
Haynes-Clark, Jennifer 121, 122, 126, 127
hegemony 147, 149
Hilal, Suraya 153–164
Hobin, Tina 78
Hollywood 129, 134, 158, 189
hybrid 4, 81, 94, 103, 112, 117, 139, 140, 142–144, 147–149, 157, 159, 181, 182, 183

identity 3, 4, 13, 19, 24, 28, 29, 48, 49, 53, 60, 61, 70, 79, 80, 103, 108, 111, 128, 135, 138, 139–141, 144, 147–149, 153, 154, 159, 161
image 3, 4, 5, 7, 8, 9, 10, 11, 13, 14, 27, 37, 39, 42, 43, 71, 72, 82, 83, 85, 86–88, 94, 99, 108, 112, 114, 121, 127, 140, 157, 158, 161–163, 165, 166, 171, 172, 174, 176, 178, 183, 185, 189, 190, 194, 200, 203, 207
imagination 3, 4, 7, 8, 9, 13, 85, 98, 102, 107–109, 116, 117, 127, 129, 144, 175, 194, 203
improvisation 6, 13, 33, 40, 140, 158, 173, 174, 202
India 8, 12, 61, 181–194
inspiration 42, 124, 126, 134, 143, 146, 159, 170, 171, 175, 188
internationality 3, 13, 49, 106, 108, 124, 147, 153, 155, 161, 164, 175, 177, 178, 182, 205, 208
internet 7, 11, 13, 89, 107, 108, 110, 112, 117, 154
Iran 5, 155, 175
Islam 5, 6, 10, 18, 19, 49, 50, 62, 65, 82
Istanbul 10, 13, 188
Italy 63

Jarmakani, Amira 8

Kamel, Randa 34, 35, 41
Karayanni, Stavros Stavrou 4, 23
kinaesthetic 4, 6, 9, 40, 110, 148, 170, 172–174
Kiwi Iwi 138, 141, 144–147, 149
Kraidy, Marwan 139

Kraus, Rachel 101
Kuhn, Annette 70
Kuipers, Joel C. 122
Kulthūm, Umm 33, 35, 40, 41–45
Kuntz, Dora 170

Laukkanen, Anu 9, 10
Lawlor, Robert 170
Lebanon 50, 55, 155, 175
Leitch, Vincent 122
lifestyle 24, 28, 29, 72, 100, 116, 128
local 9, 10, 12, 113, 114, 19, 20, 23, 24, 28–30, 58, 65, 94, 103, 106, 117, 138, 139–144, 146, 153, 178, 197, 198
London 154–158, 160, 161, 163
Lorde, Audre 9

Malik, Meher 181, 185, 191, 192
Maori 138, 141–149
Maslow, Abraham 94, 99, 101, 102
Massad, Joseph 23
Mazumdar, Ranjani 182–184
Mediterranean 157
memory 36, 41, 42, 43, 163
Middle East 3–6, 8–14, 18, 19, 33, 34, 48–52, 54, 56–62, 64, 65, 69, 81–85, 93, 95, 96, 113, 116, 121, 123, 127, 133, 138–144, 148, 149, 152, 155, 156–159, 162, 164, 175, 176, 190–192, 205, 206
migration 12, 108
Mishkin, Julie 69, 75, 77, 79, 80, 82–84, 87
Mitchel, Timothy 23
Morgan, Robin 8
Morocco 158
multiculturalism 49, 84, 138, 142
music 4, 6, 7, 8, 12, 13, 17, 18, 21, 22, 27, 28, 33–46, 50, 52, 55, 57, 58, 61–65, 81, 84, 98, 100, 106, 109, 112, 117, 123, 124, 127, 128–134, 139, 142, 143, 146, 147, 149, 155, 156, 163, 169, 171, 172–176, 187–189, 201, 202, 203

Najmabadi, Absaneh 23
nation 3, 11, 13, 14, 38, 42, 49, 52, 63, 106–109, 112, 113, 117, 138, 139, 154, 175, 176, 183, 184, 191
network 21, 49, 70, 134, 140, 144, 187, 198, 199
New Zealand 12, 93, 95, 103, 138–149
nostalgia 13, 121, 124, 135, 163
Nour, Aida 12, 34–36, 45

orientalism 3, 4, 5, 8, 11, 13, 14, 23, 49, 68, 70, 82, 83, 127, 129, 133, 135, 142, 149, 152, 154, 157, 185
O'Shea, Janet 12
Osweiler, Laura 148
Ottomania 10
Outka, Elizabeth 128, 129

Pacific 138, 141, 149, 174, 175, 177
Pakeha 138, 141, 142, 147
Paris 158, 161
Parker, Jill 123
performative 3, 4, 12, 14, 79
philosophy 176, 177
physical 5, 9, 21, 35, 37, 39, 40–45, 55, 72–75, 77, 83, 87, 88, 99, 101, 141, 145, 163, 174, 188, 197, 198, 200, 204, 207
post-colonial 3, 4, 97, 159, 164
Potuoğlu-Cook, Okyu 9, 10, 194
primitive 13, 87, 96, 99

Racy, Ali Jihan 33, 35, 39, 43
Racy, Barbara 35, 39
Ramzy, Yasmina 34, 35, 43
Raqs al-baladi 17–30
Raqs sharqi 5, 13, 57, 122, 123, 124, 126, 129, 133, 134, 153, 155, 157, 158–161, 163, 192, 197
reality 121, 129, 132, 192, 193, 207
ritual 6, 8, 9, 13, 62, 99, 101, 109, 172, 174, 179, 192, 200
Russo, Mary 11, 86, 87

sacred 78, 79, 94, 101, 163, 174
Said, Edward 3, 8, 18, 37, 49, 81, 83
Saidi 37, 38, 39, 40
St. Denis, Ruth 3, 8, 172
San Francisco 13, 106, 112, 123
Savigliano, Marta 7, 10, 23, 122
Schechner, Richard 4, 130
Schill, Marta 69, 75, 77–80, 82–84, 87
Seattle 169–180
Second Life 197–207
sensuality 3, 5, 8, 74, 80, 85, 88, 94, 95, 114, 127
sexuality 21, 23, 38, 58, 80, 85, 86, 88, 94, 116, 130, 181, 182, 183, 187–190
sha'bi 17, 24, 25, 28
Shay, Anthony 3, 5, 6, 7, 19, 23, 49, 69, 81, 138, 149, 152, 185, 190, 192

spectator 73, 74, 98, 104, 186
spiritual 78, 79, 83, 85, 86, 93, 94, 99, 101–104, 170, 173, 183, 205
stereotype 7, 11, 24, 38, 49, 69, 85, 181, 193
Stone, Merlin 78
subculture 69, 121, 127, 128, 132, 207
subjective 4, 12, 22, 94, 97, 100, 102, 104
symbol 9, 10, 11, 50, 71, 78, 79, 84, 127, 172, 177, 178, 182, 183
Syria 60, 156

Tamra-henna 34–39, 41
tarab 12, 33–46, 176
tattoo 114, 126, 145, 146
tourism 4, 8, 10, 13, 40, 140
tradition 6, 8, 14, 17, 19, 24, 33–40, 49, 61, 62, 64, 72, 79, 81, 82, 84, 95, 103, 107, 110, 111, 115, 116, 121–126, 128, 129, 132–135, 138, 142, 146, 148, 152, 153, 158, 159, 163, 164, 182, 183, 191, 192, 197, 201
transculturalism 138, 189, 140
transgressivism 11, 70, 71, 129, 132
transnationalism 7, 13, 48, 49, 66, 109, 129, 134, 135, 159, 197
travel 8, 49, 50, 63, 108, 126, 140, 158, 172
tribe 65, 144
Tunisia 49, 63–65, 152, 158, 160, 161
Turing, Alan 204
Turkbas, Ozel 69
Turkey 9, 10, 14, 81, 82, 140, 188, 194, 206
Turner, Victor 13

Ukraine 107, 110, 115
United Kingdom 201
United States 9, 10, 68–70, 140–143, 149, 152, 179, 198
urban 4, 8, 10, 21, 22, 23, 24, 28, 29, 124, 158, 161, 177

vamp 127, 134, 182–184
Van Nieuwkerk, Karin 18, 19, 23, 24, 29, 159, 192
vaudeville 126, 127, 128, 130, 133, 152, 157, 161
Victorian 73, 127, 128
vintage 121, 124, 126, 127
virtual 13, 106, 109, 115, 117, 197–207

Warren, Karen 78
Washington 107, 176, 177
wedding 6, 8, 20–21, 28, 29, 36, 52, 53, 58, 169
Wilson, Serena 69, 75, 76, 80–85
Wood, Leona 5, 7

Yellis, Kenneth 71, 72
Young, Iris Marion 88

YouTube 12, 89, 106, 107, 108, 112, 116, 117, 198, 200, 201, 204

Zay, Julia R. 123
Zonana, Joyce 82
Zuhur, Sharifa 4

www.ingramcontent.com/pod-product-compliance
Ingram Content Group UK Ltd.
Pitfield, Milton Keynes, MK11 3LW, UK
UKHW041956140426
5217IPUK00015B/822